Mission Impact

Mission Impact

Breakthrough Strategies
for Nonprofits

ROBERT M. SHEEHAN, JR.

WILEY

John Wiley & Sons, Inc.

Published by John Wiley & Sons, Inc., Hoboken, New Jersey.
Published simultaneously in Canada.

For general information on our other products and services or for technical support, please contact our Customer Care Department within the United States at (800) 762-2974, outside the United States at (317) 572-3993 or fax (317) 572-4002.

Wiley also publishes its books in a variety of electronic formats. Some content that appears in print may not be available in electronic books. For more information about Wiley products, visit our web site at www.wiley.com.

Library of Congress Cataloging-in-Publication Data:

Sheehan, Robert M.
Mission impact: breakthrough strategies for nonprofits/Robert M. Sheehan, Jr.
    p. cm.
Includes bibliographical references and index.
ISBN 978-0-470-44980-6 (cloth/website)
    1. Nonprofit organizations–Management.   2. Strategic planning. I.   Title.
HD62.6.S497 2010
658.4'012–dc22

                                                                    2009037491

Printed in the United States of America

10 9 8 7 6 5 4 3 2 1

The AFP Fund Development Series

The AFP Fund Development Series is intended to provide fund development professionals and volunteers, including board members (and others interested in the nonprofit sector), with top-quality publications that help advance philanthropy as voluntary action for the public good. Our goal is to provide practical, timely guidance and information on fundraising, charitable giving, and related subjects. The Association of Fundraising Professionals (AFP) and Wiley each bring to this innovative collaboration unique and important resources that result in a whole greater than the sum of its parts. For information on other books in the series, please visit:

www.afpnet.org

THE ASSOCIATION OF FUNDRAISING PROFESSIONALS

The Association of Fundraising Professionals (AFP) represents over 30,000 members in more than 197 chapters throughout the United States,

Canada, Mexico, and China, working to advance philanthropy through advocacy, research, education, and certification programs.

The association fosters development and growth of fundraising professionals and promotes high ethical standards in the fundraising profession. For more information or to join the world's largest association of fundraising professionals, visit www.afpnet.org.

2008-2009 AFP Publishing Advisory Committee

Chair: Nina P. Berkheiser, CFRE
Principal Consultant, Your Nonprofit Advisor
Linda L. Chew, CFRE
Development Consultant
D. C. Dreger, ACFRE
Senior Campaign Director, Custom Development Solutions, Inc. (CDS)
Patricia L. Eldred, CFRE
Director of Development, Independent Living Inc.
Samuel N. Gough, CFRE
Principal, The AFRAM Group
Audrey P. Kintzi, ACFRE
Director of Development, Courage Center
Steven Miller, CFRE
Director of Individual Giving, American Kidney Fund
Robert J. Mueller, CFRE
Vice President, Hospice Foundation of Louisville
Maria Elena Noriega
Director, Noriega Malo & Associates
Michele Pearce
Director of Development, Consumer Credit Counseling Service of Greater Atlanta
Leslie E. Weir, MA, ACFRE
Director of Family Philanthropy, The Winnipeg Foundation
Sharon R. Will, CFRE
Director of Development, South Wind Hospice

John Wiley & Sons, Inc.:
Susan McDermott
Senior Editor (Professional/Trade Division)
AFP Staff:
Jan Alfieri
Manager, New Product Development
Rhonda Starr
Vice President, Education and Training

To my Dad, the dreamer, and my Mom, the pragmatist.
Together you've encouraged me to bring dreams into reality.

With Love,
Rob

Contents

Introduction

We need a breakthrough in the quality of life for millions of people on our planet. A few examples:

Hunger

- An estimated 12.4 million children in the United States live in food–insecure households and are at risk of experiencing hunger on a daily basis.[1]
- Nearly 3 million seniors in the United States access food pantries annually to meet their emergency food needs.[2]

Housing

- More than 700,000 people in the United States are homeless.[3]
- More than 30 million U.S. households either pay excessively for housing, live in overcrowded conditions, or have physically inadequate housing—such as no hot water or no electricity.[4,5]

---

[1]John Cook, John. Feeding America. Child food insecurity in the United States: 2004–2006. November 2008.

[2]Mathematica Policy Research. Feeding America. Hunger in America 2006. February 2006.

[3]Mary Cunningham, Mary and Meghan Henry. 2007. Homelessness counts. Washington, DC: National Alliance to End Homelessness.

[4]Harvard University's Joint Center for Housing Studies, *The State of the Nation's Housing,* 2004.

[5]The U.S. Census Bureau's 1993 American Housing Survey.

Education

- Up to one-third of school children in the United States begin kindergarten not fully prepared for a successful learning experience.[6]
- Only about half (53 percent) of high school students in the largest U.S. cities graduate on time.[7]

Health

- Cancer, heart disease, mental health, and other health issues continue to plague legions of Americans.
- HIV/AIDS continues to be a major problem in the United States; every 9 1/2 minutes someone in the United States is infected with HIV and for African-Americans and other blacks, HIV/AIDS is a leading cause of death.[8]

And these are just examples from the United States. The challenges for our fellow citizens across the globe are multiplied many times over by comparison.

While nonprofit organizations cannot and should not solve all of these problems, we do play a significant role in making a difference in the quality of life for millions of people. Children, families, and adults are living in conditions that are unacceptable, and we need to make more of an impact. And we need to do better than incrementally more. We need to somehow create breakthrough improvements in these intolerable conditions.

Staff and volunteers in the nonprofit sector already work very hard. The questions this book considers are: How can we work together even more creatively and strategically? How can we invent breakthrough improvements for those we serve through our missions? The intention of this book is to provide a process that nonprofit organizations can use to create breakthrough strategies that will make very significant improvements in our collective mission impact to improve the quality of life for others.

---

[6]Reach Out and Read National Center, 2007. Reading across the nation: A chartbook.

[7]Cities in crisis 2009: Closing the graduation gap, prepared for America's Promise Alliance by the Editorial Projects in Education Research Center.

[8]www.cdc.gov/hiv/ and www.nineandahalfminutes.org/get-the-facts.php.

While we do work very hard, I believe that we in the nonprofit sector still have tapped only a tiny portion of our collective creativity and that great ideas are out there—waiting to be invented—that can help us make even more of a difference than we are currently.

And, of course, the preceding examples just begin to touch the myriad of other causes and issues that nonprofit organizations serve to make a difference for others, including those serving the environment, disaster relief, cultural interests, public interest groups, religious commitments, member associations, and more.

The strategy development process that is explained in this book is based on my more than 30 years of experience in the nonprofit world as a practitioner, academic, volunteer, and consultant. My unique blend of experiences gives me a practical perspective on strategy while also applying cutting-edge concepts—such as strategic intent and systems thinking—that are used primarily in the corporate world.

Much has been written about strategic planning for nonprofits. My approach is much different, and it is unique for three key reasons:

1. It shows nonprofits how to measure their mission impact and focuses the creation of strategy around increasing that impact to fulfill unmet needs, which is the organization's mission gap.

2. It uses an aspirational mind-set to set vision and strategic stretch goals, which lead to the development of a breakthrough strategy—a strategy to close the mission gap as effectively as possible. Most strategy processes result in plans for incremental improvements.

3. It provides a clear definition of what strategy is and, more importantly, what nonprofit strategy is—a coherent, integrated explanation of how the organization is going to guide its performance toward a breakthrough in mission impact. Most strategy processes result in a collection of goals and activities that are not integrated or even connected in any way.

If your organization is committed to a breakthrough—a dramatic improvement—in the impact you are making for those you serve through your mission, then this strategy development process was designed for you. My distinct perspective on strategy derives from my unique blend of experiences with nonprofits during my career, including:

- Eighteen years as CEO of two different nonprofits in which each organization experienced breakthroughs in performance
- PhD from Ohio State focused on the study of organization development, leadership, and nonprofit organization performance
- A lifelong commitment to philanthropy as a donor, volunteer, and board member for a wide variety of nonprofits
- Numerous consulting engagements with a spectrum of nonprofits across the country
- Continuing academic research on nonprofit strategy and performance
- Executive education experiences with corporations, government entities, and nonprofits through the James MacGregor Burns Academy of Leadership and the Robert H. Smith School of Business, both at the University of Maryland, College Park

The result of these experiences is a perspective that has produced a Strategy Development Process that brings together the very best ideas on strategy and performance from all sectors into an approach that addresses the distinctive circumstances that nonprofits face.

This book is written primarily for nonprofit practitioners—staff and volunteers—to empower them to design, develop, and implement breakthrough strategy to make an increased mission impact. Graduate students who are or intend to be practitioners will find it very useful. In addition, there are enough academic citations and recommendations for additional reading to satisfy the curious practitioner, serious graduate student, and practice-minded academic. As a special bonus, board members who work for corporate and/or government organizations will find that many of the ideas in the book can be applied to their sectors as well.

LAYOUT OF THE BOOK

The book is a guide for designing and carrying out a strategy development process for a nonprofit organization. As an aid to help understand how to apply the concepts within each chapter, examples are provided through the creation of three hypothetical organizations. These organizations include a food bank, a housing services organization, and a literacy council—each with their own unique circumstances.

Chapter 1 is the conceptual setup for the book and answers the question, "What is nonprofit strategy?" Chapter 2 explains the factors an organization should consider as it designs its strategy development process. Chapters 3 through 7 explain the key steps that a strategy development group would go through in creating a strategy. These include establishing mission accomplishment measures, a mission gap, an organization vision, strategic stretch goals, completing an organization assessment, and developing an organization strategy narrative. Chapter 8 provides an overview of issues for senior management to consider as it implements strategy.

Appendix A includes a reprint of the Capacity Assessment Grid that was developed for Venture Philanthropy Partners by McKinsey & Company. I am very pleased that we were given permission to include this helpful assessment tool in the book. Appendix B includes summaries of the actions taken by the three hypothetical organizations discussed in Chapters 1 through 7.

One theme that continues throughout the book is the importance of taking the time to go through this entire process thoughtfully, rather than trying to do strategy in an afternoon or in the midst of an emergency. Crafting breakthrough strategy takes time and the involvement of key stakeholders.

Following are more details on what is included in each chapter.

Chapter 1: What Is Nonprofit Strategy?

This chapter provides the definition of nonprofit strategy that will guide the strategy development process. Nonprofits differ from their counterparts in the for-profit world, and these differences must be made clear as they set out to create strategy. While for-profit organizations are primarily concerned with producing profits and beating their competition, nonprofits are primarily concerned with accomplishing their missions—making a difference for society. Therefore, the objective of nonprofit strategy is to guide the organization on its way to mission accomplishment.

Chapter 2: Designing the Strategy Development Process

The design of the strategy development process can take many forms and must fit the organization's situation. This chapter explains the factors that an organization should consider as it is designing its process. It is important that stakeholders are meaningfully involved and that those most intimately involved have credibility and organizational wisdom—an understanding of the dynamics that can lead an organization to high performance. The organization's board of directors and its CEO, along with other senior staff management, need to collaborate and agree upon the design of the strategy development process.

Chapter 3: Your Mission Impact

The first action item for the strategy development group (SDG) to address is the review of the mission and its intended impact. By the conclusion of this step in the process, the SDG will make sure that the mission statement contains impact language, that mission accomplishment measures are set, and that its mission gap—an identification of unmet needs—has been articulated. In subsequent steps, a vision, strategic stretch goals, and the new strategy will all be designed to close the mission gap as effectively as possible to maximize mission impact.

Chapter 4: Vision for Your Organization

The next step in the process is for the SDG to set a vision for the organization. With their mission gap in mind, the SDG is asked to create a future picture of what their organization would be like if it was ideally designed to fill the mission gap as effectively as possible. An inspiring, aspirational vision of the organization provides focus and momentum for strategy development.

Chapter 5: Strategic Stretch Goals

In this step of the process the SDG sets five strategic stretch goals, which are designed to catapult the organization toward its vision. The goals sharpen the organization's focus for the strategy development process and spur creativity. Working toward the accomplishment of the goals begins to bring the vision into reality. In this way, the goals are strategic and their completion point is at the end of the strategy time frame being used (three to five years out). They are outcome based and SMART: specific, measurable, almost impossible, relevant, and time bound.

Chapter 6: Organization Assessment

A clear strategic understanding of the organization's current reality is essential in order to craft breakthrough strategy from that current reality toward the strategic stretch goals and vision. This chapter explains how the SDG can effectively identify the organization's strengths, weaknesses, opportunities, and threats in the context of the organization's commitment to achieve the strategic stretch goals, pursue the vision, and close the mission gap.

Chapter 7: Strategy Development and Management

Chapter 7 integrates all of the prior steps into the process to create the strategy. Strategy development is a creative process that results in a statement of the general themes, a strategy narrative, which will guide the organization's performance for the coming three to five years. The strategy narrative generally explains how the organization will leverage its strengths, fortify its weaknesses, seize its opportunities, and block its threats as it pursues its strategic stretch goals, vision, and mission accomplishment.

Chapter 8: Strategy Implementation and Management

Now that the organization has developed a breakthrough strategy, it is time for implementation. This begins by making sure that all aspects of the organization, especially the culture, are aligned with the strategy. The strategic stretch goals are then integrated into the annual planning process, while the strategy guides the development of the action plans. The organization and external environment are continually monitored for changes—and the organization prepares itself to engage those changes. Implementing and managing the strategy requires comprehensive effort from everyone within the organization. Concepts and tools to help support the implementation are provided at the end of this chapter including ideas on quality management, the balanced scorecard, and strengths-based management.

FOR MORE INFORMATION

I have developed a Strategy Development Workbook as a complement to this book, which organizations can use to follow the strategy development process. The Workbook is available at no cost and can be found on my web site www.SheehanNonprofitConsulting.com in the Resources section. You may make as many copies as you would like for your planning and strategy development purposes.

Also on the web site, you will find additional strategy examples from more hypothetical organizations to complement what is already in the book. These include organizations representing cultural missions, member associations, public interest groups, and more.

Some people will read this book and say that I have made strategy too simplistic. I have, indeed, intended to make a complex concept as practical as possible. Having said that, if, as you read along there is anything in the book that is unclear to you, please email me at BreakthroughImpact@gmail.com. I will create an FAQ section on my web site for the book as questions come in, so please check there first. But if you have other questions, please let me know so I can build out more FAQs.

Thank you for your commitment to the nonprofit world and for taking the time to learn how your organization can make even more of an impact for those you serve. I am committed to philanthropy—as a volunteer, donor, consultant, and researcher—and I believe that our collective philanthropic efforts play an important role in creating a more just, equitable, and thriving society for all.

Rob Sheehan
College Park, Maryland
July 2009

Acknowledgments

Writing this book has been like distilling the learning from my 30-year nonprofit career into a readable package. That has included academic learning and on-the-job training.

I learned a great deal about organization performance, strategy, leadership, and nonprofit organization effectiveness during my graduate work at Ohio State. While many people influenced me there, I give special thanks to Jeff Ford, Bob Backoff, and Astrid Merget.

As powerful as these formal educational experiences were, I have learned even more through my practical experiences. Board members and staff at Alpha Sigma Phi Fraternity and Alpha Sigma Phi Educational Foundation, where I served as CEO of both entities from 1981 to 1990, taught me many things during those years. I want to particularly thank Ralph Burns, Evin Varner, Stan Miller, Bob Sandercox, Jeff Schwind, Jeff Hoffman, Al Wise, Kevin Garvey, Bev Moody, Merilyn Sipes, Hazel Dargatz, Randy Lewis, Bob Simonds, Gale Wilkerson, and Steve Zizzo for training me there in my first nonprofit assignment.

My practical learning continued and expanded during my years as CEO of LeaderShape, Inc. from 1992 to 2001. Board and staff members who especially influenced me during those experiences include Gene Hoffman, Alice Faron, Anne Humphries Arseneau, Paul Pyrz, Mike McRee, Barb Frahm, Bob Baney, Bob Brucken, and Maureen Hartford.

In more recent years, I have been fortunate to work on a variety of executive education projects through the James MacGregor Burns Academy of Leadership and the Robert H. Smith School of Business at the University of Maryland, College Park. This has continued my exposure to more cutting-edge ideas in strategy, leadership, and organization performance. I extend special thanks for this continued learning to Judy Frels, Gerald

Suàrez, Hugh Courtney, Scott Koerwer, Steve Feld, Carol Pearson, Nance Lucas, Jeff Kudisch, Cindy Stevens, Joyce Russell, Paul Tesluk, Susan Taylor, Russ Ackoff, Doug Smith, and Anand Anandalingam.

I started consulting on a part-time basis more than 20 years ago and have had the pleasure to work with a wide variety of nonprofits from whom I have learned much through the years. I have also had the opportunity to teach nonprofit executives in various settings, including training programs sponsored by NeighborWorks America. The NeighborWorks America people are doing important work in the arena of affordable housing and I have learned much from them. Special thanks for all of this goes to staff and consultants there with whom I have had the pleasure to work, including Randy Gordon, Chris Deady, Paul Kealey, John McCloskey, Carilee Warner, Mark Levine, Tom Adams, Karen Gaskins-Jones, and Mark Robinson.

I have also learned a lot about nonprofit performance and strategy from years of experience as a volunteer and Board member for a variety of organizations. I especially acknowledge learning with and from Carla Poanessa, John Thies, Pat Chapel, Tim Deuitch, and Bill Kitson through these experiences.

As cosponsors of this book and as colleagues, I also want to thank the Association of Fundraising Professionals. I have been a member of AFP since 1986 and have served as president of two different AFP Chapters—Central Ohio and East Central Illinois. I believe that AFP does very important work in bringing much-needed, quality educational programs to nonprofit executives through chapters all across the country. Special colleagues there have included Nina Berkheiser, Jim Weidman, Gene Hunckler, Kelly Godshall, Bob Fogal, Mark Neville, and many more.

There are many people who have also been specifically helpful to me in writing this book as resources for information and supporters. This first includes Susan McDermott and Judy Howarth at Wiley who have very helpfully guided me through the process of writing the book. Others include Julie Scofield, Jeff Eaton, Maggie Grieve, Barbara Edmonston, Ron Johnston, Lyn Hang, Steven Miller, Gary Cook, Ed Leonard, Paul Niven, Irv Katz, Susan Phillips Bari, Claire Walden, Lynn Brantley, Ross Fraser, Marla Bobowick, Jan Pruitt, Heath Courtney, and many colleagues within ARNOVA who have given me helpful ideas.

Finally, and most importantly, I want to thank my family—my all-time greatest fans—for their love and support, as well as the many friends who are so wonderfully caring and supportive.

This book is an extension of my commitment to philanthropy, which is grounded in my faith in God as well as my love for humankind.

My apologies to the many people who have helped me along the way but whom I have inadvertently left out.

About the Author

ROBERT M. SHEEHAN, JR.

Rob Sheehan is currently the academic director of the Executive MBA program at the Robert H. Smith School of Business at the University of Maryland, College Park, where he is also a lecturer in the Department of Management and Organization. In this capacity, he directs the academic aspects of the Executive MBA and teaches in the program. He also assists with custom-designed executive education programs for various client organizations.

Rob also is principal of Sheehan Consulting, where he provides consulting services in strategy development and implementation, leadership and teamwork development, board development, and succession planning for nonprofits, businesses, and government entities.

His background and experiences have included serving as CEO of LeaderShape, Inc., a nonprofit that provides ethics-based leadership programs to young adults, from 1992 to 2001. He served as CEO of Alpha Sigma Phi Fraternity and Alpha Sigma Phi Educational Foundation from 1981 to 1990. From 2001 to 2004 he served as Director of Executive Education at the James MacGregor Burns Academy of Leadership at the University of Maryland, College Park.

He received his master's degree (1989) and PhD (1994) from The Ohio State University. While at Ohio State he directed the *Excellence in Philanthropy* research project, which became the basis for his dissertation, *Mission Accomplishment as Philanthropic Organization Effectiveness*. His BA is from Westminster College, PA (1979).

Rob is an active member of ARNOVA (Association for Research on Nonprofit Organizations and Voluntary Action) and the Academy of Management. He has published research in both leading nonprofit academic journals, *Nonprofit and Voluntary Sector Quarterly* and *Nonprofit Management & Leadership*. He is an active member of the Association of Fundraising Professionals, having served as president of both the Central Ohio and East Central Ohio chapters. He attained the association's CFRE (Certified Fund Raising Executive) designation in 1986.

Rob has been an active volunteer and donor for a wide variety of nonprofit organizations, and currently serves as chair of the board of trustees of LeaderShape, Inc.

CHAPTER 1

What Is Nonprofit Strategy?

N onprofits differ from their counterparts in the for-profit world, and these differences must be made clear as they set out to create strategy. While for-profit organizations are primarily concerned with producing profits and beating their competition, nonprofits are primarily concerned with accomplishing their missions—making a difference for society. Therefore the objective of nonprofit strategy is to guide the organization on the way to mission accomplishment.

WHAT IS STRATEGY?

The concept of strategy is often misunderstood in all sectors—corporate, government, and nonprofit. Hence the plethora of strategy consultants and books (here's another) abound. So let's begin by simplifying.

Strategy is an integrated and coherent explanation of how an organization is going to guide its performance in the future. It explains how its essential operations will interact with one another, and within the organization's environment, to produce effective performance.

We'll now look at the different parts of this definition.

An Integrated Explanation of Performance

Many authors point out that the historic roots of strategy come from the military. For example, "The term *strategic* is derived from the Greek *strategos,* meaning 'a general set of maneuvers carried out to overcome an enemy during combat'" (Nutt & Backoff, 1992, p. 56). Using the same military mind-set, Hambrick & Fredrickson (2005) call strategy "the art of the general" and explain that "Great generals think about the whole. They have a strategy; it has pieces, or elements, but they form a coherent whole. Business generals . . . must also have a strategy—a central, integrated, externally oriented concept of how the business will achieve its objectives" (p. 52). Others build on this militaristic concept to describe strategy more generally for organizations as "determining *what* an organization intends to be in the future and *how* it will get there" (Barry, 1986, p. 10).

When many organizations discuss their strategy, they end up listing pieces or elements without an explanation of how these are integrated into a whole. For example, organizations will list goals, initiatives, and/or plans without an explanation of how these are connected to one another. In fact, any connection between these various elements is often unclear. It's not that goals and initiatives and plans are bad, it is just that without an explanation of how they fit and interact together to move the organization forward, they do not constitute a strategy.

Explaining a strategy is like telling a story that has a beginning, middle, and end. As we think back to the example of generals, we can imagine them talking with their troops to explain what they are about to do: "First, we are going to . . . then some of you will . . . which will then allow others of us to . . . and that will give us the opening to . . . which will lead us on to victory." Note how the actions in this simple example are connected with one another. Many people refer to strategy as a cause-and-effect story that describes the journey from the present to the desired future. Certain actions create certain effects, which then allow new actions to be taken, and so on. The strategy story becomes the guiding narrative for the organization's future activities.

In order for a strategy to work well, the various strategic actions taken need to have positive interactions. They need to produce a positive reinforcing cyclical effect upon one another so that the collective result of the actions propels the organization into the future. We know that organizations can find themselves in vicious downward spirals. Good strategy creates a virtuous positive spiral toward high performance (Senge, 1990).

The importance of these positive interactions is central to the concept of systems thinking. Systems thinking seeks to understand an organization as a whole. It looks at how the different parts of the organization interact and affect one another. Rather than analyzing each part of the organization separately, the parts are looked at synthetically. Russell L. Ackoff, one of the leaders of the systems thinking approach, describes one of the tenets of this approach: "A system's performance is the product of the interactions of its parts" (1999, p. 33) rather than the sum of the performance of the parts or "how they act taken separately" (1999, p. 9).

Crafting strategy, this cause-and-effect story, is a creative act, not an analytical function. It is a process of considering the organization's current situation, such as its SWOTs (strengths, weaknesses, opportunities, and threats), looking at the organization's desired future, and designing a set of actions which will catapult it forward. Typically, an organization will want to leverage strengths, seize opportunities, fortify weaknesses, and block threats. These orchestrated actions all make up the cause-and-effect story. In this sense, there is no such thing as a right or wrong strategy and a strategy cannot be figured out. It needs to be generated from the strategist's understanding of the current situation and commitment to pursuing the organization's future intentions. This is what Henry Mintzberg refers to as "strategic thinking" as he compares it to the analytical function of "strategic planning": "Strategic thinking, in contrast, is about *synthesis*. It involves intuition and creativity. The outcome of strategic thinking is an integrated perspective of the enterprise, a not-too-precisely articulated vision of direction . . . " (1994, p. 108).

While a strategy may not necessarily be right or wrong, it can be sufficient or deficient. If the strategy does not coherently explain how the various strategic actions it is going to take are integrated with one another and/or does not explain how these actions will work together to create a virtuous cycle of performance, then it will serve as little future guidance to the organization.

In order to further understand the essential elements of the strategy story, it is helpful first to understand the essential elements of the means of organization performance.

Essential Elements of Performance

Many different aspects of an organization need to work together well in order for it to achieve high performance. This is true regardless of the type of organization it is—for-profit, government, or nonprofit. The strategy definition we are working from states that strategy *explains how its essential operations will interact with one another, and within the organization's environment, to produce effective performance.* The "essential operations" of an organization are its primary means of performance.

In his book *Make Success Measurable!* (1999), organization expert Doug Smith outlines the essential elements of an organization's operations, which it needs to integrate in order to be successful. These activities are essential for organizations from all three sectors. The categories of activities can be thought of as financing, staffing, and provision of products/services/programs of value.

These categories of activities will make intuitive sense to most people who are familiar with running an organization. The categories cover essential questions:

1. What products/services/programs of value are we going to provide and to whom?

2. Who do we need to hire to provide the products/services/programs?

3. How do we finance all of this activity?

The specific ways the activities are carried out will vary within different sectors, but answering these questions is essential to each. Smith explains that organizations must create a "reinforcing cycle" of actions that connects the three categories of activity so that they build upon one another to create a "cycle of sustainable performance."

For the for-profit entity, the cycle includes shareholders who provide opportunities and rewards to people of the enterprise and their partners who provide value to customers who generate returns to shareholders . . . and the cycle continues (see Figure 1.1). Each of the three parts of the cycle benefits from the other two and contributes to them as well. Smith then changes the terminology slightly to demonstrate how the same logic works for government and nonprofit organizations. In government, shareholders are taxpayers, while in nonprofits they are funders. In each case, though, the function is about financing the operation. Customers become citizens in the government model and beneficiaries in the nonprofit model. In this case, it is all about providing products/services/programs of value regardless of the sector (see Figures 1.2 and 1.3).

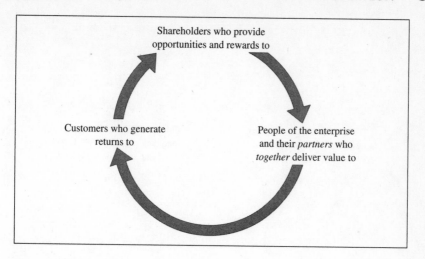

FIGURE 1.1 **Cycle of Sustainable Performance (a)**

Source: Douglas Smith, *Make Success Measurable!* (1999). Reprinted with permission of John Wiley & Sons, Inc.

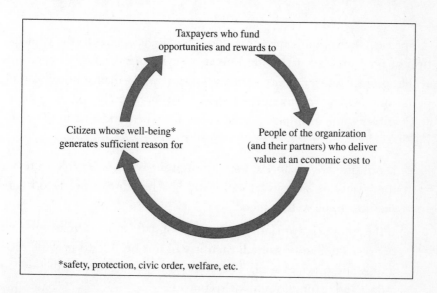

FIGURE 1.2 **Cycle of Sustainable Performance (b)**

Source: Douglas Smith, *Make Success Measurable!* (1999). Reprinted with permission of John Wiley & Sons, Inc.

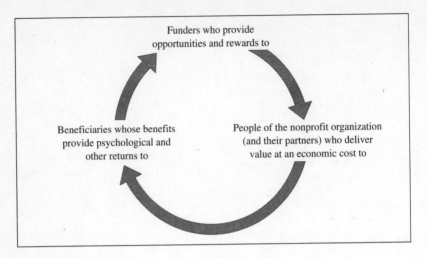

FIGURE I.3   **Cycle of Sustainable Performance (c)**

Source: Douglas Smith, *Make Success Measurable!* (1999). Reprinted with permission of John Wiley & Sons, Inc.

For each sector, the same cause-and-effect logic applies to the explanation of how strategic actions in one area of the organization's operations will impact the others. Smith calls this logic a "performance story," and he points out the "cyclical interdependence" that each area has on the others.

Consider some examples of this cyclical interdependence in the nonprofit world:

- If not properly financed, then a nonprofit will not be able to retain the quality or quantity of staff it needs. Therefore, it needs to figure out how to be well financed.

- If the appropriate quantity and quality of staff (and/or volunteers) are not attracted and retained, then it will not be able to provide programs and services well. Therefore, it needs to figure out how to attract and retain staff and/or volunteers.

- If programs and services are not provided well, then funders (which can include those paying fees for service) will not renew their support. Therefore, it needs to figure out how to provide programs and services well.

Without all three of these areas of activities working well and positively feeding off of one another, the cyclical interdependence breaks down and performance is not optimized.

So as organizations answer the three questions posed at the outset of this section, they need to be sure that their plans in each category positively interact with their plans in the other categories. Since the answers to these questions are essential to the organization's performance, they are also essential to the organization's strategy and need to be included in the organization's strategy story.

The three essential elements of staffing, financing, and products/services/programs are the "means" of performance, and they need to be addressed by organizations in all three sectors. However, an important way that the for-profit, government, and nonprofit sectors differ is by their core purpose—why they exist. Therefore, while they have similar categories of means of production and performance, their ends are quite different—and this will impact how they craft strategy.

STRATEGY GUIDES PERFORMANCE

The purpose of having a strategy is to guide the organization toward its desired future. In other words, the strategy guides the organization's performance. With this in mind, we can examine the different ways in which for-profit and nonprofit organizations think about performance and then look at implications for strategy.

For a number of decades, consultants and authors have taken the general idea of strategy—built upon its militaristic past—to design methods for corporate organizations to craft and implement strategy. In more recent years, nonprofit organizations have begun seeing the value of strategic planning. They have attempted to take methodologies used in the for-profit world and apply them to nonprofits.

The results of these efforts have been mixed. The difficulty in translating for-profit methods of strategy development into the nonprofit world was one of the motivating forces behind a research forum sponsored at Harvard in 1998. From their work with nonprofit practitioners, the conveners stated, "The feedback from these practitioners was that strategy models developed for for-profit organizations were relevant for their purposes, but these models required significant modification or adjustment to work in nonprofit settings" (Backman, Grossman, & Rangan, 2000, p. 2).

While numerous books and articles on nonprofit strategy have been produced since this conference was held more than 10 years ago, nonprofit executives still find difficulty in applying for-profit methods to their unique situations. The development of modifications and adjustments that need to be made in for-profit methodologies of strategy development, in order for them to work for nonprofits, begins by examining the key differences between the two types of organizations—their reasons for being and their notions of performance.

For-Profit Performance

For-profit organizations typically judge their performance by various perspectives on how much profit they make. They have investors who expect a return on that investment. Many companies will also monitor metrics such as customer and/or employee satisfaction, but most do this as a means to the important end of making profit. Some companies may take a shorter-term view of profits (e.g., most companies listed on the New York Stock Exchange) while some may focus on the longer term (e.g., Berkshire Hathaway). Some may look at different permutations of profit, such as price of traded shares or return on invested capital. But, essentially, the idea is to make a profit.

Certainly, many for-profit entities are also concerned about the "social value" they produce for society and they are increasingly concerned about their impact on other various stakeholders. However, for most, these are secondary to their interest in making a profit and returning value to shareholders. A statement from the Business Roundtable, an association of CEOs of leading U.S. companies, reinforces this in its 2005 version of its Principles of Corporate Governance:

> Corporations are often said to have obligations to shareholders and other constituencies, including employees, the communities in which they do business and government, but these obligations are best viewed as part of the paramount duty to optimize long-term shareholder value. (2005, p. 31)

This statement is not as blunt as renowned economist Milton Friedman's famous article "The Social Responsibility of the Corporation is to Increase its Profits" (1970), but it makes the same point.

The definition we are working from states that strategy *explains how its essential operations will interact with one another, and within the organization's environment, to produce effective performance.* We see that *effective performance* means making profit for the for-profit organization (aptly named). But it is also important here to comment on the *environment* in which for-profit organizations operate.

A key challenge that for-profit organizations face is that they exist within a highly competitive environment where other organizations also exist to make a profit. Once they start making a good profit on a particular product or service, then other organizations will enter their market to make a profit by selling a similar service or product to the same types of customers. Therefore, the for-profit world is understandably preoccupied with the problems of competition. A leading expert on corporate strategy is Michael Porter, whose *Competitive Strategy* (1980) is perhaps the most widely read book on the subject. In Porter's view, "Strategy is making trade-offs in competing" (1996, p. 70). This is why the military roots of strategy apply so nicely to the for-profit world. A military general may want to take territory, while a business general may want to take market share. They are both very much concerned with the others in their competitive space and take their actions accordingly.

It is understandable, then, that people refer to the "competitive paradigm that is one of the drivers of the business world" (Kearns, 2000, pp. xiv–xv). Since making profit is its purpose and competition is an important aspect of the environment in which it operates, a for-profit organization needs to address these issues in its strategy story. Next, we look at how the purpose and environment for nonprofits differ.

Nonprofit Performance

While for-profit organizations are accurately labeled according to purpose, using the term *nonprofit* does not describe the purpose of these organizations. People have tried to promote other labels, such as charitable or philanthropic organizations, but none of these have caught on, and we seem to be stuck with the *nonprofit* term for at least a while longer.

Nonprofit organizations are formed for different purposes than for-profit organizations. By definition and by charter, they are given permission by the federal government to exist as organizations that do not pay taxes on their net revenues because their purpose is to make a difference in society. Some nonprofits may also accept contributions, for which donors may receive a federal tax deduction. Nonprofit organizations need to be financially viable, but they do not judge their success by how much their revenue exceeds their expenses. In the absence, though, of profit as a performance criterion, we find that notions of nonprofit performance can become much more complex.

Much has been written and researched regarding nonprofit performance (or in other words, effectiveness) to try to clear up this complexity (Forbes, 1998). Yet, after many years of research and writings by many people, the concept remains elusive. Recently, two of the most notable contributors to the nonprofit effectiveness research literature stated, "Nonprofit organization effectiveness remains a complicated and challenging construct for researchers and practitioners alike" (Herman & Renz, 2008, p. 412).

The view on this issue that I have long advocated—and used as a nonprofit CEO and consultant—is the "Mission Accomplishment as Nonprofit Organization Effectiveness" approach (Sheehan, 1994, 1999, 2005, 2009). Essentially, this approach says that the core purpose of a nonprofit is to carry out its mission—to make a difference for society. The extent to which it is accomplishing its mission is its level of performance. Therefore, the focus of its strategy should be to maximize mission accomplishment.

A number of scholars and authors support this idea:

- James Phills, in *Integrating Mission and Strategy for Nonprofit Organizations*, suggests "For a for-profit organization, performance is typically defined in terms of profitability or economic returns to its owners. For the nonprofit (as well as for some for-profits), performance is defined more broadly, typically in terms of achieving the mission" (2005, p. 17).

- In their review of a collection of articles on nonprofit strategy, Backman et al. conclude that "The most important and perhaps most obvious theme that emerges from these articles is that mission and values, rather than industry structure or internal capacities, are the starting points for strategy development in the nonprofit sector" (2000, p. 6).

- Paul Light, in his survey of 250 executive directors of nonprofits identified as "high performing," found that "three in five equated effectiveness with being focused on or accomplishing a mission or goals" (2002, p. 39).

- Mark Moore, in "Managing for Value: Organizational Strategy in For Profit, Nonprofit, and Governmental Organizations," states that "Just as financial performance becomes the touchstone for gauging past and planning future performance in the for-profit sector, so mission performance becomes the touchstone for gauging past and planning future performance in the nonprofit sector" (2000, p. 194). He suggests that the key calculation for public-sector strategy should be to "find better ways to achieve mission" (p. 189).

- Numerous other researchers have suggested effectiveness approaches consistent with the mission accomplishment approach (e.g., Stauber, 2001; Sawhill & Williamson, 2001a, 2001b; Singh, 2005).

While the mission accomplishment approach seems very straightforward to numerous practitioners, consultants, and researchers, there are those who promote other approaches. Three other popular perspectives are the goal approach, the internal process approach, and the social construction approach. Each of these provides interesting viewpoints.

The goal approach was preferred as a method of assessing effectiveness of all types of organizations for many years (e.g., Price, 1968). This approach considered an organization effective to the extent that it met its goals. But problems persisted with this approach. First, organization goals are often not clear, and this makes it difficult to tell if they have been met. Next, even when they are clear, conflicting goals often exist within the same organization, and it is difficult to tell which ones are more important. And finally, goals may or may not be relevant to the organization's core purpose. Goals can play a vital role in the development and implementation of an organization's strategy—as we will see in forthcoming chapters. However, on their own, they may or may not provide a reliable indication that an organization is fulfilling its purpose.

The internal process approach has been used by researchers who want to study the internal operations of an organization to determine if some optimal set of internal processes may end up predicting effectiveness (e.g., Etzioni, 1964). A great deal of research, for example, has focused on organizational decision-making processes (e.g., March & Simon, 1958). Again, knowledge gained from these approaches can be helpful in the implementation of strategy, but these approaches are more concerned with the means of performance than the ends. If an organization has efficient internal operations, for example, we still cannot determine the extent to which it is fulfilling its purpose.

A more recent development is the social construction approach developed by Herman & Renz (1997, 1998, 1999, 2004, 2008). Their research demonstrates that various stakeholders of organizations have different perspectives on whether an organization is effective and/or the extent to which it is effective. They have recently concluded that "Nonprofit leaders need to recognize that NPO effectiveness is socially constructed, that it is not a stable construct, and that different stakeholders will judge it differently" (2008, p. 410). This is very good advice, and it makes sense that various stakeholders with their own set of values and perspectives would judge performance differently.

Contrasting the mission accomplishment approach with the social construction approach, we see that even when an organization chooses to judge its own performance by the extent to which it accomplishes its mission, it cannot control how various stakeholders will judge that performance. Stakeholders may (and some surely will) have their own criteria that differs from what the organization's board and senior management team chooses. Therefore, when an organization sets out to craft strategy toward accomplishing its mission, it must keep in mind that its performance will be judged differently by various stakeholders. This will be particularly important to remember in Chapter 3 as we look at operationalizing the mission accomplishment approach. In this way, the social construction approach provides a valuable perspective to judging performance and crafting strategy.

While the goal, internal process, and social construction approaches provide helpful perspectives on performance, the mission accomplishment approach is the most appropriate perspective to use as the organization sets out to develop strategy. The mission accomplishment approach captures the core purpose of the nonprofit organization—to make a difference for society. To think of this in the same terms as the Conference Board's earlier commentary on the paramount importance of shareholder value, we could say that "While goals, internal processes, and stakeholders are all important, they are best viewed as part of the paramount duty of the nonprofit to optimize mission accomplishment."

And what about the environment in which nonprofit organizations operate? The strategic opportunities and threats in a nonprofit's environment are even more complex than that of a for-profit. This has been pointed out by many researchers, including Jim Collins in his "social sector" supplement to *Good to Great* (2001). Nonprofits must carefully consider all of their complex environmental factors when they develop strategy—including the possibility of competitive issues.

Depending on the nonprofit, issues of competition may or may not be vital environmental factors to consider. For example, nonprofits that rely heavily on fees for service in environments where other service providers are active will certainly need to consider competition when crafting strategy. Importantly, though, they will consider the competition within their broader commitment to accomplish their mission—not to make a profit. With this in mind, we can imagine the strategic move of two nonprofit competitors to collaborate in order to maximize mission accomplishment for the good of a community. This type of cooperation would be less likely in the for-profit world and may even be deemed as collusion—subject to the violation of law. Therefore, while competition may be something for a nonprofit to consider in its environment, beating its competition is not its overriding concern. It is concerned with making a difference for society.

NONPROFIT STRATEGY

With the preceding discussion in mind, following is the definition of nonprofit strategy, which will be used in the rest of this book:

> Nonprofit strategy is an integrated and coherent explanation of how a nonprofit organization is going to accomplish its mission of making a difference for society in the future. It explains how its essential operations (funding, paid & unpaid staffing, programs/services for beneficiaries) will

interact with one another, and within the organization's environment, to accomplish its mission. (Sheehan, 2009)

This compares to the more general definition provided at the outset of this chapter.

Strategy is an integrated and coherent explanation of how an organization is going to guide its performance in the future. It explains how its essential operations will interact with one another, and within the organization's environment, to produce effective performance.

The nonprofit definition adds specific language that tailors it for these organizations. The first change is that it replaces the term *performance* in both sentences with language that acknowledges that performance for a nonprofit means accomplishing the mission.

Next, it adds specific language to amplify essential operations. This language is connected to the examples provided by Doug Smith earlier in the chapter. The financial category of the operation is referred to as "funding" and may include fees for service, donations, grants, and/or other income. The people of the enterprise category are more specifically named "paid & unpaid staffing" to acknowledge the important role of volunteers in the operation of a nonprofit. Finally, in the customers or beneficiaries category, the term has been somewhat expanded to "programs/services for beneficiaries." This sharpens the role of the activities generated from this category.

Using this definition and these new terms, the strategy story that a nonprofit will tell will include an explanation of how it will arrange for funding to retain paid and unpaid staff and make a difference for beneficiaries through programs/services that will accomplish the mission. It will explain how those different essential parts of the operation will positively interact with one another—and their environment—in a way that creates a virtuous positive cycle of performance toward mission accomplishment.

We will look at more specifics of how this strategy story is crafted together in later chapters. With this understanding of what nonprofit strategy is, the rest of the book will explain how a nonprofit organization can design and carry out a process to create a strategy. The next chapter will discuss how to design a process to fit the needs of an organization. This will be followed by chapters that explain steps that an organization's strategy development group can go through in preparation for developing the strategy: setting mission impact, creating a vision, establishing strategic stretch goals, and completing an organization assessment. The final two chapters, then, cover strategy development and strategy implementation. As the strategy development process is explained, examples of how the process can be applied in different organizations will be provided.

HYPOTHETICAL EXAMPLE ORGANIZATIONS

Throughout the rest of the book, examples of the strategy development activities discussed will be provided by referring to three hypothetical non-profit organizations. These organizations do not exist, but are a composite of various organizations like them. Following are general descriptions of the organizations.

Large City Metro Food Bank

Location: LCMFB is located in a metropolitan area of more than one million residents. It has a main administration office, which is co-located with its food distribution center. The population of the area is 47 percent White, 29 percent African-American, 18 percent Hispanic, and 6 percent other. Median family income is $47,391.

Mission: The mission statement of LCMFB is: "To obtain and distribute food through a network of providers."

Staff: The total staff includes 47 people. The senior staff consists of a chief executive officer and three vice presidents: Development, Finance, Human Resources. The CEO is 55 years of age and is starting his third year in that position. He came to LCMFB from a similar organization in another city where he had served as the vice president of Marketing & Development. The VPs of Finance and Human Resources are in their 60s, while the VP of Development is in his 40s. Beyond the senior staff, other program director positions exist. By board policy, staff compensation and benefits are at the 80th percentile for the U.S. nonprofit sector. Volunteers are used extensively.

Board: The board of directors has 18 people, mostly professionals: three attorneys, two CPAs, two MDs, a clergyperson, a university professor, and nine senior business executives. Board members serve a maximum of three three-year terms. There is an executive committee made up of five board members. The executive committee meets monthly, and the board meets every two months.

Programs/Services: LCMFB collects food from a wide variety of sources and then distributes it to community partners, including food pantries, soup kitchens, shelters, after-school programs, and senior housing sites.

Funding: $55 million annual budget, with a $250,000 net surplus for the most recent fiscal year. Revenue is 80 percent in contributed food, 10 percent from contributions and grants, and 10 percent other. The organization has $8 million in net assets.

Big River Regional Housing Services

Location: BRRHS serves a five-county region that is mostly rural. It has its main administrative offices in the largest city in the area, with satellite offices in two of the other counties. The region includes 500,000 residents, and the population is 80 percent White, 9 percent African-American, 7 percent Hispanic, and 4 percent other. Median family income is $41,940.

Mission: The mission statement of BRRHS is: "To enhance the quality of life of our communities by providing housing services."

Staff: The total staff includes 38 people. This currently includes an interim CEO, Pat, who was brought in to serve temporarily until a new permanent CEO is hired. The most recent CEO, Jeff, accepted a position on the domestic policy team of the Obama White House. There is a chief operating officer, a director of finance, a director of operations, and a number of other program directors and line staff. The chief operating officer and director of operations are both in their early 60s, and the director of finance is in her 50s. Compensation and benefits are generally at the 40th percentile for the U.S. nonprofit sector, although the former CEO was paid at the 65th percentile level. Volunteers are used sporadically for programs.

Board: The board of directors has seven people, including a bank vice president, two residents of the organization's housing units, an attorney, a retired county government worker, a social worker, and a realtor. Board members serve three-year terms with no limits.

Programs/Services: Develop and construct affordable housing units, which are then either sold or managed by the organization. Currently 360 units, mostly multifamily, are managed and three to four units per year are built and sold. They also conduct other neighborhood revitalization programs.

Funding: $6 million annual budget that includes 15 percent in government funding and most of the rest from fees for service. The most recent fiscal year ended with a $93,000 surplus. The organization has $1.2 million in net assets.

Merrill County Literacy Council

Location: MCLC is located in a county of 125,000 residents. It has a main administration office in the largest city in the county. The population is 68 percent White, 18 percent African-American, 9 percent Hispanic, and 5 percent other. Median family income is $52,628.

Mission: The mission statement of MCLC is: "To provide literacy educational services to citizens in Merrill County."

Staff: The total staff consists of five people—a CEO, a now vacant director of programs position, a part-time director of finance, and three program staff. The CEO is 33 years old. When the previous CEO moved out of state during the past year, she was promoted from her post as director of programs. Compensation and benefits for staff are at the 30th percentile for the U.S. nonprofit sector. Volunteers are used extensively as teachers, child care providers, and tutors.

Board: The board of directors currently has five members, but could have as many as eleven. Members include the founding chair of the organization, who is a retired elementary school principal, a clergy-person, an assistant superintendent of one of the county school districts, an attorney, and one of the organization's volunteer tutors who is a homemaker.

Programs/Services: Classes for adults in reading and mathematics literacy, as well as tutoring for adults in the classes. Child care services are also provided for adults who need to bring children to classes.

Funding: $195,000 annual budget and the most recent year ended with a $3,000 deficit. Funding includes 10 percent from individual contributions, and the rest in grants from United Way, local corporations, school districts, and various government entities. The organization has $40,000 in net assets.

CHAPTER 2

Designing the Strategy Development Process

The rest of this book will explain how an organization can design and implement a strategy development process that will guide its performance for its near-term future—three to five years. Outputs of the process include mission accomplishment measures, a mission gap, a vision for the organization, strategic stretch goals, an organization assessment, and an organization strategy narrative. As a part of strategy implementation, the organization then develops more specific plans to accomplish the strategic stretch goals, pursue the vision, and close the mission gap as effectively as possible.

The design of the strategy development process can take many forms and must fit the organization's situation. It is important that stakeholders are meaningfully involved in the process and that those most intimately involved have credibility and organizational wisdom—an understanding of the dynamics that can lead an organization to high performance.

The organization's board of directors and its CEO, along with other senior staff management, need to collaborate and agree upon the design of the strategy development process.

ARE YOU READY?

This chapter assumes that your organization is about to undertake a complete strategy development process, which I suggest organizations implement at least every five years. Choosing the right time to implement the process and making sure that the organization—especially the board—is ready for the process is an important first step.

The Right Time

When is the right time to develop a new strategy? Here are some signs that it is time to start thinking about implementing a new strategy development process:

- You think that your mission or your vision needs to be revisited.
- Your situation has changed very significantly—this includes your external environment and/or changes within the organization itself.
- You read Chapter 1 and realize you don't really have a clear strategy (don't worry, you are not alone).
- You feel that your organization is adrift; for example, goals are fuzzy or nonexistent, the annual planning process is clumsy.
- It has been at least five years since you did your last formal strategy development process.

Mission and Vision   Mission is your organizational touchstone, which articulates the difference you intend to make. Vision is your ideal picture of how your organization would exist so that it can carry out that mission most effectively. More about both of these issues will be discussed in subsequent chapters. However, if you have concerns that your current mission or vision may not be relevant—or that different interpretations of either exist within the board or staff—then it is definitely time to begin organizing a new strategy development process. Without agreement on why your organization is here and where you are heading, you will be unable to operate the organization effectively.

Your Organization's Situation   If you did a SWOT (strengths, weaknesses, opportunities, threats) analysis the last time you did a strategy development process, then check to see if they are still accurate or have changed significantly. If you don't have anything formal to review, then think about what your external environment was like the last time you created your strategy and consider how much has changed from then until the current time. Then consider your organization itself and think about how it has changed. Have there been changes in senior staff, funding, types or levels of services and programs? If you find that there have been considerable changes either externally or internally, then—at minimum—you want to review the vision, goals, and strategy you had developed earlier to see if they still fit your current situation. If they do not, then it is time to organize a new strategy development process.

Your Current Strategy   As mentioned in the previous chapter, many organizations—for-profit and nonprofit—do not have a well-articulated strategy. If, based on your reading of the previous chapter, you don't think that you have a well-articulated strategy, then you are going to need to keep reading for a while to know whether you should actually go through an entirely new strategy development process. If, as you read, you discover that you feel good about your mission, vision, goals, and so forth, then you may just need to sharpen the articulation of your strategy. Alternatively, if you think that a number of these important aspects of your organization need to be reviewed or rethought, then implementing a completely new process may be the thing you need to do.

Your Organization Seems Adrift   If your organization's goals seem unclear, are nonexistent, or change frequently, then you may need a new strategy process to revisit mission, create a new vision, set specific goals, and craft a new strategy. Other symptoms may include the observation that the organization seems whipsawed by changing circumstances—changing directions erratically—or that the annual planning process is clumsy and includes few performance metrics of any type.

It's Been Five Years   If it has been at least five years since you last did a formal strategy development process, then it is definitely time to begin designing the next iteration of your strategy. Too many things change in five years—opportunities and challenges within the environment, staffing, board membership, stakeholders, and so on.

If any of these factors are true for your organization, then it may be time for a new strategy. Of course, this all assumes that the organization is prepared to put in the time and resources necessary to do the work thoroughly. Strategy development does not have to be a laborious, drawn-out process, but it also can't be done properly in an afternoon without any preparation. It needs to be done thoughtfully in order to effectively guide the organization into the future.

If you are reading this book because, as a staff or board member, you have been assigned to design the strategy development process for your organization, then your first step should be to assure that there is strong commitment from the CEO and from the board of directors to undertake the process. The CEO and board will need to allocate time and other resources to the process. Gaining this commitment is an essential first step. If this commitment does not exist, then it is definitely not the right time to do strategy development.

Organizations that find themselves in the midst of staff leadership transitions, particularly if it is the CEO, often wonder if they should recruit a new CEO before starting a new strategy development process or do the strategy work first, then search and hire. More and more organizations will find themselves in this situation in coming years as Baby Boomers reach traditional retirement age. While opinions on strategy first or hiring first may vary, I contend it is actually ideal to do the strategy work first. If at all possible, the organization should hire an external person to serve as the interim CEO or, if that is not feasible, identify an internal staff person to take on the role temporarily.

The reason for waiting to hire until the strategy process is complete is that the new strategy may suggest opportunities that the organization can more effectively seize if the new CEO has a certain skill set and/or if the entire senior staff team requires a particular collective skill set. So long as regular operations can continue in an uninterrupted fashion, then allowing an interim to take over while the strategy process is completed will allow the organization to go about making a hire most strategically. Of course, organizations that find themselves in a CEO transitional situation may end up deciding to complete their strategy development work more quickly than those who are fully staffed. This will be another factor in deciding what the overall process will look like. Organizations should also be aware that some funders, sympathetic to this perspective, have been known to provide grants to support interim staffing as well as the overall strategy development process.

Board Readiness

Boards have important roles regarding strategy because not only are they expected to work with senior management to develop strategy, as they are with for profit organizations, but they also play a key role in the implementation of the strategy. They are important as linchpins to the external environment where opportunities often exist. These opportunities could include raising funds, raising community awareness, developing collaborative partnerships, and more. Therefore, making sure that the board is ready for and engaged in the process is of importance.

Board Membership   What does the ideal board look like for your organization, and how closely does your current board match that ideal? If this is not a question that your board has addressed recently, then now—before the strategy development process begins—is the time to do it. Admittedly, in some ways this is a classic chicken or the egg question. After all, how do you know what kind of board you need until you know what your strategy is going to be? This is a fair question, and it is not unusual for a board to identify specific changes it wants to make to its membership as a result of creating a new strategy. The questions to ask at this stage—before strategy development begins—are: Are these the people that can likely lead us into the future? Are we lacking in some key areas of skill, talent, or knowledge? Are we lacking some important stakeholder representatives? Do we have people on the board who have access to the resources that we will likely need to implement our strategy?

Again, the answers to these will be clearer at the end of the strategy process, but thinking through obvious potential changes to membership at this stage can be very helpful. If one or two new members who fill obvious needs can be recruited and added to the board without delaying the strategy process too long, then it will be helpful to have them as a part of creating the new strategy that they will be expected to help implement.

If some obvious needs are identified, but there is simply not the time to add new people to the board (or there are no currently available positions) then another approach would be to add potential board members to the strategy development group as at-large volunteers. They can be involved in the strategy process and then added to the board later as time permits.

Adding one or more board members prior to the beginning of the strategy development process can be especially helpful if the organization identifies the need to recruit more people who have access to funding sources. Strategizing ways to bring in more funding with people on the board who actually have access to funds is usually far more effective!

Board Development   Boards exist at various developmental stages. In their book *Governance as Leadership* (2005), Chait, Ryan, and Taylor distinguish three different modes or types of nonprofit boards:

- Type 1: Fiduciary: "stewardship of tangible assets" (p. 6)
- Type 2: Strategic: "creating a strategic partnership with management" (p. 7)
- Type 3: Generative: "providing a less recognized but critical source of leadership for the organization" (p. 7)

Chait, Ryan, and Taylor suggest that boards that reach the generative level will provide the most value to their organizations, as they will carry out the generative function as well as the fiduciary and strategic functions. While the first two types of boards may seem rather self-explanatory, the generative type requires some additional discussion.

According to the authors, some of the hallmarks of the generative thinking that these types of boards have are: noticing cues and clues to understand the deeper meaning of data, reframing problems and issues from various perspectives, and thinking retrospectively—providing an understanding of the past in a way that sheds light on possibilities for the future.

A board that employs this type of generative thinking would provide great value to an organization. Insights gained from this type of thinking would be of especial value during strategy development. In some ways, generative thinking is an advanced type of strategic thinking. It would be ideal for any board that is about to become involved in strategy development to have reached the generative developmental stage, and boards should work together to achieve this developmental level.

While a strategy development process cannot be put on hold until a board reaches the generative level, there are steps it can take prior to doing the strategy work that can help move its development along. For example, copies of the *Governance as Leadership* book can be purchased for board members and time at meetings can be set aside to discuss implications for the board.

In addition, a tool often used to promote board development is a self-assessment. Board self-assessment involves board members reflecting on their behaviors and then comparing them to an ideal of how a board should act. Comparing the perceived actual behaviors to the ideal then gives the board data to consider as it makes plans for improvement. While numerous self-assessment tools exist, the one that is probably most widely used was created by BoardSource, a national nonprofit organization founded in 1988 to provide resources for improving nonprofit board performance. For a reasonable fee, boards can access this tool through BoardSource (www.BoardSource.org), take the self-assessment confidentially, and allow the board to review the collective results while maintaining the anonymity of individual respondents. Often, boards employ an outside facilitator to review the results and work with them to make specific plans for improvement.

It is generally a good idea for boards to do a self-assessment every two years or so to gauge how well members are working together and to identify areas for improvement. This is even more important to implement prior to a strategy development process if the board has not gone through a self-assessment in the prior two years. It helps ensure that the board is operating as effectively as possible prior to taking on the important strategy work.

In addition to having board members read the *Governance as Leadership* book and do a self-assessment, they may also want to consider learning more about systems thinking. Generative thinking and systems thinking have a great deal in common. Systems thinking pioneer Russell Ackoff describes an attribute of systems thinking as the ability to think synthetically rather than just analytically. Synthetic thinking encourages asking more *why* questions than the *what* questions of analytical thinking. Ackoff's book *Re-Creating the Corporation* (1999) is a good place to start for those interested in this.

All of these board developmental activities will create better board members, better strategists, and—most likely—more effective employees back in their full-time jobs.

Using Consultants

One of the purposes of this book is to empower staff and board leaders with knowledge about designing and implementing the strategy development process. Far too often, organizations leave too much of the strategy process up to consultants which can result in a feeling of "it's the consultant's strategy." This is a result that is not helpful to anyone.

It is ideal for an organization to retain a consultant if at all financially feasible. The organization and consultant should be partners in designing and implementing the process. Consultants can provide significant value to the process, including some or all of the following:

- Assist with designing the strategy development process.
- Conduct stakeholder interviews, town hall meetings, focus groups, and/or implement survey research.
- Serve as source of knowledge on strategy, nonprofit performance, and specific domain areas of importance such as fundraising, management, finance, marketing, and board development.
- Facilitate sessions of the strategy development group.
- Help ensure accountability on tasks leading up to and following the strategy development process.

It is possible that one consultant or consulting firm can provide all of these services in an integrated fashion. It is also not unusual for individuals or firms with more expertise in one area or another to be retained to work with the organization on the overall process. For example, a firm with more experience in marketing may be better suited for work on stakeholder focus groups and surveys, while a firm more focused in strategy may provide those consulting services.

Consulting fees can be costly, and organizations will want to balance the costs and benefits of these services. At minimum, though, it is especially helpful to have a knowledgeable outside consultant help with the design of the process and to facilitate the strategy development group sessions.

Stakeholder Identification and Involvement

Types of Stakeholders

A stakeholder of an organization is literally defined as any person or organization that has a stake in the organization's performance and activities. For most organizations, stakeholders will include:

- Recipients of services and programs
- Volunteers
- Board members
- Staff
- Individual donors
- Funders
- Potential funders
- Elected officials
- Community leaders
- Collaborators and/or potential collaborators
- General citizenry

It will be important for the organization to create a list of all potential stakeholders as they consider how to involve them. It is far better to ask people to be involved who may have a limited interest than to ignore a person or group that ends up having more interest than imagined.

Methods of Involvement

It is important for the organization to design specific activities for the involvement of stakeholders in the strategy development process. But even more important than these activities, it is important for the organization to commit to creating a culture of meaningful stakeholder involvement that is continuous, not episodic. If the organization has not developed a pattern of meaningful involvement for stakeholders in the past, then this will not happen overnight. The strategy development process can provide a beginning point for that kind of involvement. However, the organization should realize that some stakeholders may be suspicious of being asked to participate in the process. They may ask, for example: "Why are they asking me my opinion now, and what are they up to?" People will need to feel that they are being asked to be authentically engaged in the process, rather than feel that they are being co-opted, for example.

Meaningful involvement can energize stakeholders. They can serve as sources of valuable data for the strategy development process, provide creative ideas for the strategy, and/or be supporters of the strategy once it is formulated. Of course, meaningful involvement takes time. Ideally, the organization will design ways to involve stakeholders before, during, and after the strategy development process is initiated.

The most direct way to involve stakeholders is to invite them to participate as a member of the strategy development group (SDG). However, as will be discussed in an upcoming section, the SDG cannot be too large. Therefore, specific stakeholders who are not asked to participate in the SDG will want to know that their views are being considered. This can be accomplished by having representatives of various stakeholder groups on the SDG or assuring that stakeholder views and opinions are communicated to and listened to by the SDG.

It may be helpful to schedule individual meetings with some of the most important stakeholders when the strategy development process is being designed to gain their input and support. This could include major donors/funders, elected officials, community leaders, and key staff.

Where geographically feasible, many organizations begin to involve stakeholders even as the entire strategy development process is being designed through the use of town hall meetings. These can be general sessions that are open to all stakeholders or can target specific groups, for example, staff at a particular location, clients of specific services, or residents of a particular community.

Two other common methods of involving stakeholders are focus groups and surveys. This book is not intended to be a resource on research methods and organizations should select consultants or other resources to learn more specifics. However, following are a few general guidelines.

Focus groups and surveys can complement one another. For example, if an organization is unclear on the types of issues that may be of importance to stakeholders, then it may want to start with focus groups to probe for these issues. Once the focus groups are completed, survey questions can be designed (sent either by mail, phone, or increasingly via the Internet) to find out how widespread some of the opinions are that were expressed in the focus groups. Thus, using the focus groups first can make the surveys more effective. Time available and budget will be key considerations for an organization to address as it determines which of these methods to use and for which stakeholder groups. You don't want to spend the entire strategy timeline and budget on collecting stakeholder data. It is a matter of finding the right balance for each particular organization as you design meaningful ways to involve stakeholders.

What type of information is typically collected from stakeholders? This can run the spectrum of topics that will be addressed during the strategy development process, as will be discussed in upcoming chapters. These could include the following types of questions, which would be formed more specifically for surveys or more generally for interviews, town halls, and focus groups:

- Does our current mission statement properly reflect our purpose and activities? Should it be changed or improved in any ways?

- We are going to explore various methods for assessing our effectiveness. Do you have any suggested criteria that we should keep in mind?

- We are going to create a vision for what our organization would look like ideally, so we are situated to accomplish our mission most effectively. What would you want to include in that kind of vision for the future?

- What ideas do you have for how we could accomplish our mission more effectively?

- What do you think are our organization's strengths and weaknesses? What opportunities do you think we should be aware of in the coming years? What threats or challenges may we want to keep in mind during the coming years?

- What thoughts do you have on what our most important goals should be for the next three to five years?

- What ideas do you have on how we can most effectively go about achieving those goals?

This is a simple sampling of questions that may be asked of stakeholders. Organizations will want to change or add to these questions depending on what they really want to know from their stakeholders.

Stakeholders should also be updated on the timeline for the strategy development process and, if possible, updated as the process progresses. Many organizations leverage technology to provide updates via email or on web sites. Of course, many stakeholders may not have access to the

Internet and it may be best to provide updates via town hall meetings and/or mailings.

Length and Scope

How long should it take to complete a strategy development process, and how many meetings should the SDG expect to have? It all depends.

First, it depends on whether the board is ready. As discussed earlier in this section, if the organization needs to add board members and/or conduct a self-assessment, then these steps should be completed before the strategy process begins.

The next factor to consider is the status of the organization's mission and whether or not it has already adopted mission accomplishment measures as a way to evaluate performance. The meaning of this is discussed in detail in the next chapter. However, if an organization thinks that it needs to take extensive time to review its current mission and/or it thinks that the development of its mission accomplishment measures will be a complex process, then it may want to appoint a special task force to complete this part of the process prior to the actual SDG being appointed. However, if a clear mission and mission accomplishment measures are already in place—or if it will be fairly easy for an SDG to update—then it can be included as part of the SDG's responsibilities.

Once these considerations are addressed and an SDG is appointed, then how long should the strategy development process take?

Too Short

A new strategy should not be developed under urgent circumstances, and shortcuts in the process should not be taken. If an organization faces an emergency situation, then it should take tactical action that will allow it to maintain its operations so it can then take the time to thoughtfully craft a new strategy.

In his book *First Things First* (1994), Stephen Covey discusses the poor decision making that can take place under urgent conditions. He suggests that highly effective people spend their time on matters that are important, without the pressures that urgency can bring. The same is true for organizations.

In the best of all circumstances, where board membership is solid, a board assessment has recently been completed, a minimal number of stakeholders exist, mission accomplishment measures are already established, and up-to-date data on the external environment has already been collected, an SDG should plan to take at least two full days of deliberation before completing the process as described in this book. But the preparations to get the SDG ready for those two days usually takes many weeks of planning. The SDG has to be chosen, meetings have to be scheduled, information has to be collected, the overall process has to be designed, and time lines need to be set. Strategy is not something that should be rushed.

Too Long

While the strategy process should not be rushed, neither should it drag on and on. The entire process can be completed by the SDG in no more than four to six full-day meetings. Only if extensive stakeholder input and external data need to be processed should additional meeting sessions be required. These sessions may be held close together or spread out over a period of months. As mentioned above, if significant work needs to be done on the mission phase, then this should be completed prior to the engagement of the SDG.

Data collection on the external environment and check-in meetings with stakeholders between SDG sessions can lengthen the strategy development process. However, once board readiness is assured and mission work is complete, even a national organization with complex data to collect and multiple stakeholder groups located across the country should be able to complete their strategy process within a year.

Just Right

Developing a new strategy should be an energizing experience with positive momentum, even though it is hard work. The pace of meetings should be upbeat. Even though the organization may face difficulties and its mission may be a challenging one, it has a noble cause and is working hard to bring its best efforts forward to make a positive difference in society. The pacing of meetings, communications, and all activities should reflect a positive attitude and not feel tedious for members of the SDG.

THE STRATEGY DEVELOPMENT GROUP

Once the considerations of board membership, board self-assessment, and mission readiness are addressed, the strategy development process is formally initiated when the board of directors appoints the SDG.

One important decision that the board needs to make before moving on to the next step is deciding on the future time frame during which the new strategy will guide the organization. It is recommended here that organizations use a five-year time horizon for planning into the future. Given the amount of time and resources that goes into the process, it is helpful to let the strategy guide the organization for this period of time. Of course, if circumstances change significantly, then the organization can always shorten the time frame later and create a new strategy. Even though five years is recommended here, an organization may choose a four- or even three-year time frame. Usually, no shorter than a three-year time frame is used.

Responsibilities

The SDG is charged by the board of directors to work together and bring back to the board recommendations, including:

- A report on a review of the mission and mission accomplishment measures with possible suggested revisions
- A statement of the organization's mission gap
- A vision of what the organization would be like if it was ideally designed to close its mission gap as effectively as possible
- Strategic stretch goals the organization will commit to accomplishing in the next five years (or three to four years if a shorter time frame is selected)
- A statement of the organization's key strengths, weaknesses, opportunities, and threats
- A recommended strategy narrative to guide the organization's performance during the next five years (or three to four years)

If there are other specific expectations that the board has for the SDG, then these should also be listed at the time the group is officially charged.

The board should also appoint a chair for the SDG—usually a senior board member—and perhaps one or two assistant chairs. One of the assistant chairs could be the CEO, for example, and another could represent another key stakeholder group (e.g., a major funder, a client, etc.).

Membership

Ideally, the SDG should be no more than 15 people, but in no circumstances more than 20. This is a nonscientific recommendation based on experience. Even with 15 members, a good facilitator will be challenged to keep a group on task. Much of the work done by the group will be more efficiently done in breakout sessions with three groups of five people each working together, and then coming back to report to the entire SDG.

In selecting members, it is important to remember that the recommendations of the SDG will need to be approved by the board of directors. Therefore, a significant number of board members—especially those with great credibility with the rest of the board—should be selected for the SDG. The process would be a major failure if a report is brought back to the board and not approved. Most organizations will make sure that a majority of their board members serve on an SDG to eliminate this scenario. If a board is too large to have a majority of members on the SDG, then it should make sure to have members on the SDG whose recommendations they intend to accept.

While the board has to approve the recommendations of the SDG, the staff and volunteers (including the board) will be tasked with implementing it. Donors and other funders will be asked to fund the strategy and clients will need to find it compelling—especially if they are fee-for-service paying clients. Therefore, these stakeholder groups and others important to the organization will want to know that their voice is being heard during the SDG meetings. This may be accomplished by selecting SDG members whom stakeholders find credible and legitimately empathetic of their views as well as by providing methods for them to have input into the process as discussed earlier in this section.

In addition to SDG members having credibility and legitimacy with various stakeholders, it is ideal if they have a good working knowledge of what it takes to operate a successful organization—especially a nonprofit organization that is committed to a breakthrough in performance. This attribute is sometimes referred to as organizational wisdom.

Preparing the Strategy Development Group

Prior to the first meeting of the SDG, a collection of materials should be provided to each member. This should include:

- A memo thanking the group for their participation in the process, which outlines their responsibilities and lists meeting dates, times, and locations
- List of SDG members and contact information
- General organizational materials, such as a brief history of the organization, the most recent audit, past year's board of directors reports and minutes, and so on
- All organization assessment data collected

Additional detail on the types of organization assessment data that may be collected is reviewed in Chapter 6. This information is typically sent to the SDG prior to their first meeting and then reviewed with them at that initial meeting.

SDG Team Charter

At the first meeting of the SDG, one of its first tasks should be to establish its team charter. A team charter is an agreement between team members that states its purpose, responsibilities, expectations, authority, and norms of behavior. Putting the charter together has also been referred to as a team launch exercise (Hackman, 2002). The board will have already outlined the responsibilities for the SDG and established meeting dates, as well as any other expectations. The main item missing will be establishing group norms. This is a task that can be guided by a facilitator or the chair of the SDG.

A simple way to begin the process of setting the norms is to ask the group to brainstorm a list of answers to the question, "What behaviors should we agree to exhibit so that we can do our work together most effectively?"

Responses can be listed on a flip chart, and the group can decide which behaviors it agrees to follow. Examples to encourage the group to consider would include:

- *Meeting norms*. Arrive and start on time, have cell phones turned off, be prepared, treat one another with respect, participate, don't interrupt one another

- *Communication norms*. Return calls and emails promptly between meetings, guidelines on confidentiality

- *Decision-making norms*. While consensus may be ideal, what process will be used if consensus cannot be reached? Facilitators or board chairs may want to make themselves knowledgeable on the use of nominal group techniques that can help groups reach agreement quickly without traditional voting. *Strategic Management for Third Sector Organizations*, (Nutt & Backoff, 1992), is an excellent resource for these techniques.

Coming to agreement on norms does not need to take a long time and can create a much more efficient meeting. Many boards of directors create these team charters to help guide behaviors during their meetings and find it very helpful.

APPLICATION TO HYPOTHETICAL ORGANIZATIONS

Following are examples of how different organizations can effectively design a strategy development process. Each organization has very different circumstances and varied degrees of freedom on how they can design their process.

Large City Metro Food Bank

The Right Time   When Tim was interviewing for the post as CEO of Large City Metro Food Bank, he learned that the organization was two years into its five-year strategic plan. He thought the plan was fine and did not see a reason to set about creating a new one right away. He had developed an appreciation of the importance of timing during his extensive career as a nonprofit executive.

During his first year, Tim did recommend that the board complete a self-assessment exercise. As a result of this, the board realized that they did not have good metrics to determine their overall performance. They also realized they needed more board members who had fundraising experience and were well connected within the community. They soon added two new board members meeting this profile.

A task force of staff, volunteers, and subject matter experts worked on a mission performance project over the period of a number of months and recommended a set of mission accomplishment measures to the board as the overarching performance metrics the organization should use to judge its effectiveness on a regular basis. The board approved the work and the metrics were adopted.

Once the task force finished its work, Tim thought that the organization was now ready to direct its attention to developing a new strategy. He felt he understood the community well enough and that the organization needed to accelerate its performance. The board of directors approved his request to retain a consultant and prepare a recommended plan for the process. The chair-elect of the board, Bob, was appointed to serve as chair of the SDG, and Tim would serve as assistant chair.

Stakeholders LCMFB has a huge number of stakeholders, which include:

- Large City Community Foundation
- City of Large City Leaders
- Board members
- County government leaders
- Numerous corporate and other funding entities
- Individual donors
- Clients of all services
- Food pantries, emergency shelters, senior centers
- Staff
- Volunteers

Length and Scope

- Week 1: Tim appoints a staff member as project manager to coordinate the process.

- Week 1: Requests for Proposals (RFPs) to consultants sent out.

- Week 2: Make lists of stakeholders and discuss ways in which they may be involved in process; discuss potential members of SDG.

- Week 3: Work with staff chief information officer to determine current availability of external data that SDG may want to review. Plan for collection of additional data.

- Week 4: Bob and Tim review RFPs and schedule interviews with consultants.

- Week 6: Meet with consultants to design overall process.

- Week 7: Board appoints SDG; provides schedule of activities and meetings.

- Week 7: Tim sends strategy process plan update to all staff, explaining the process and how they will be involved.

- Week 8: Consultants begin interviewing key stakeholders in individual meetings; also begin scheduling focus groups with staff, volunteers, clients, and individual donors.

- Week 10: Orientation breakfast meeting held with SDG. Consultants are introduced and detail of process is discussed.

- Weeks 10–12: Focus groups held; begin drafting survey instruments.

- Week 12: Tim holds town hall meeting for staff with update on strategy process and encourages participation in surveys.

- Week 13: Update to SDG on preliminary analysis from focus groups and individual interviews.

- Week 13: Online surveys sent to staff, volunteers, previous individual donors.

- Week 14: Staff report on external data collected sent to SDG.

- Weeks 15–16: Results of surveys tabulated; final report prep.

- Week 17: Report from consultants sent to SDG with synthesis on individual interviews, focus groups, survey results.

- Week 18: Day 1 SDG session: Report from consultants on findings, report from staff on external data collection, report from leaders of mission task force and update on mission accomplishment measures, review mission gap data.
- Week 20: Day 2 SDG session: Create draft vision for the future LCMFB and strategic stretch goals.
- Week 21: SDG surveyed for SWOTs.
- Weeks 21–23: Individual meetings and/or focus groups held with other board members, staff, and other selected stakeholders regarding draft vision and strategic stretch goals.
- Week 23: SDG SWOT results sent to SDG.
- Week 24: Days 3–4 SDG sessions, weekend retreat at State Park: Report on feedback from stakeholders on vision and strategic stretch goals, finalize vision and strategic stretch goals, complete SWOT analysis, create strategy narrative. Hold picnic with families at the end of retreat.
- Week 25: SDG presents final report to board of directors.

Strategy Development Group   The SDG appointed by the board included:

- All five executive committee members (Bob, Al, Stan, Andy, Doug) and two additional board members (Christine, Hugh)
- Four staff: Tim, the Vice President of Development (Brian), two program directors (Merilyn & Bev)
- Kevin, the president of the Large City Community Foundation
- Richard, a County Commissioner
- Steve, Director of Large City Human Services
- Randy, an individual major donor
- Evin, director of one of the food pantries served by LCMFB
- Jeff, director of one of the homeless shelters served by LCFMB

Analysis of LCMFB Process Design   Tim was wise to wait two years into his tenure to initiate this process. He was able to complete a board self-assessment early on that led to the addition of new board members and improvements in mission performance metrics. His patience allowed him to set the organization up nicely for the new strategy development. All too often, new CEOs want to march in and put their stamp on an organization by creating a new strategy right away when that is not necessary.

The RFP process in this situation gives LCMFB some flexibility. Depending on how they write the RFP, they could retain one consulting firm for all the work or end up hiring one firm for the marketing aspects—interviews, focus groups, surveys—and another for the overall strategy design and facilitation. Sometimes organizations will write an RFP in such a way that it gives them this flexibility.

There will be those who think that this LCMFB process drags on, but there are certainly organizations which take much longer to complete their strategy. Members of the SDG are appointed in week 7 and have an orientation breakfast in week 10. Sitting at that breakfast, they understand that they have agreed to four full days of meetings during the next 15 weeks, and that their work will be completed with a final report to the board of directors by that time. It is a big commitment, but the work is spaced out in a way that the process can maintain a positive momentum while making sure that the work done is thorough. The picnic for families at the end of the retreat is a nice symbol of appreciation for the work of the SDG as well as a good community-building activity.

This process spends a significant amount of time making sure to gain input and feedback from stakeholders. This should serve the organization particularly well when it comes to the support of stakeholders when the final report is presented. The organization is large enough to have data collection experts on the staff who can provide and collect the information needed by the SGD. Tim was also fortunate to have a staff person available whom he could appoint as project manager for the process. For an organization this large, and with the number of activities involved, the process is very complex to coordinate.

The SDG includes 7 of the 18 board members. While it is not a majority of the board, it does include the entire executive committee, and one would think the rest of the board would be inclined to support the report the SDG proposes. Still, Tim and the board members on the SDG will be wise to keep the others informed as the process unfolds. By forgoing the temptation to have more board members on the SDG, the organization is able to keep the group to 15 members and still have representation from the staff, volunteers, clients, and the community.

In sum, this process balances the needs to move the process along at a reasonable pace with the importance of involving stakeholders through interviews, focus groups, a staff town hall, and surveys. It even builds in a check-in point with some stakeholders once the vision and strategic stretch goals are set. This helps give the SDG some feedback to fine-tune their work on the vision and goals. However, if this process had stretched out much longer, one can imagine that members of the SDG could begin getting burned out with the process or disengaged.

Big River Regional Housing Services

The Right Time   Shortly before Jeff was appointed to his position in the Obama White House and had to leave his CEO post at Big River Regional Housing Services, he had the board complete a self-assessment process. Having done this, the board was working very well together and handled his sudden departure quite effectively. They quickly decided to hire an interim CEO rather than do a search, so that they could develop a new strategy for the organization that would inform their hiring.

The board retained a consulting firm that would provide them with an interim CEO, provide a consultant to assist them with the strategy development process, and work with the board to do the search for their new CEO once they were ready.

Pat, an experienced nonprofit executive and former CEO of two other nonprofits, had decided to devote the rest of his career to serving organizations as an interim CEO. He had served as the interim CEO of a number of nonprofits during the past eight years and appreciated the difference he could make in helping organizations prepare for new, permanent leadership.

One of Pat's primary mandates from the board was to help design a strategy development process. It was helpful that the organization had a strong COO, so Pat could devote energy to this effort. The board chair, Kendra, would serve as chair of the SDG and would work closely with Pat as assistant chair on the process. Working with their strategy consultant, Pat and Kendra determined that their mission and performance metrics were in good enough condition that they would not require a lengthy review. This was something that could be included in the work of the SDG.

Stakeholders

- Housing residents
- Volunteers
- Board members
- Staff
- Individual donors
- National association funder
- Elected officials from regional cities and counties
- Community leaders
- Big River Regional Community Bank
- Other corporate donors

Length and Scope

- Week 1: Pat serves as coordinator of the process; Pat, a consultant from his firm, Tom, and Kendra begin designing overall process.
- Week 2: Make lists of stakeholders and discuss ways in which they may be involved in process; discuss potential members of SDG.
- Week 3: Begin identification of external data that SDG may want to review. Plan for collection of data.
- Week 3: Board appoints SDG; provides schedule of activities and meetings.
- Week 4: Staff town hall meeting to announce the process, time line, and how they will be involved.
- Weeks 5–6: Consultants begin interviewing key stakeholders in individual meetings; also begin scheduling focus groups with staff and residents, and individual donors.
- Weeks 5–6: Housing residents town halls.
- Week 6: Staff and board surveyed by consultants using assessment tool.

- Weeks 6–8: Focus groups held.
- Week 9: Staff report on external data collected sent to SDG.
- Week 10: Consultant report with synthesis on individual interviews, focus groups, and assessment tool results sent to SDG.
- Week 12: Day 1 and 2 SDG sessions, weekend retreat: Report from consultant on findings, report from staff on external data collection, review mission, set mission accomplishment measures and mission gap, draft vision, draft strategic stretch goals, draft SWOTs.
- Weeks 13–14: SDG members check in with constituents regarding draft vision and strategic stretch goals.
- Week 15: Day 3 SDG session: Finalize vision, strategic stretch goals, and SWOTs; create strategy narrative.

Strategy Development Group   The SDG appointed by the board included:

- Pat, the interim CEO; Troy, the COO; Erin, the director of operations
- Kendra, the board chair; Elaine, the vice-chair of the board and the five other board members (Amber, Lauren, Samantha, Gale, and Don)
- Two residents of BRRHS housing, Dale and Joyce
- Representatives from the housing offices of two of the largest cities in the five county area, Allison and Cynthia
- Scott, vice president of Big River Regional Community Bank

Analysis of BRRHS Process Design   The only way that BRRHS is able to get as much done on its strategy this quickly and thoroughly is because they were able to retain one consulting firm to provide them with an interim and fulfill all of their consulting needs. Even with that, it is a very aggressive schedule. If Pat did not have a strong COO to run operations while the strategy process was going on, then there certainly would have been numerous operational breakdowns while the strategy process was implemented.

This process does not allow for widespread input from stakeholder groups via surveying of any kind. It will be difficult for the SDG to be sure how pervasive any of the comments from the interviews and focus groups are. But they saved money and time in not doing this.

One trade-off that this design makes is including all seven board members on the SDG. This is understandable, as with a board that size nobody wants to feel left out. However, it is not always advisable or necessary. By taking seven slots on the SDG, this only left eight spots for others— assuming that the organization wanted to keep the group to the size of 15. This limits the number of staff and clients that can participate. Perhaps more importantly, other community stakeholders are left with little representation. While having all seven members on the SDG guarantees approval of the plan, the same would be true for four or five members serving on the SDG.

The three full days of strategy sessions is enough for them to complete all of the steps, but they will be fast-paced days to get everything done well. They built in an opportunity to have some check-in time with stakeholders between the second and third day. This will give them an opportunity to check some of their assumptions and ideas with others.

Merrill County Literacy Council

The Right Time   Colleen had aspired to be a nonprofit CEO and felt it was a calling. While she loved the direct contact with clients and volunteers, she found herself musing about new and better ways the organization could be operated. She was a natural strategist.

With the board's support, Colleen took two swift actions in her first 30 days as CEO. First, she announced that they would not now fill the open director of programs position. The organization had run a deficit in the prior year and needed to stop the bleeding. They would all have to pitch in extra to support their programs.

Next, Colleen recommended an additional member to the board who was then approved. Colleen had met Donta' at Rotary when he was transferred to the community just weeks before she was appointed as CEO. He was the new president of the regional office of a major bank located in the community. A young, energetic African-American, he was being quickly promoted through the ranks of the bank since completing his Executive MBA at the Robert H. Smith School of Business at the University of Maryland.

Colleen knew that the organization needed a new strategy badly, but she also knew that the board was not functioning well. She had learned about the value of board self-assessment at a program sponsored by the local chapter of the Association of Fundraising Professionals. As she related her thoughts about the need for a self-assessment to Donta', he quickly offered for his bank to fund the project. Still in her honeymoon period, the board easily agreed to do the self-assessment. It was an eye-opening experience for the board as they realized they had not been carrying out many of their key responsibilities for years—including strategic planning.

Colleen and the founding board chair, Ellen, went to one of their long-time funders, the Merrill County Community Foundation, to tell their program officer of their recent insights and to ask for strategic planning funding. Impressed with the new spark she was seeing in an organization with an important mission, she agreed to a small grant to fund the strategy process and to serve as a member of the SDG. She provided a couple of names of potential facilitators for the process.

While Colleen knew that the organization was also deficient in the area of performance metrics, she felt this could be addressed during the strategy development process. The board appointed Ellen as chair of the SDG, along with Colleen and Donta' as assistant chairs. They set about selecting a facilitator and designing their strategy process.

Stakeholders

- Alumni, students, and potential students of MCLC programs
- Volunteer teachers, tutors, and child care providers
- Board members
- Staff
- Individual donors
- United Way of Merrill County
- Merrill County Community Foundation
- Corporate and governmental funders
- County and city government officials
- Merrill County Community College

- Merrill County School Districts
- Merrill County employers

Length and Scope

- Week 1: Ellen, Colleen, and Donta' contact two facilitators suggested by Community Foundation and choose one.
- Week 1: Colleen serves as coordinator of the process.
- Week 1: Ellen, Colleen, and Donta' design overall strategy development process.
- Week 1: Make lists of stakeholders and discuss ways in which they may be involved in process; discuss potential members of SDG.
- Week 2: Board appoints SDG; provides schedule of activities and meetings.
- Week 2: Staff meets to discuss process, time line, and how they will be involved.
- Weeks 2–4: Identify and collect external data that SDG may want to review, such as benchmarking programs of other literacy councils across nation.
- Weeks 2–4: Ellen, Colleen, and Donta' conduct individual interviews with key stakeholders: funders, company officers and HR managers, community leaders, individual donors.
- Week 3: Colleen surveys staff and board for SWOTs.
- Week 4: Town hall for program alumni and current students (child care provided).
- Week 5: Reports sent to SDG from Colleen, Ellen, Donta' on external data collected, SWOTs, synthesis on individual interviews, and town hall.
- Week 6: Day 1 and 2 SDG sessions, Friday and Saturday with no overnight stay: Report review on external data, individual interviews, town hall; review mission, set mission accomplishment measures and mission gap, set vision, set strategic stretch goals, select SWOTs, create strategy narrative.
- Week 7: SDG presents final report to board of directors.

Strategy Development Group   The SDG appointed by the board included:

- Colleen and Kristen, the longest serving of the program staffers
- Ellen, Donta', John, the assistant superintendent of schools; and Pam, volunteer tutor
- Paul, vice chair of board of United Way of Merrill County
- Mike, vice president of the Merrill County Chamber of Commerce
- Alice, director of human resources for Merrill County General Hospital
- Two volunteers, Janelle and Anne
- Two graduates, Kiersten and Roger
- Suzanne, program officer, Merrill County Community Foundation
- Keith, Vice President of Academic Affairs, Merrill County Community College

Analysis of MCLC Process Design   Approaching Donta' to join the board when he was just a new arrival in the community was a bold and strategic move on Colleen's part. She may or may not have been able to convince the rest of the board to do the self-assessment process without his support and funding. And the board may not have self-discovered the need to do a new strategy if they had not done the self-assessment. Had Colleen waited too long to approach Donta' he might have been scooped up by other nonprofit boards. Her move set in motion the right timing for the organization to address strategy.

The schedule that Ellen, Colleen, and Donta' created completes a strategy development process that is ready for presentation to a board in six weeks. If it seems rushed, that's because it is! But MCLC is operating under a number of constraints including a small staff and limited funding. During the six-week period, Colleen and other staff are spending so much time on the strategy process that operations may surely suffer. Perhaps some classes will have to be postponed or other activities put on hold. These six weeks will consume nearly all of Colleen's time—and require a significant investment of time from Ellen and Donta'.

Still, they do—at least minimally—work through each of the steps of the strategy development process, though they are sure to feel rushed at certain points. Their facilitator will have to assertively move the process along during their two-day session.

One downside of this process design is that the organization only had enough funding to retain a facilitator to come in for the two days of planning sessions, rather than have them involved in designing the overall process and overseeing it. This means that process design had to be done by Colleen, Ellen, and Donta'. We'll hope they got their hands on a good book on nonprofit strategy.

Another downside of this design is that Colleen did the collection of the SWOT analysis. This is not ideal, as respondents may not feel comfortable being totally candid if they cannot be assured that their responses are confidential. It may have been better for them to have spent a little additional money to hire someone outside the organization to collect and summarize the results.

It also would have been ideal if the SDG could have gotten away together for the weekend somewhere to focus on the strategy development process, rather than having to go home and come back the next morning. Again, funding was the issue here, but the quality of the discussions and decisions may have suffered without the ability to get away, immerse the SDG in the process, and focus together.

The SDG includes four of the six organization board members, so passage of the final recommendations created should be assured. By not including all six board members on the SDG this allowed some open spots to include other stakeholders while keeping the group to 15 members.

A positive sign for the future of this organization is the appointment of Donta' as the assistant chair for the SDG. The fact that the board was willing to embrace this young newcomer and that he agreed to take on the post will send a positive message to the community. It probably helped them recruit some leaders to the SDG who seem well positioned to help the organization move forward.

CHAPTER 3

Your Mission Impact

The first action item for the Strategy Development Group (SDG) to address is the review of the mission and its intended impact. By the conclusion of this step in the process, the SDG will make sure that the mission statement contains impact language, that mission accomplishment measures are set, and that its mission gap has been articulated. In subsequent steps, a vision, strategic stretch goals, and the new strategy will all be designed to close the mission gap as effectively as possible to maximize mission impact.

THE MISSION ACCOMPLISHMENT APPROACH

As discussed in Chapter 1, the perspective on nonprofit performance used in this book's strategy development process is the mission accomplishment approach. This approach says that the core purpose of a nonprofit is to carry out its mission—to make a difference for society. The extent to which it is accomplishing its mission is its level of performance. Organizations need to establish performance metrics that correspond to the intended impact of their mission in order to track their progress in accomplishing the mission. These metrics are called mission accomplishment measures—measures that serve as registers to indicate the level of mission accomplishment attained.

I first learned about the mission accomplishment approach when I was working on my PhD at Ohio State (Ford & Ford, 1990). By that time, I had already served one nonprofit as a CEO for nine years. The approach appealed to the practitioner in me. Of course, how else would you assess your performance but by the extent to which you are accomplishing your mission? Certainly, the idea of outcome-impact measures had been around for a while for assessing individual programs (e.g., Rossi & Freeman, 1985). But this was the first time I had heard about applying an impact approach at the organizational level.

I adopted the mission accomplishment approach for a research project at Ohio State called the *Excellence in Philanthropy Project,* which was the basis for my dissertation (1994) and later wrote an article on some of the findings (1996). I adopted the approach as a practitioner in the organization I served as CEO from 1992 to 2001 and have used it in my consulting, teaching, and research (Ford, Sheehan & Ford, 1994; Sheehan, 1999, 2005, 2009).

Since the early 1990s, many others have written about using similar approaches in organizations and/or discussed the importance of organizations using performance metrics that correspond to their missions.

For example, in a 1995 article entitled "Measuring What Matters in Nonprofits," John Sawhill, then CEO of the Nature Conservancy, and David Williamson, director of communications there, stated:

> Most nonprofit groups track their performance by metrics such as dollars raised, membership growth, number of visitors, people served and overhead costs. These metrics are certainly important, but they don't measure the real success of an organization in achieving its mission . . . . Our research on 20 leading nonprofit organizations in the United States—as well as our firsthand experience with one of them, the Nature Conservancy—shows that this problem is not as intractable as it may seem. Although nonprofits will never resemble businesses that can measure their success purely in economic terms, we have found several pragmatic approaches to quantifying success, even for nonprofit groups with highly ambitious and abstract goals. The exact metrics differ from organization to organization, but this thorny problem can be attacked systematically." (p. 1)

In a more recent example, The Bridgespan Group, a consulting firm, has reported using a similar approach. In a 2008 *Harvard Business Review* article ("Delivering on the Promise of Nonprofits"), Bradach, Tierney, and Stone state that more nonprofits are moving to a mission impact approach. They have found that a key question these organizations are asking themselves is "Which results will we hold ourselves accountable for?" (p. 90). The organizations then create a "strong intended-impact statement," which "identifies both the beneficiaries of a nonprofit's activities and the benefits the organization will provide. . . . " (p. 91).

The idea of utilizing metrics to assess mission accomplishment is growing and there are a variety of ways to implement the approach. In my view, the way to operationalize the mission accomplishment approach for an organization's practical use is to first review its mission statement, to next set its mission accomplishment measures, and finally to identify its mission gap. The following sections will explain the steps the SDG should go through to be prepared to use the mission accomplishment approach as its guide to strategy development.

THE MISSION STATEMENT

The first step of making the mission accomplishment approach of practical use to a nonprofit is to review its mission statement. The intent here is not to devote an inordinate amount of time into wordsmithing the mission statement, but to consider sharpening its stated impact and aim.

Impact and Aim

Getting the mission right is a key to success for nonprofits and for profits alike. Management guru Peter Drucker (1974, p. 75), suggests that:

> Only a clear definition of the mission and purpose of the business makes possible clear and realistic business objectives. It is the foundation for priorities, strategies, plans, and work assignments. It is the starting point for the design of managerial jobs and, above all, for the design of managerial structures.

Drucker elaborates on this point in his self-assessment tool for nonprofits (1999, p. 40):

> The results of social sector organizations are always measured *outside* the organization in changed lives and changed conditions—in people's behavior, circumstances, health, hopes, and above all, in their competence and capacity. To further the mission, each nonprofit needs to determine

what should be appraised and judged, then concentrate resources for results.

One way to think about a mission statement is that it is a stated intention to make a difference for a person, place, or thing. In fact, in *Boards That Make a Difference* (1990), John Carver suggests that stating this difference explicitly is a Board's number one responsibility.

So the first question for the SDG to ask in reviewing the mission is "Does our mission statement specify the difference we are committed to making in a person, place, or thing?"

In the *Excellence in Philanthropy Project,* referenced earlier, we reviewed more than 100 mission statements from a broad variety of nonprofits. To generalize, most of them were something like this fictitious example of the mission statement of the Charles County Homeless Services, Inc. organization:

> *To provide services to the Homeless in Charles County.*

Most of the mission statements we reviewed discussed the fact that the organizations were providing services. They were clearly intending to make a difference, but they did not specify what that difference was. One way to add impact specificity to this mission statement would be to change it to something like:

> *To provide services to the homeless in Charles County that enhance their economic self-sufficiency.*

It is important to note that this is not the "right" answer. Maybe the organization has a different intended impact in mind. Maybe they want to make sure that all people who are homeless have a safe, decent place to sleep every night. It is hard to tell from the first statement what their intention might be.

The next question for the SDG to ask itself is "Does our mission statement specify the persons, places, or things we aim to impact?"

In the preceding example, the organization seems clear on its aim— "homeless in Charles County." But is it? Does it only intend to operate in particular areas within Charles County? If so, it may consider changing its mission statement to be more specific. Many nonprofits are rather vague regarding the specific persons, places, or things they intend to impact.

Inspirational

Another aspect of a mission statement that is often mentioned as important is that it should be inspirational. While different people will have causes that inspire them differently—as well as different words that they find to be inspirational—there is an exercise that organizations can complete to see if they might make their mission statements more inspirational. Peter Senge provides some insight to this point when, in *The Fifth Discipline* (1990), he talks about the value to organizations and individuals in identifying their "ultimate intrinsic desires." While an organization may state an impact that it wants to make, this may or may not express its ultimate desire.

So the next question that the SDG can ask as it reviews its mission statement is "Does our mission statement express our ultimate intrinsic desire?"

Okay, that sounds a bit ethereal. Here's the way to think about it. Look at the impact, as per above, that the organization states it wants to make and let's use the Charles County example again. If we begin with the statement:

> *To provide services to the homeless in Charles County that enhance their economic self-sufficiency.*

then the first thing we want to look at are all of the ripple effects of making that impact. You can ask, "What additional impacts are we making?" or "What are we building with that?" or "Why do we want to do that?" For example, once we enhance the economic self-sufficiency of people who are homeless, here are some of the ripple impacts that may occur:

- Increase self-esteem of people who are homeless.
- Increase opportunities of people who are homeless to find a job.
- Increase the number of people who are homeless who find jobs.
- Increase the personal income of people who are homeless.
- Increase the number of people who were homeless but who now can afford safe, decent, housing.
- Decrease the number of people who are homeless.
- Significantly decrease the number of people who are homeless.
- Eliminate homelessness.
- Improve quality of life for all in our county.

And you see how the list could go on and on.

Once the SDG lists the ripple effects, then the questions for the SDG to ask itself are: "As we look at the list of ripple effects, what inspires us most? What will inspire our stakeholders most? What statement do we want to make to the world about why we are here? What do we want most?"

Again, there is no right or wrong answer here—organizations have to look at the list and choose the particular level of impact that they want to focus on. Regarding this specific example—when I read "eliminate home-lessness," I get chills. That would be a sign of an ultimate intrinsic desire. If the SDG for the Charles County Homeless Services organization felt the same way, then they might recommend changing the mission statement to:

> To end homelessness in Charles County.

The SDG should not spend an overabundance of time on this mission step. If an organization wants to more deeply consider these mission issues, then it may want to assign a task force to do the work prior to the beginning of the strategy development process. In addition to the preceding steps, some organizations will conduct focus groups of people who don't know anything about the organization to see if their mission statements communicate to those outside the organizations' influence. This can be helpful as often organizations, for example, fall into the trap of using jargon that may not communicate as well as they assume it does.

These actions in the mission review process set up the organization for the next two steps of establishing mission accomplishment measures and mission gap. But they are also valuable exercises on their own. By specifying impact and aim, a mission statement can communicate more effectively to potential donors, supporters, volunteers, funders, and other potential collaborators. Identifying the ripple effects can also be a very powerful thing to discuss with potential supporters as the organization identifies all of the far-reaching impacts that every dollar of support and every hour of volunteer time makes. Many times people who are not close to the organization are not aware of these important additional impacts or just don't think of them.

MISSION ACCOMPLISHMENT MEASURES

Having completed the preceding activities, the SDG is now ready to look at the organization's mission accomplishment measures. To recap briefly, the mission accomplishment approach states that the core purpose of a nonprofit is to carry out its mission—to make a difference for society. The extent to which it is accomplishing its mission is its level of performance. Therefore, organizations need to establish performance metrics that correspond to the intended impact of their mission: mission accomplishment measures. The measures serve as registers to indicate the level of mission accomplishment attained.

A good way to get started with this process is for each SDG member to write down his or her individual answer to the following question:

"Explain how you determine whether our organization is or is not accomplishing our mission. List any results, outcomes, and specific evidence you look at to make this determination."

We asked this same question of CEOs of nonprofits who participated in the *Excellence in Philanthropy Project* and then had research analysts review their responses at three levels. First, they analyzed each response to see if it was a "reliable measure." Then they reviewed each of those responses to see if it was also a "reliable impact measure." And a final step was to see if those measures represented an impact at the organization mission level.

A reliable measure collects evidence that could be confirmed by an objective observer. With the Charles County Homeless Services organization in mind, examples could include:

- Amount of dollars raised
- Number of program participants
- Number of new volunteers recruited
- Number of educational materials distributed
- Number of programs held
- Cost per participant

While all of these are reliable measures, none of them are reliable *impact* measures. Reliable impact measures are reliable measures that represent an impact—a difference made in the condition of a person, place, or thing. Again, with Charles County Homeless Services in mind, examples could include measures such as:

- Number of participants who complete a job-training program and secure a job for a year after attending the program

- Number of participants who complete a drug rehabilitation program and are "clean" for at least one year after completing the program

- Number of participants who complete a literacy program and demonstrate an ability to read, write, and do mathematics at a sixth-grade level

The final step is to see if these measures represent an impact simply at the program level or at the organization mission level. In the case of Charles County Homeless Services, we can see that it depends on how they decide to state their mission. If they left it as "increase economic self-sufficiency," then one could argue that each of the preceding measures is an indicator of that intention. However, if they stated their intention as impacting "the number of homeless people who attain their own safe, decent, affordable housing," then these measure would not be indicators at the mission level. They would need to use something like "Number of participants in programs who attain their own safe, decent, affordable housing." And, further, if they stated their intention as "ending homelessness," then they would need to use something like "the number of homeless people in Charles County, as reported by county officials." The measure used needs to match the intended mission impact.

In the *Excellence in Philanthropy Project,* mission data was analyzed and 13.86 percent of the organizations in the study listed results that were judged to be reliable impact measures at the mission level. The vast majority did not have mission accomplishment measures.

Another question in the research study asked the CEOs who answered the surveys if their senior staff and Board members also used the same criteria to judge mission performance as they—the CEOs—did. While 90.10 percent of the CEOs said "yes" other organization leaders use the same criteria to judge performance, follow-up surveys and interviews within these organizations found that "no" they do not. In none of the organizations that had mission accomplishment measures did even a majority of the senior staff and Board members report using the same criteria to judge performance.

Why is this important? An organization without widely agreed-upon mission accomplishment measures does not have a reliable way of knowing if it is accomplishing its mission. It will have a number of problems and challenges, some of which include:

- It will be unable to coordinate action toward producing its most important results. Different people will rely on their own opinions of the most important results. Imagine a football team on which each player has his own opinion of the direction of the goal line—it makes coordinating action difficult.

- Without knowing its results, it will not have a reliable basis on which to judge expanding, cutting, or eliminating certain programs or activities.

- It will make learning from mistakes and successes much more difficult.

- Since it cannot manage for results, it will be managing opinions—an all-too-often time-consuming, no-win situation.

- Resource allocation decisions will be based on opinions rather than reliable data.

- Increasingly, funders and donors at all levels want to see measurable results.

- Since the performance of the CEO is often linked to the performance of the organization, it makes CEO performance evaluation problematic.

When mission accomplishment measures are not used to judge performance, mischief and misinformation can be injected into organizational decision making. In this vacuum, individuals will attempt to assert their own criteria as the most important performance measures.

For example, many accounting professionals encourage nonprofits to keep their overhead or indirect costs low as a percentage of their overall expenses. While efficiency is worth considering when organization budgeting decisions are being made, there are some people who will assert that when a high percentage of an organization's expenses go toward direct program costs that this is evidence that it is fulfilling its mission. Obviously, given the preceding discussion, this is not true. It is simply evidence of an allocation of spending. Whether the spending of the allocated funds is producing mission impact is a totally different matter.

In the *Excellence in Philanthropy Project,* interviews were held with board members of some of the organizations who were part of the study. In response to the question, "How do you determine whether your organization is or is not accomplishing your mission?" one respondent, a judge, stated "Well, I get invited to a lot of cocktail parties and I ask people how they think we are doing. If they think we are doing well, then great. If they ever express concern, then I get concerned." Is the judge's positive response an indication that the mission is being accomplished or that the judge is attending a really, really good party?

At some point, without mission accomplishment measures, an organization may be relegated to asserting, as in Brian O'Connell's fictional *Our Organization* in *The Board Members Book* (1985), that "any organization made up of such bright people, who are so dedicated and who have worked so hard, must be doing a great deal of good" (p. 204).

Let's consider a hypothetical example to review some of these implications.

So What? Hypothetical Example of Mercer County Literacy Council

So what if an organization does not have mission accomplishment measures? Let's consider the following scenario.

We are using the fictitious organization, Merrill County Literacy Council, in this book to demonstrate some examples. Let's imagine that this organization's founding chair, Ellen, has a brother, Bob, who lives in another part of the country. One day Bob is very excited to learn that he has won the state lottery. He gave his dreams a chance and his ship has come in with $350 million in winnings. But before Bob and his wife head off to their new home in Bermuda to enjoy the glow of their retirement years, Bob acts on a passion he shares with his sister. He decides that he, too, should start a literacy council in his home area with a mission to end illiteracy there.

Bob hires an attorney to set the organization up. He recruits a top-notch board of directors for the new Mercer County Literacy Council and contributes $50 million into an endowed fund to get the organization up and rolling. The board hires a top-notch CEO, Judy, to launch the new organization. With confidence that the organization is going to do well and make a difference, Bob and his wife head to Bermuda. One year later, Bob returns to see how things are going.

BOB: "Hello there Judy, how are things going?"

JUDY: "Bob, good to see you, and things are going great here. The budget is balanced, the board is happy with what we are doing, we hired a highly qualified staff, and we are very popular in the community. Your gift has attracted lots of other donations and we are being featured next month in the *Chronicle of Philanthropy*."

BOB: "Good, are people learning how to read?"

JUDY: "Well, more than 300 people have participated in one of our programs, and another 500 are currently enrolled for future programs. We are growing! And the participants love the programs. It is heartwarming to see the smiles on their faces in the classes. Besides that, have I mentioned how efficient our programs are? We have a very low cost per person. And you will be proud to know that our organizational administrative costs are a small percentage of our overall expenses.

BOB: "Good, are people learning how to read? How many people have learned how to read and do essential math? Have we reduced illiteracy in this county?"

JUDY: "Well, Bob, that is difficult to say. But with the commitment level of our staff and all of the hard work we have put in, I'm sure we have made some kind of difference. And you would be so proud of our participants and our teachers—many of whom are dedicated volunteers. Why don't we drop in on a class this evening?"

So is this organization accomplishing its mission? There are certainly some positive things going on. But the fact is that they don't know if they are accomplishing their mission. They could be making a big difference, or maybe not. Without mission accomplishment measures, all they have to go on are their thoughts and feelings about their activities.

Well, so what?

In this case, obviously, they owe it to Bob to know. It is a stewardship responsibility to use his gift in a way to maximize the accomplishment of the mission. But don't they also owe it to the participants in their programs to know? And how about all of the volunteers? Are they spinning their wheels with all of the time they are putting in or are they making a difference? Wouldn't they like to know one way or the other? And the same goes for the staff. Actually, the organization owes it to itself to know if it is accomplishing the mission, and to what extent. If it is making significant progress, then everyone involved deserves some positive recognition for that. If it is not making as much of a difference as it would like, then it can reassess its programs and activities.

An organization needs to know if it is accomplishing its mission.

Designing Your Mission Accomplishment Measures

Perhaps your organization already has mission accomplishment measures. If so, then the SDG will want to review them either to make some improvements or to confirm that they are still relevant. If mission accomplishment measures do not exist, then the SDG will need to create them. As mentioned earlier, if it is anticipated early on in the design phase that this will be a lengthy process, then the board may want to appoint a task force to focus on this part of the process even before the SDG is engaged.

The process of creating the mission accomplishment measures is made easier once impact language is added to the mission statement, as discussed earlier in this chapter. The SDG will need to identify reliable measures that indicate a change in the condition of the persons, places, and/or things that the organization wants to impact.

This can be much more difficult for some organizations than for others. Organizations that have a single area of focus and a few programs may be able to identify a mission level indicator rather easily. In these cases, impact measures for programs may even serve as measures at the organizational level. Alternatively, organizations with multiple areas of focus will find this to be more complicated and may end up with a set of three to five mission accomplishment measures that capture the collective impact of a number of programs.

When organizations are just starting the process of identifying mission accomplishment measures, they should not try to be too perfect too quickly. You don't need immediate, iron-clad, scientific proof that you can present to your harshest critic to prove your results. At the beginning, you want to find some measures that you, as an SDG and board and staff, believe give you reliable data on the impact you are committed to making. It is likely to be a little rough at first. It is best to choose some reliable measure that gives you a good start and then let your work evolve over time.

In some cases, organizations find that reliable measures exist in data that they are already collecting or that governmental organizations collect. In many other cases, they find that they need to create instrumentation (e.g., surveys, questionnaires) for the measures.

Let's take the fictitious example of the charter school, Hillkirk Academy for Excellence, with a mission:

> *To prepare young people from low income families in the Hillkirk School District for excellence in postsecondary education.*

One mission accomplishment measure the Academy adopted was:

> *The percentage of students enrolled as ninth graders who graduate and enroll in a post-secondary institution.*

The SDG for the Academy thought this was a good start. But how would they know that they had prepared the students for "excellence"? As a simple next step, they decided to ask the students. So they added another measure:

> *Satisfaction of preparation survey scores of graduates two years following graduation.*

The Academy would now have to create the surveys and collect the data on a regular basis to see how well they were doing. This is a good start. Imagine if many students reported that they found themselves to be not nearly as well prepared for postsecondary work than their peers. Now that would be an important for the Academy to know, since they are committed to excellence. Alternatively, maybe they find out that they are preparing the students very well.

Do these two measures prove that the Academy is preparing their students for excellence, and should they add other measures? No, it does not prove that these students are prepared for excellence. And yes, they may consider adding other measures. But what they are measuring now can be helpful and they can consider doing more later. Perhaps they add another survey once students are four years out of the Academy. Or, to get beyond self-reported data, they survey or even conduct telephone interviews with faculty of their students. Maybe they consider focus groups of graduates at some point. You can see how quickly the process of creating measures and collecting data can get complex and expensive. This is why it is most important for the data to satisfy the organization that they are making the impact they intend to make—not to provide irrefutable proof to outsiders.

Of course, funders may ask for better data—either at the program level or organizational level—that an impact is being made. In this case it is fully appropriate for the organization to ask funders to assist in funding this type of research. When I was CEO of LeaderShape, Inc. (1992–2001), the W. K. Kellogg Foundation was interested in assessing the impact of their funding of the leadership development program for young adults we were running. We worked with them to design an extensive project, which was conducted by external researchers and fully funded by Kellogg. The research resulted in the LeaderShape program's being named as an "exemplary program" by the Foundation.

Organizations with complex programs will likely need to retain subject matter experts to design measures and/or collect data. Again, this will require organizations to balance their need to reliably measure their impact with the cost necessary to collect this data. The good news for nonprofits these days is that the interest in collecting impact data has increased especially during the past 15 years due to the efforts of many foundations, and other organizations such as Grantmakers for Effective Organizations and United Way of America. Due to this interest, many more consultants and researchers now exist who specialize in this type of work, especially within graduate programs for nonprofit management, which have proliferated in recent years. Many resources exist to assist nonprofits with the design of their mission accomplishment measures.

Mission accomplishment measures provide organizations with the foundation for coherent and coordinated action of all of their functions. The value of having the measures goes far beyond strategy. They inform all actions of the organization.

One of the organizations studied in the *Excellence in Philanthropy Project* was the Central Ohio office of Mothers Against Drunk Driving (MADD). MADD's mission statement, as reported in their 2006–2007 Annual Report, is "to stop drunk driving, support victims of this violent crime, and stop underage drinking." One of the questions I asked every staff member and board member I interviewed there was, "Explain how you determine whether our organization is or is not accomplishing our mission. List any results, outcomes, and specific evidence you look at to make this determination." Each person quickly responded, as if speaking from a script, "The reduction of deaths from alcohol-impaired traffic crashes." Talk about a team who understands exactly where the goal line is! In the course of these interviews, it was clear that everything this organization was doing or considered doing had to pass the litmus test—how it was going to help eliminate drunk driving and deaths from alcohol impaired traffic crashes. I would assert that the single-minded, laser focus of this organization on that mission accomplishment measure is one key reason the United States has seen a reduction in deaths from drunk driving crashes, from 26,173 in 1982 to 12,998 in 2007. And if you have the opportunity to meet people associated with this organization, it will become quickly clear to you that they will not rest until that number is zero.

With the importance of mission accomplishment measures in mind, let's imagine how our earlier hypothetical example might have played out if the organization had mission accomplishment measures.

So What? Hypothetical Example of Mercer County Literacy Council—Revisited

Same scenario: Bob wins the lottery, starts the organization, recruits the board, makes the donation, and they hire Judy. But this time, before heading off to Bermuda, Bob makes sure that the board and Judy establish mission accomplishment measures. And now Bob returns one year later to see how things are going.

BOB: "Hello there, Judy, how are things going?"

JUDY: "Bob, good to see you, and things are going great here. The budget is balanced, the board is happy with what we are doing, we hired a highly qualified staff, and we are very popular in the community. Your gift has attracted lots of other donations and we are being featured next month in the *Chronicle of Philanthropy*."

BOB: "Good, are people learning how to read?"

JUDY: "Well, some are. We had more than 400 people sign up for our 16-week, three-nights-a-week course. But we only had the resources to fit 200 of them into the course. Those 200 all showed improvement in their reading and math, with 80 percent of them reaching the minimum sixth-grade level we were shooting for.

BOB: "That's impressive. What happened to the 200 people you couldn't fit into the course?"

JUDY: "That's our current challenge. We didn't want to turn them away, so we put together enough resources for a four-week, two-nights-a-week course for them."

BOB: "How did that work?"

JUDY: "It didn't. There was very little improvement in their reading and math skills, and only 5 percent got to the sixth-grade level."

BOB: "Sounds like the longer program is the way to go."

JUDY: "Right. Even though it is more expensive, it is producing the results we are committed to. So the board and staff are working on a new fundraising initiative to generate the resources for the expanded program."

BOB: "Well, Judy, I sure am impressed with what you are doing. And, you know, a person can only drink so many dirty martinis. You can tell the board that I'll match every dollar contributed to your new campaign $50 to $1 to a maximum gift of $5 million more to the endowment. That should motivate some new gifts quickly. We would hate to have people waiting on that new program. Keep up the good work."

It could happen.

YOUR MISSION GAP

The creation of mission accomplishment measures allows an SDG to identify the organization's mission gap. *Mission gap* is a term I created (2005) and have used with organizations in my consulting and teaching. The first step in identifying a mission gap is to use mission accomplishment measures to articulate the current state of the persons, places, and/or things for whom/which the organization wants to make a difference. Next, the SDG would choose what their/its condition would be in an ideal world. The difference between the current reality and the ideal is the organization's mission gap—the gap the organization is committed to closing. The driver of strategy becomes the commitment to closing the Mission Gap as effectively as possible.

As an example, let's look at the recent example of MADD.

- *Current condition:* 12,998 deaths from alcohol-impaired traffic crashes
- *Ideal condition:* Zero deaths from alcohol-impaired traffic crashes
- *Mission gap:* 12,998 deaths

Some people find the identification of the mission gap to be unsettling. "Wouldn't it feel better to focus on successes and progress, rather than this mission gap?" Yes, it would feel better, and it is important to acknowledge successes from the past—as in this case the reduction in deaths from alcohol-impaired crashes over the years. However, crafting strategy is about pointing the organization in a future direction. So, while there is an important time and place to celebrate progress from the past, there is also the time and place to look to the future. Organizations committed to accomplishing their missions use their mission gap as an important step in this process.

Admittedly, focusing on the mission gap can be emotionally troubling. Some mission gaps are so huge they are more like mission "chasms." This is an indicator of some of the very difficult social situations in which many people live today. As people committed to making a difference in the quality of life for others, it is our challenge—in the nonprofit world—to channel our emotional energy into designing more creative ways to close these gaps as effectively as we can.

It's not your fault you have a mission gap!

Of course you have a mission gap. You didn't create the conditions that caused it. Your organization was founded to close the gap. And, maybe, while you are working tirelessly to close the gap, other forces in the external environment are at work to widen it. In fact, for some organizations, the focus is to first slow down the widening of the gap before it can begin closing it.

So it is not your fault that you have a mission gap, but you have chosen it as your challenge. This is why you want to work to invent a new breakthrough strategy that will help you close the gap as effectively as possible.

The important role of the mission gap for creating strategy will be discussed in future chapters. But it can be a helpful concept to utilize in other arenas of the organization's operations as well. Many people are simply unaware of the current magnitude of many of our social problems, which have been around for a long time. And they can become somewhat complacent about it, for example, "Haven't we been working on that poverty thing for a while?" The stark identification and explanation of a mission gap can, for example, help create more of a sense of urgency among potential funders, donors, and potential volunteers.

APPLICATION TO HYPOTHETICAL ORGANIZATIONS

Following are examples of how the hypothetical organizations have applied the ideas presented on mission statement review, mission accomplishment measures, and mission gap. Some representative dialogue is presented here—and in future chapters—to provide some insights into how the process might unfold. The complete dialogue on these matters would, of course, take much longer in each situation.

Large City Metro Food Bank

Mission Statement   As mentioned in the prior chapter, a task force of staff, board members, and other stakeholders was appointed to do the mission review work prior to the initiation of the strategy development process. Their full report and recommendations were made directly to the LCMFB board of directors. The approved report was then provided to the SDG for their use in strategy development.

When the task force was assembled, the mission statement of LCFMB was:

> *To obtain and distribute food through a network of providers.*

The task force thought the mission statement was fine, but decided it would be improved by putting the direct impact up front by saying "To feed those who suffer from hunger" and then talking about the collection and distribution of food. It was also suggested that they add some specifics about their distribution channels so people would understand how widespread their impact is.

The task force then discussed the ripple effects of its various services. It listed:

- Shelters, pantries, churches, and others who provide meals have food to distribute.
- People who go to these places have at least one healthy meal that day.
- More people who need a meal hear about the meals that are available.
- As more meals are provided, fewer people in the metropolitan area go hungry for a day.
- Ultimately, no one needs to go hungry for even a day.
- Children who are well fed do better in school.
- Adults who are well fed do better at work.
- The quality of life in the community is enhanced.

The task force discussed all of the various ripple impacts they make in the community by providing their services. And while they realized that their impact was far reaching, they were most interested in those immediate needs that they were meeting. "We are focusing on the emergency needs of people who are hungry and need a meal," said Bev, the director of programs, "We want them to be able to change their life in a way that they don't need a meal, but we serve an immediate need. That's our role in the spectrum of services within the community. And we want everyone who is hungry to have food."

With all of these discussions in mind, the mission statement was updated and proposed to the board of directors, which approved it.

> To feed those who suffer from hunger in the Large City Metro Area by obtaining food and distributing it through a network of providers including food pantries, soup kitchens, shelters, after-school programs, and senior housing sites.

Mission Accomplishment Measures   Tim knew of some pioneering work being done in the area of mission accomplishment measures at the North Texas Food Bank and he suggested that some of the task force schedule a site visit there. The focus from the mission statement conversation helped the task force quickly identify that they would need a measure on how many emergency meals people in the area needed and how many they were getting. Hugh, a university professor and board member, was a co-chair of the task force and reported to the SDG:

"Our mission is to feed people who are hungry. So we needed to figure out the gap—how many meals people needed that they were not getting.

The people at the North Texas Food Bank have developed a model for determining this that looks at food provided by a variety of sources and then can state what the hunger gap or meal gap is for a community. It is a robust model that we found to be well thought out and applicable to our situation. So, with some minor modifications we have adopted it. Our mission accomplishment measure is:

> The number of meals reaching people living in poverty in the Large City Metro area compared to (divided by) the number of meals they need.

Mission Gap   The mission gap for LCFMB then looked like this:

- *Current condition:* Forty million emergency meals are needed by people in the Large City Metro Area annually and 13 million meals are reaching them.
- *Ideal condition:* Everyone in the Large City Metro area has access to emergency food when they need it.
- *Mission gap:* Twenty-seven million meals per year.

Big River Regional Housing Services

Mission Statement   Just as soon as Tom, the consultant, had finished briefing the SDG on the work they were about to do on the mission, three or four people nearly shouted out at once "We have to improve our geographic aim!" "Well, I guess that has been stewing for a while," Tom thought.

When the process started, the mission statement of BRRHS was:

> To enhance the quality of life of our communities by providing housing services.

Additional comments from members of the SDG made it clear that the organization's name and general mission statement had created confusion among many people about the reach of the organization's service area. "It sounds like you are saying we should either change the name or list the counties we serve in the mission statement," observed Kendra. "Even as a newcomer to this community, I can tell you I have heard a number of comments about this," said Pat. "The Big River is so big that it is not easy to tell where our coverage area stops and starts."

While everyone on the SDG seemed to agree with the comments being made, there was not a lot of enthusiasm with changing the name of the organization.

"Why don't we list the name of the counties in the mission statement and keep the name the same," said Kendra. "If we ever expand our coverage area we can just add county names to the mission statement. That's easier than changing the name of the organization." Everyone seemed to agree.

"It looks like we also need to improve our impact language," said Troy, the COO. "We just say we are going to provide services."

"We want everyone to have good housing," said Lauren, one of the Board members. "That's the point of everything we do, right?"

"I think that's right," said Erin, the director of operations. "We want people to have housing that is safe, decent, and affordable."

"In the mission statement, do we have to say that our efforts are focused on people of low and moderate incomes?" asked Allison, one of the representatives from a city housing office.

"Not necessarily," said Tom. "You could say in the mission statement that you want everyone in the region—or in the counties you want to list—to have safe, decent, affordable housing. When it comes time to design the mission accomplishment measures, then income levels may come into play."

"It sounds like we are coming to some agreements here, let's make a list of those ripple effects that Tom mentioned and see if that tells us anything," suggested Kendra. "If, as a result of our activities, people have safe, decent and affordable housing, then what are the ripple effects from that?" Following is the list that the group came up with:

- Individuals and families living in the housing will have more safe and healthy lives.
- Individuals and families will have more disposable income.
- Increased savings rates for individuals and region.
- Improved economy for the region.
- New homeowners will be more effective citizens.
- Individuals and families in housing will have a higher quality of life.
- Overall quality of life of people in the region will improve.

After discussion of these various ripple effects, the SDG decided upon the following new mission statement:

> *To ensure that all citizens within the Big River Region (currently defined as Franklin, Yates, Thompson, Mercer, and Allegheny Counties) have access to safe, affordable, and decent housing.*

Mission Accomplishment Measures   When the board reconvened it directed its attention toward the design of measures that would capture the extent to which it is accomplishing its mission.

"I have some ideas to get us started here," said Pat. "In the transition memo that Jeff left for me, he said that he had mentioned the possibility to some of you of BRRHS using Success Measures®. Have you all discussed that recently?"

"It sounds familiar. But please refresh our memories on Success Measures, Pat," asked Kendra.

"Great," said Pat. "I have had some experiences with this at other organizations. Success Measures is a social enterprise operated by Neighbor-Works® America that provides outcome evaluation tools for community development organizations. They have a wide range of tools, many of which relate directly to our mission. For example, they have a set of measures for housing affordability, another for housing quality, and yet another for safety. The measures have been tested and refined during the past decade to help community-based organizations gauge the impact of our work in a systematic, credible, and practical way."

"Sounds interesting," said, Elaine, the board vice chair. "Tell us more about how it would work exactly."

"We would want to do baseline assessments first," replied Pat. "Then, for each measure we would want to set our goals based on that initial data. For example, we may decide to follow HUD guidelines for affordability or set our own even higher standards. And for the economic impact, we would only do that again after we put new units in service."

"That sounds like it is exactly what we need and we don't have to reinvent the wheel," said Elaine. "Is it expensive?"

"I can get the exact costs for us," replied Pat. "But if we want to start out with just the three tools I mentioned, then it can definitely fit our budget for this coming year and we can get a baseline. Then we could update the

reports every 18 months or so to track changes. And we can consider adding measures if we want to track other outcomes."

"It sounds like it will take a lot of staff time, Pat," said Amber, a board
member. "We wouldn't want this to be a burden on them."

"It's a great point and I am sure everyone agrees," replied Pat. "My experiences have been that it is not onerous for staff; it takes some time but is
well worth it."

"That pretty much closes the deal for me," said Scott, the vice president
of Big River Community Bank. "I am all about leveraging resources. I
propose that we set our mission accomplishment measure as:

> *Percentage of households within the Big River Region (currently defined as Frank-
> lin, Yates, Thompson, Mercer, and Allegheny Counties) which meet the stan-
> dards we set for affordability, quality, and safety using the Success Measures
> surveys.*

"How does the rest of the group feel about that?" asked Tom. All heads
nodded and Tom added "Okay, I will tell you that I am familiar with Success Measures® as well, and I think you will be pleased with your
decision."

Mission Gap   "One question, though," asked Scott. "When we do this
baseline, does anyone have any idea how many households are going to fall
below our standard of affordability, quality, and safety?"

"Well," said Pat, "the records I have been going through indicate that
there are approximately 250,000 households in the five counties we serve.
What percentage of those would you all estimate don't have safe, decent,
affordable housing—according to the definitions we are using?"

"We have good documentation on that through the Regional Planning
Commission," said Troy. "I attended a number of meetings when they were
doing the work on this. We have about 80,000 households who do not
have what we would consider to be safe, decent, affordable housing."

"That's the number I remember," said Allison.

"You mean to tell me that there are 80,000 households in this region
that do not have safe, decent, affordable housing?" said Scott. "That is
unbelievable!"

"Yep," said Troy, "that's what we're saying."

"I had no idea it was that many," said Scott, "I mean I knew housing was an issue, but 80,000 households . . . that's just huge."

"That's a mission gap," said Tom.

"Scott," said Kendra. "we're glad you're here to work with us on a strategy to fill that gap."

"If everyone is comfortable with these estimates, then we can use them as a working draft of our mission gap and perhaps Allison and Troy can work together between now and the next meeting to get more specifics," suggested Tom.

Allison, Troy, and the SDG agreed. The draft mission gap for BRRHS then looked like this:

- *Current condition:* 80,000 of 250,000 households have housing that is not safe, decent, and affordable.

- *Ideal condition:* All households in our region have housing that is safe, decent, and affordable.

- *Mission gap:* 80,000 households.

Merrill County Literacy Council

Mission Statement   As indicated earlier, the mission statement of the Merrill County Literacy Council is:

To provide literacy educational services to citizens in Merrill County.

Under the guidance of their facilitator, Mark, the MCLC Strategy Development Group reviewed this mission statement using the guidelines outlined earlier in this chapter. They first realized that they could sharpen the aim language in the statement as their focus is on adults, sixteen years of age and older—not all citizens in Merrill County. But they did confirm that they wanted to target the entire county—not just specific neighborhoods.

Next the SDG looked at its impact language and noted that this was lacking. The intent of their services was to assist adults to become literate. So, it updated the statement to read:

To provide literacy educational services to adults age sixteen or older in Merrill County which result in them becoming literate.

Then they took the final step of identifying the various ripple effects that this mission impact would make:

- Graduates would get jobs or better jobs.
- Families of graduates would have an improved quality of life.
- Graduates and their families would need fewer government subsidies.
- Organizations in the county would have a more effective workforce.
- County economy would be more robust.
- State and national economy would improve.
- Fewer people would be illiterate.
- Fewer and fewer people would be illiterate.
- All people in the county would be literate.

After reviewing their list, Mark asked the group which of the impacts were most meaningful for them.

Mike, from the Chamber of Commerce, suggested, "Maybe we should restate the mission is to say we are here to improve the economy of the county. We certainly make that impact."

Donta' responded, "I'm so glad that we are taking time to discuss mission, as that is the key to our success, but I'm not sure that's it, Mike."

Then Janelle, one of the volunteer tutors, spoke up. "I have worked as a volunteer with these people for years and it breaks my heart that anyone in this county can't read to their children or grandchildren or not to be able to figure out their bill at the grocery store or to be unable to figure out what bus to take. I want everyone in the county to be literate."

After a few moments of silence, Donta' looked around the room and said, "Okay then, I suggest we restate our mission as":

> The mission of Merrill County Literacy Council is to assure that all adults age sixteen or older in Merrill County are literate.

And there was unanimous agreement.

Mission Accomplishment Measures   The new mission statement set MCLC up nicely for the creation of its mission accomplishment measures. Colleen informed the SDG that, annually, a National Assessment of Adult Literacy was conducted through the U.S. Department of Education and that the MCLC could obtain county specific estimates from the assessment. While somewhat rough, as it relies on sampling various households, the data could provide an indicator of literacy in the county. Colleen explained that people who were judged to be at Level 3 literacy would typically be considered literate for their purposes.

"I would love to have more detailed and reliable data," said Suzanne, from the Community Foundation. "but I just don't think that we could justify the expense."

"This sounds like a good start to me," said Ellen, "But, Keith, going forward, why don't we talk with some of the faculty in your social work department who might be willing to create some student projects around collecting better data for us?"

"Great idea, Ellen" said Keith. "I was thinking the same thing myself and I agree. Let's use the NAAL data for now and see if we can augment it inexpensively in the future."

And so the SDG adopted the following mission accomplishment measure:

> The percentage of adults in Merrill County, age sixteen and older, who are literate as measured by the NAAL survey.

Mission Gap   The newly clarified mission statement and the new mission accomplishment measure gave the SDG clear direction on their next steps. "We're going to need to know the number of adults, sixteen and over, who live in the county," said Mike. "Our folks over at the Chamber have that data from the census reports. I'll make a quick call over there." "And while you are doing that," said Colleen. "I'll look up the county data from the latest NAAL report."

The group had their data pretty quickly. There were an estimated 100,000 adults of age sixteen or older in the county and the NAAL data estimated that 20 percent were assessed at below Level 3 literacy.

"Now it's a just a simple math problem to calculate the gap," said Ellen.

"Right," said Janelle. "A simple math problem that 20,000 people in this county probably can't solve."

That sobering reality sunk in with the group for a few moments and then Donta' broke the silence. "Okay, 20,000 people. We have our work cut out for us. Let's remember our mission and get to work on the next step—creating a vision of an organization that can serve those 20,000 people and eliminate illiteracy in this area. Let's get it going! We want people to be able to read to those grand-babies and figure their grocery bills."

The mission gap for MCLC then looked like this:

- *Current condition:* Twenty percent of 100,000 adults age 16 and older in Merrill County are not literate at NAAL Level 3.
- *Ideal condition:* All adults age 16 and older are literate at NAAL Level 3 or higher.
- *Mission gap:* 20,000 adults, age 16 and older.

A Note about Examples

The issues discussed in the hypothetical organizations are real, and they are complex. By providing the scenarios above on how these organizations have determined they will judge their mission accomplishment, I am in no way saying that this is way that all organizations of these types should be doing so. The most important point is that the boards, staff, and other stakeholders of these organizations should engage in a conversation with one another about the metrics they think are most appropriate for them. They should make their choice and then communicate it so they may co-ordinate action within their organizations.

The North Texas Food Bank example discussed earlier in the chapter is real and, from my discussions with people there, they are finding this to be very helpful in guiding the performance of their organization (see Figure 3.1 for their meal gap logo). But their hunger/meal gap method is not the one that every food bank *should* use. Different food banks across the

FIGURE 3.1   North Texas Food Bank Meal Gap Logo

country are exploring their own methods of determining mission accomplishment.

The Success Measures mentioned above are real and are used extensively in community development organizations. They have a wide variety of measures that organizations and communities can use. But again, I am not suggesting that they are the *right* answer.

And finally, the NAAL data is also real but may not provide the type of information that a literacy council would want to use to determine mission accomplishment.

Most important is for organizations to discuss these matters and come to an agreement within the organization on how they will judge their mission performance. Without a reliable, agreed-upon measure, they will not know if they are making a difference.

CHAPTER 4

Vision for Your Organization

The next step in the process is for the strategy development group (SDG) to set a vision for the organization. With their mission gap in mind, the SDG is asked to create a future picture of what their organization would be like if it was ideally designed to fill the mission gap as effectively as possible. An inspiring, aspirational vision of the organization provides focus and momentum for strategy development.

WHAT IS VISION?

Vision is a term that is frequently used in organizations and in strategy development efforts. However, exact definitions vary. A simple way to think about a vision is that it is a "future picture."

The concept of a vision can be applied in a wide variety of ways. An individual can use the concept to create a future picture of the kind of career they want or the type of home they want to live in, for example. Or citizens in a city can use the concept to create a future picture of what they want their community to be like.

During the process of identifying a mission gap, discussed in the prior chapter, the SDG is asked to identify the ideal condition of the people, places, and/or things that they intend to impact. When they do this they are creating a future picture of those people, places, and/or things under ideal conditions. In fact, in their book on strategic planning, Allison and Kaye call this an "external vision"—"how the world will be improved if the organization achieves its purpose" (2005, p. 101).

In this chapter, we are applying the concept of vision at the organization level. With their mission gap in mind, the SDG is asked to create a future picture of what their *organization* would be like if it was ideally designed to fill the mission gap as effectively as possible.

The specific question they are asked to answer is:

With your *current environment* in mind—including your "mission gap"— think about how you could make "quantum leap" progress on your "mission gap" if your organization existed in an "ideal state." Answer the question:

"If you could have it any way you wanted it, what would your organization be like? Describe it in detail."

It is important for the SDG to keep the current environment in mind when they do this exercise. We aren't making the mission gap or the problems in the external environment go away in this exercise. We are dreaming up what the ideal organization would be like so that it can close that mission gap as effectively as possible in the current environment. I have had people say "Here is my vision—homelessness no longer exists and therefore my vision for the organization is that we are out of business!" That's not the exercise here. The exercise is to create the ideal organization that could most effectively close the homelessness mission gap—in that example—and eventually close the gap all the way.

As the SDG takes on this exercise, it is encouraged to use an aspirational mind-set in creating the vision.

ASPIRATIONAL VISIONS

There are two distinctly different mind-sets, or mental models, from which one can create a vision. One is an analytical mind-set and the other is the aspirational mind-set.

In the analytical mind-set, a vision is a future predictable picture.

In the aspirational mind-set a vision, is a future ideal picture.

Most visions in organizations are created using the analytical mind-set. Organizations study their current situation and the environment and then try to figure out their "best case scenario" for the future. Specifically, they:

- Analyze their internal capabilities and predictable changes to those capabilities.

- Analyze the external environment and predictable changes there.
- Forecast a reasonable, predictable future.
- Establish vision as best case scenario.

This should sound familiar, as it is the process used most commonly in organizations. For example, Nutt and Backoff (1992) suggest that strategic planning should include a description of the organization's future that is "extrapolated" from its current reality as a "projection" into the future, based on the constraints of the environment and the organization's SWOTs. They suggest that the constraints provide a lens through which an organization can foresee its future.

The aspirational mind-set is quite the opposite of the analytical mind-set. The aspirational approach begins not with analysis, but with dreams. The process looks like this:

- Dream of possibilities with no constraints.
- Create an ideal future picture, based on inspiration, passion, and commitment to the mission.
- Create new internal capabilities.
- Search the environment for opportunity.

The intent of the aspirational approach is to lead organizations toward transformational changes—to create breakthrough improvements in performance. The analytical approach is not "incorrect," and—as suggested earlier—is used quite commonly in organizations. However, the analytical approach will not lead an organization toward transformational improvements. Since the intent of this book is to lead organizations toward creating breakthrough strategy, the aspirational approach is a better fit for this strategy development process. Once an organization identifies a massive mission gap, it is acutely aware of the need for a new breakthrough strategy.

But why base a vision on a dream that may seem impossible to achieve?

When I served LeaderShape, Inc., as CEO (1992–2001) I learned that our founding board chair had a favorite saying: "Great leaders have a healthy disregard for the impossible." We thought this was such a great quote that it was added to the curriculum for our leadership program for college-age students. After all, how do any of us know what is really possible or impossible?

Any of us can think of things that have happened in our lifetimes that people once said was impossible: space travel, running a sub-four-minute mile in track, cellular phone technology, personal computers, the fall of the Berlin Wall, President Nelson Mandela (remember when we hoped that he would maybe get out of prison before he died; but president of apartheid South Africa?). These things would never have happened if someone had not first dreamed about them as a possibility.

While the "I Have a Dream" speech by Dr. Martin Luther King Jr. has been roundly celebrated, there are others who criticized it as being unrealistic. This is because it was a *future ideal picture*, not a prediction. And while we still have far to go to achieve Dr. King's dream, progress has been made—too slowly, but there has been progress. Just a few years ago, many people would have said that electing an African-American president of the United States of America in 2008 was impossible. Dr. King's vision established a future ideal picture of America toward which we can all aspire.

Many people resist the idea of creating an aspirational vision. "We're afraid that if we do that we will disempower the staff, board, donors, and other stakeholders when we don't achieve it."

This is an important issue to manage in how the vision is communicated. It needs to be clear that the vision is an ideal, a dream. It may or may not come into reality—but it is worth working toward to try to make that happen. And the time frame could be a long one. Dr. King did not say "I have a promise for you about what we are going to achieve in the next 5 to 10 years." It was a dream.

The first step in the aspirational visioning process is to freely dream about the ideal future. In an SDG, it is often good to let people do this on their own in silence first, and then do group brainstorming to take the dreams and turn them into a specific future ideal picture.

One small caveat here. When the SDG creates its vision, it should invoke a "no science fiction" rule. The main office should not be located on Mars, telepathy should not be the way the staff communicates, and the volunteers cannot sprout wings to fly out to where people need assistance following a recent natural disaster. You want to have a healthy disregard for the impossible without the surrealism.

Two concepts related to aspirational visioning that are used in corporate America, though not so often in nonprofits, are Idealized Design and Strategic Intent.

Idealized Design

Dr. Russell Ackoff has been a pioneer in applying the concept of systems thinking to organizations for more than 50 years. He is professor emeritus at the Wharton School at the University of Pennsylvania. The university has established the Ackoff Collaboratory for the Advancement of the Systems Approach there. Dr. Ackoff has consulted with a wide variety of corporate, government, and nonprofit entities across the globe during his illustrious career. The following summary of his approach to Systems Thinking and Idealized Design are taken from his books *Re-Creating the Corporation* (1999) and *Idealized Design* (2006) as well as numerous seminars I have had the opportunity to hear him teach during the past five years.

Systems Thinking seeks to understand organizations as whole systems, rather than viewing them from more narrow perspectives. This is valuable because it gives us a deeper understanding and appreciation of the complexities of organizations. To understand an organization, one must understand the system of which that organization is a part, as well as the parts of the organization itself. As briefly mentioned in Chapter 1, a central tenet of Systems Thinking is that: "A system's performance is the product of the interactions of its parts" (p. 33) rather than the sum of the performance of the parts or "how they act taken separately" (1999, p. 9).

Systems Thinking alters the way we think about organizations and solving the problems we perceive within them. Dr. Ackoff suggests that "problems should be viewed from as many different perspectives as possible before a way of treating them is selected" (p. 18). And he goes on to point out: "It is not uncommon for problems to be best solved in domains other than the one in which they were first identified. Headaches are a simple example. They are not usually treated by performing brain surgery, but by putting a pill in the stomach. Understanding the way the parts of a system interact enables one to find a better place to enter the system" (1999, p. 16).

Most problems are actually systems of problems with strong, complex interactions among their parts. Dr. Ackoff aptly calls these systems of problems "messes."

When applying the ideas of Systems Thinking to an organization's overall performance we can see that we are presented with a complex challenge. Rather than trying to solve, resolve, fix, or tinker with the "messes" within an organization to improve it, Dr. Ackoff recommends that it be completely redesigned for optimal performance. He calls this process Idealized Design.

Dr. Ackoff's first experience with Idealized Design was in 1951, when he was coincidentally able to sit in on a meeting at Bell Labs where a vice president declared to other leaders within the organization that "the telephone system of the United States was destroyed last night." The vice president went on to challenge the group to design a new telephone system with which they would replace the one that had been destroyed the night before. It was a dramatic way to get the group's attention, but it worked. From that initial meeting, various work groups generated ideas that have resulted in many of the telephone advances we have seen in the past 50 years including touch-tone, speaker phones, call waiting, voice mail, caller ID, and more.

With this initial experience as his benchmark, Dr. Ackoff describes Idealized Design as a process in which the designers assume the organization being planned for was completely destroyed last night, but its environment remains exactly as it was. Then they try to design an organization to replace the existing organization right now, if they were free to replace it with any organization they wanted.

While extensive Idealized Design work has been done with corporations, two nonprofit examples of Idealized Design successes include the Academy of Vocal Arts and Community Home Health Services, both of Philadelphia. At the Academy of Vocal Arts:

> Board members were completely sold on the exciting possibilities the design presented, and their energy was evident to foundations and other potential providers of funds. The school not only increased the number of funded programs, but also was able to double its endowment. (2006, p. 91)

At the Community Home Health Care, a provider of nursing services in homes, the results included (2006, p. 95):

- Earned income doubled
- Went from negative to positive cash flow
- Operating and equipment funds increased significantly

- Salaries and employee benefits increased
- Overhead decreased
- Attrition rates and absenteeism significantly decreased

The aspirational visioning aspects of the Idealized Design process are so powerful that they have even been able to impact governmental bureaucratic processes—including those at the White House.

Appointed as director of the Office of Process Improvement for the White House Communications Agency in 1992, Dr. Gerald Suàrez had worked to make improvements to the organization. While these incremental improvements were helpful, the agency realized it needed a total organizational redesign. Dr. Ackoff and his colleagues were engaged to facilitate an Idealized Design process. By the conclusion of the process, the agency had dramatically improved efficiencies, reduced bureaucracy and hierarchy, and more fully engaged the staff.

Reflecting on this experience, more than ten years later, Dr. Suàrez—now the Associate Dean for External Strategy at the Robert H. Smith School of Business at the University of Maryland, College Park, remarks:

> You are referencing the story about this that is in Russ's book, but there is another article about it as well entitled "Transformation and Redesign at the White House Communications Agency," (1999) and that is what this was—a transformation. You know that for a number of years I had the opportunity to work closely with one of the giants in quality management, Dr. W. Edwards Deming. So, the first thing I tried when I came to the White House was to utilize some of Dr. Deming's approaches. But it was clear that we needed much more than that. We really needed redesign.
>
> So that is how I met Russ Ackoff and had the opportunity to work with him. And I will tell you, Deming and Ackoff—I think that both of them border on being geniuses. They have each shaped me in their own special ways.
>
> As far as the effort at the White House goes, you know the two toughest things you can try to do in an organization are to start something new or to stop something old. In Idealized Design, you do both. The methodology guides you, but you need a compelling reason to do it. Ours was an appreciation for the responsibility of being an institution that shapes the direction of the nation and in some cases, the free world. So the stakes are

high, the impact is enormous, and the complexities are abundant. You can surrender to the complexities or let your personal commitment to excellence drive you and seize the opportunity to take the organization to new levels of performance and set an example of being a good steward of public funds.

And the power of Idealized Design is that when you say the system was destroyed last night, you not only destroy the system, you destroy all of the constraints along with it. That is freedom and that is what leads to transformation." (Interview, June 24, 2009)

Strategic Intent

In 1989, Gary Hamel and C. K. Prahalad published their *Harvard Business Review* article entitled "Strategic Intent," and later followed up with another article and book (1993, 1994) reinforcing the concept. Very soon, corporations across the globe were using the term, though it is uncertain how many were using it correctly. This is because it truly is a radical notion, compared to how strategic planning has been done and is done in organizations. They created the term *strategic intent* based on their research of companies that had become global leaders during the 1980s such as Canon, Kamatsu, and Honda:

> Companies that have risen to global leadership over the past 20 years invariably began with ambitions that were all out of proportion to their resources and capabilities. But they created an obsession with winning at all levels of the organization. . . . We call this obsession "strategic intent." (1989, p. 64)

Hamel and Prahalad contrast their strategic intent approach with the traditional concept of "strategic fit" between resources and opportunities—a concept they believe has "often abetted the process of competitive decline" (1989, p. 63).

> Strategic intent implies a sizable stretch for an organization. Current capabilities and resources will not suffice. This forces the organization to be more inventive, to make the most of limited resources. Whereas the traditional view of strategy focuses on the degree of fit between existing resources and current opportunities, strategic intent creates an extreme misfit between resources and ambitions. Top management then

challenges the organization to close the gap by systematically building new advantages. (1989, p. 67)

They go on to say that strategic intent is, essentially, a new "strategy frame" and suggest that "the essential element of the new strategy frame is an aspiration that creates by design a chasm between ambition and resources" (1993, p. 84).

Regardless of their resources, organizations practicing strategic intent create aspirational visions of what they want to accomplish and then set out to create that future. Again, simply setting these visions was not a guarantee that these companies would become the leaders of their industries. Hamel and Prahalad reinforce this: "Leadership cannot be planned for, but neither can it happen without a grand and well-considered aspiration" (1993, p. 84).

Written for a corporate audience, their book *Competing for the Future* (1994) seeks "to help managers imagine the future and, having imagined it, create it" (1994, p. 25). In the competitive corporate environment, companies that do not compete effectively are taken over or go out of business. In challenging leaders of companies, they pose questions that are paraphrased below (1994, pp. 4–6):

- Do you have a keen sense of urgency about how to reinvent your organization as the world changes?

- Are you investing your time as an architect of your organization's future, rather than as today's problem solver?

- Would you describe yourselves as proactive, rather than reactive?

- Are you seen by other organizations as an innovator?

- Are your employees hopeful and excited about the future, rather than anxious about the present?

If an organization's leaders cannot answer most of these questions with a "yes," then Hamel and Prahalad suggest that their future may be in jeopardy.

How would the leadership of your nonprofit organization respond to similar questions? Most nonprofits won't get taken over or even go bankrupt. But they can linger in mediocrity and irrelevance. In what direction is your organization headed? It may be time for an aspirational vision and a breakthrough strategy.

ROLE OF ASPIRATIONAL VISIONS

Aspirational visions play an important role in the strategy development process, but they also play a vital role in other aspects of the organization. These include leading change, fundraising, transformational leadership, and goals.

Leading Change

One of the most important skills that organizations of all types are looking for in executives is the ability to lead organizations through change. Given the rapid changes going on in our economy and environment, the ability to lead change has become more and more important.

The most frequently used model of leading organizations through transformational change is John Kotter's eight-step method (1995, 1996), which he developed through extensive studies of organization change successes and failures.

The first step of the process is to establish a sense of urgency about why change is necessary. For nonprofit executives who want to utilize the Kotter model of change, the mission gap presents a way to describe urgency in very specific terms. As mentioned in the previous chapter, many people are unaware of the magnitude of many of our societal problems. An explanation of mission gap can help them gain this understanding.

The next step is to recruit a guiding coalition of others who are willing to assist in leading the change. This is where both formal and informal organizational leaders and stakeholders are recruited to help lead the change effort. It is important that this group operates as a team and that each person has a sense of urgency about the change.

The third, and in my view, crucial step in the process is creating a vision and a strategy for implementing the change. This is a crucial step because it shifts the energy of the change effort into a positive direction. Typically, in the first and second stages, leaders seek to get the attention of others in the organization by pointing out problems that are looming if the organization does not take quick action. While this is a helpful way initially to get people's attention, relying on it for the long term does not work. Kotter says that he has never seen a successful organizational transformation that tried to rely only on urgency and a discussion of problems. The change effort has to be about more than just averting an emergency:

> We haven't seen fear used in a single successful transformation effort as a sustaining force. What we've sometimes found is fear used as a surprise element. It's the "hit them upside the head with a board" approach to getting their attention. But then you've got to move quickly to convert it into something positive or you get all of the drawbacks of fear. (Kotter, 1998)

If this third step is done well, then the rest of the process has a strong chance of succeeding. If, however, an inspiring aspirational vision is not created in step three, then the change effort can run out of steam.

The final five steps in the process include communicating the vision, empowering others to act, planning for and creating small wins, consolidating and creating more change, and anchoring the change in culture.

Each of these final steps in the process relies on a vision that inspires others to change and it is the key to sustaining the change.

Fundraising

Nonprofits are depending more and more on their ability to raise funds in order to carry out their missions. Certainly, any nonprofit with a sizable mission gap knows that additional resources are going to be a part of what they will need in order to close that gap more effectively. An aspirational vision is essential to fundraising success.

There are many excellent books and courses on fundraising to help nonprofit executives learn how to raise funds more effectively. Following is a very basic model I have used for years, which will explain the role of vision in the fundraising process.

The three words I always make sure to keep in mind when I discuss a possible gift with a prospective donor are *problem, opportunity,* and *challenge*. This is a very simplistic approach, but I have found it to be helpful. I have used it personally and in teaching fundraising, especially to volunteers. A conversation about making a gift should be sure to cover:

- *Problem.* This is where the mission is discussed, and it is the perfect place to discuss the mission gap. "You may not be aware of this, but . . ." and insert your own explanation of your organization's mission gap.
- *Opportunity.* This is where the aspirational vision is discussed. You explain what you are doing now, but you then paint a picture of what you want to do so you can close that mission gap more effectively.
- *Challenge.* "We understand the problem. And we have a vision for what needs to be done to address it. Our challenge is that we do not have the resources at this time to begin making that vision a reality. Will you invest (insert your vision of their gift) to help us make that vision come true for the benefit of those we serve?"

The nonprofit executives who do a lot of fundraising know that I am simplifying a lot here, but it is amazing to me how many people skip one or more of these basic steps.

There are many who chitchat and then go straight to the challenge ("We need money!") and ask for a gift. The prospective donor is not given the opportunity to understand the magnitude of the problem and, worse, they are not given an opportunity to dream about helping to solve the problem.

Perhaps still worse, there are those who explain the problem in excruciating detail and then go directly to challenge, without discussing the hope of the vision. Talk about a depressing conversation. Talk about feeling hopeless!

Vision provides opportunity. Vision provides hope. With vision, we have a chance to make a difference. Creating an aspirational vision for an organization that can help close the mission gap is vital to any fundraising effort.

Transforming Leadership

Effective leadership is understood to be an important ingredient in the performance of organizations. Yet, many different definitions of leadership exist as do a variety of theories on what makes a leader successful. One type of leadership, transforming leadership, is held up as an example of how leaders can work with others in communities and organizations to produce change that positively transforms them.

In his seminal book, *Leadership* (1978), James MacGregor Burns first identified this type of transforming leadership, which has the potential to produce significant positive change in society, communities, and organizations. He contrasts transforming leadership with transactional leadership.

Transforming leadership is a process in which "leaders and followers raise one another to higher levels of morality and motivation" (1978, p. 20). Transforming leadership involves a dynamic relationship between leaders and followers. In a sense, both parties become leaders even though the one who initiates the process is referred to as the leader. They engage one another for the benefit of a common purpose. It is a shared, two-way relationship with a moral dimension.

Transactional leadership occurs "when one person takes the initiative in making contact with others for the purpose of an exchange of valued things" (1978, p. 19). It may involve bargaining and the leader will appeal to the self interest of the follower. It is a one-way process in that the leader is only interested in what the follower has to say in order to complete a negotiation that satisfies the self-interest of the leader.

In transforming leadership, leaders listen to understand—to really hear and consider what is being said by the other. In transactional leadership, leaders listen to respond—to help them figure out how to argue effectively and/or complete the bargain.

When organizational leaders gather together to collaboratively create an aspirational vision they are engaging in a transforming leadership activity. The SDG can have this transforming experience as it creates vision, so long as they work together in a truly collaborative and transforming way.

Once the SDG creates the vision for the organization, however, it needs to be careful in how it communicates the new vision to others within the organization. A recent study (2009) by leadership researchers James Kouzes and Barry Posner reports:

> Constituents want visions of the future that reflect their own aspirations. They want to hear how their dreams will come true and their hopes will be fulfilled. . . . The only visions that take hold are shared visions . . . and you will create them only when you listen very, very closely to others, appreciate their hopes, and attend to their needs. (p. 21)

This study reinforces the points made earlier about assuring that the members of the SDG have legitimacy with the various stakeholder groups. When stakeholders read about a vision, they want to know who has represented their voice in the creation of the vision. It also reinforces the need to give as much voice to stakeholders directly into the strategy development process when it is designed.

Even with a representative SDG and opportunities for input by stakeholders into the process, the SDG and the board of directors need to take care in communicating the vision, strategic stretch goals, and strategy when they are complete. If possible, I often suggest a preliminary "draft report" be circulated for comment and dialogue. I find that people respect being asked and often some helpful suggestions are made to make improvements to the vision, strategic stretch goals, and/or strategy.

Without these demonstrated opportunities for people to provide voice, the organization leaders run the risk of falling into a fateful pitfall that consultant and author Peter Block calls leadership by *lamination*. This is the mistake that leaders make when they go to a mountaintop retreat and come back with a new vision that they print on the back of every employee's business card, and then laminate it. Think of it. If you had an idea of how to make a slight improvement to the vision, you can't write on the card—it's laminated. "Once a vision is laminated, it loses life," says Block (2000, p. 252).

Rather than leading by lamination, be a catalyst. Ask people what they think, how they feel, and what they want. Truly listen to them and a collaboratively created aspirational vision can be transforming for all.

Goals

There are people who say "I don't want to waste time with our heads in the clouds dreaming about visions when there is work to be done." And I appreciate that—there is a lot of work to be done. But before we take action, we want to make sure we have the right goals, and before we have the right goals we have to make sure we are heading in the same direction together. Vision gives us that future picture to tell us where we are going. Then we can set specific goals for specific time frames that will take us toward the vision. And the goals will allow us to make action plans that will guide activities—yearly, quarterly, weekly, and daily. Setting strategic stretch goals that are connected to the vision is the subject of the next chapter.

Vision not only provides a direction that allows us to set goals. It also gives us a context of action. A vision that is created for the purpose of closing the mission gap empowers action. Let's consider an example.

Amanda goes to work Monday morning after a great weekend with the family, to be met with a seemingly endless number of new emails. Her YMCA is located on the West Coast, and there are already emails from the national office in Chicago as well as from other Y colleagues on the East Coast with whom she is serving on a national task force. And then there are the usual emails from volunteers who are early risers and have had the weekend to think of questions to ask her. She slogs through email for 30 minutes until it is time for the weekly staff meeting.

Patty opens the staff meeting. "Okay, good morning everyone and let's dive into our first weekly agenda item—mission and vision updates. Does anyone have anything cool to report on something that has happened recently to remind us of our mission and vision?"

"I've got one," said Ron. "It was Learn to Swim graduation on Saturday morning and that is always a great event. We had two little boys who literally did not make it across the pool for the first time until that morning—and, boy, were they excited. So that was cool. And then I noticed that a parent seemed especially emotional about the whole event. I asked if she was okay and she told me she was so happy that her daughter had learned to swim. She, the mom, has always been terrified of the water and does not know how to swim. She was afraid that her daughter would not ever learn to swim either. She was very happy. But I saw the opening, so I told her about our adult Learn to Swim classes that are designed for people just like her. She was so excited about the graduation that she signed up while her daughter was getting dressed. And she even paid in full so it would make it harder for her to back out! It was a very exciting morning."

"That's great, Ron, and thanks," said Patty. "Anyone else?"

"I had one that just happened this morning," said Chris. "Some of you who lifeguard in the morning know Mrs. Pascoli who comes in for the early adult lap swim. She must be 80, right? Well after she was done with her swim this morning, she said, 'Woo hoo, Miss Lifeguard,' and I said 'Yes, good morning, Mrs. Pascoli,' and she said, 'I just want to thank you for lifeguarding this morning. My morning swim gets my day off to a great start and I certainly couldn't afford to go anywhere else.' It just really made me feel good."

"That's another great one," said Patty. "Mrs. Pascoli is one awesome woman. I think she has been doing that morning swim as long as any of us have worked here. Okay, great mission and vision updates. Now on to the next agenda item. What are important upcoming activities that everyone should have on their radar screen this week?"

Following the meeting, a newly invigorated Amanda headed back to her office and thought, "Cool stories this morning. I help make those kinds of great YMCA experiences available for children, families, and adults of all ages. And to make that happen, email has to be answered, phone calls need to be returned, and other things on my To Do list need to be checked off. That's just what needs to be done. Email, here I come."

Daily activities without vision and mission can be tedious. With a perspective on the vision and mission in mind, however, goals and even routine tasks can be empowering.

REAL-WORLD APPLICATIONS OF ASPIRATIONAL VISIONS

The Kleinoeder Gift

My first CEO role (1981–1990) was with Alpha Sigma Phi Fraternity and the Alpha Sigma Phi Educational Foundation. I inherited an endowment fundraising campaign that was having a difficult time. But by 1985, after a lot of hard work by a lot of people, we eventually raised $1.1 million. This was a lot of money for us, as we previously had no real endowment to speak of.

During the next year we realized that we needed to plan more for the future. We didn't know much about strategic planning, but we stumbled into an aspirational visioning exercise. We thought it would be helpful to bring in various leaders and stakeholders for a weekend of brainstorming to get creative about what new programs we should create in the future. By the end of the weekend, we had come up with a great set of ideas for new programs. Once we put price tags on them, they came to about $750,000 in additional annual costs—requiring at least an additional $15 million to endow them. We didn't plan to start a new campaign again soon, but we wanted to have some ideas about the direction we wanted to go in for the future.

That's the background for the story.

I started my work day one morning by reviewing the results from a volunteer phonathon from the night before. I saw a note that said a Mr. Howard Kleinoeder had made a $1,000 pledge and that he wanted to talk with someone about making a bequest. I phoned him and he reiterated his interest and added, "You shouldn't wait too long. My health is not so good." In my wisdom, I made an appointment with him right then and scheduled my flight.

Mr. Kleinoeder lived on a thoroughbred horse farm in Florida. Other than that, I knew he was a member of our fraternity at the University of Washington in the 1930s and that he had only recently started making gifts to the Educational Foundation. I didn't know much more about him. Our fundraising operation was not very sophisticated, especially when it came to research. It was only recently that we had found out that Warren Buffett was an alumnus, but that's another story.

I met Mr. Kleinoeder at his home. I started the conversation by thanking him for his previous gifts and updating him on some of the things that we were doing. After we talked for a while, he said something to me like "How much money do you fellas need anyway? You just raised a million dollars." "That's true, Howard," I said, "but that was just the beginning. Some of our leaders got together recently and came up with a list of programs we need that will require an additional $15 million in endowment." I went on to describe some of the programs we had on the drawing board and how they would make a difference for our students. He didn't jump up and cheer at the ideas or anything, but he seemed satisfied that we had some good ideas we were working on.

I made a few additional visits to see Howard over the next couple of years. When we started our planned giving society, he agreed to sign a statement confirming that he had provided a bequest for the Educational Foundation in his estate. But he declined to list the amount. All he wrote was: "Depends on the value of stock." The last time I saw him, he took me to dinner at the Elks Club where they had the fish dinner special that night. I think my meal cost about $7.00. He was a frugal guy. I had no idea how much he had in mind for the Educational Foundation in his will, but I thought maybe six figures—a lot of money.

I was out of town when the phone call came. Actually, I was in India-napolis at the Center on Philanthropy for a conference entitled "Taking Fundraising Seriously." When I phoned in for messages, I was told that an attorney had called and that Mr. Kleinoeder had passed away. I returned the call to the attorney and he told me he estimated that the Educational Foundation would receive about $5 million once all of the stock and prop-erty was sold.

It turned out to be $6.4 million—"Taking Fundraising Seriously," indeed.

This was a very generous gift, to say the least. And it turns out that Howard Kleinoeder gave his entire fortune of $20+ million to different philanthropic organizations when he died. Now, who knows what he had in mind when he asked to speak to someone about making a bequest to the Educational Foundation? Maybe he was thinking about giving us the entire $20+ million, but he was so unimpressed with me that he cut it in one-third. Who knows? But here is what I wonder. I wonder about when he asked how much money "we fellas" really needed. I wonder what he would have done if I had said "You're right, Howard. We are finally in decent shape financially. But we are hoping to keep increasing our annual fundraising results by 5 to 10 percent a year." I wonder that if I had said something like that whether he would have given anything at all to the Educational Foundation from his estate.

The lesson: If you really want to "take fundraising seriously," you will create aspirational visions that can attract people with the resources to make some dreams come true.

Postscript: Warren Buffett. Yes, I did have an opportunity to visit with Mr. Buffett. One of our alumni volunteers knew him and arranged for the meeting. Mr. Buffett very politely listened to me share the same kinds of aspirational visions for the Educational Foundation as I had shared with Mr. Kleinoeder. He kindly asked a few questions. And then he nicely declined the opportunity to make a gift. He said that he had other priorities.

So what went wrong? It was the same aspirational vision each time. Did I somehow say it incorrectly to Mr. Buffett? I think not. I think the lesson here is that different visions inspire different people. And as we have learned in recent years, Mr. Buffett seems inspired by what the Gates Foundation is doing—and they have some pretty terrific aspirational visions of their own. All we can do is dream our dreams, share them broadly, and work together with those who are inspired to pursue those dreams with us.

Google

In 1994, Google cofounder Larry Page was a student at the University of Michigan. He was selected to attend a session of The LeaderShape Institute held by the university for student leaders.

A few years later, while I was serving as CEO of the LeaderShape, Inc. organization, one of Larry's classmates—also a LeaderShape graduate—emailed me and told me about a company with a cool new search engine that Larry and some others had started up. Larry and Google were on my radar screen—and wow, did they skyrocket.

By the summer of 2001, Google was a household name and rumors of the company's going public were ongoing. Amid all of the growth of the company, we were pleased that Larry was able to come to Champaign, Illinois, for one of our national sessions of The LeaderShape Institute to serve on a panel of guest speakers for a group of students who were participating in the program that week. When asked how he learned to be a leader, he said, "Everything I know about leadership I learned at LeaderShape." And he told them he had the statement "Have a Healthy Disregard for the Impossible" on his office door.

A few months later I was traveling in the San Francisco area and Larry agreed to show me around the Googleplex. It is hard to describe how a place can feel like it is bursting with innovation, but that's how it felt to me. *Fast Company* magazine, in naming Google the world's number one most innovative company, simply said about the Googleplex, "What's special is elusive. . . . It's in the air, in the spirit of the place" (Salter, p. 74).

I enjoyed having Larry show me around, and we concluded our tour with lunch in the cafeteria. We sat down with some of his colleagues and he introduced me, telling them that he had attended this leadership program and that's how we knew each other. "What did you learn there, Larry?" one of them asked. "I learned to have a healthy disregard for the impossible," he replied. And they just laughed and laughed. "Yeah, you learned that, all right."

So, what has Google done to earn this title of the world's number one most innovative company? Some include:

- *Google Maps.* A web mapping service that provides detailed information on street addresses as well as a route planner. It works online as well as on cell phones.

- *Adwords.* A major source of revenue that allows advertisers to select words that, when searched on Google, produces a sponsored link for the advertiser.

- *Google Calendar.* An online calendar and to-do list system that is similar to other desktop calendars, but stored online and then viewed from anywhere. It boasts ease of use and is integrated into other Google applications, such as Gmail.

- *Google Custom Search Engine.* Allows users to create a search engine exclusively for their own web site or for a special set of web sites, while utilizing Google's search technology.

- *Gmail with Google Talk.* The Gmail email system has been upgraded to allow chat features, talking via the Internet, and voice mail.

- *Google Checkout.* A payment processing system that allows users to store their payment methods so that making purchases via the Internet is much easier.

In May 2009, Larry Page was the University of Michigan's commencement speaker. And he was still at it, encouraging people to have a healthy disregard for the impossible:

> I have a story about following dreams. Or maybe more accurately, it's a story about finding a path to make those dreams real.
>
> When I was here at Michigan, I had actually been taught how to make dreams real! I know it sounds funny, but that is what I learned in a summer camp converted into a training program called LeaderShape. Their slogan is to have a healthy disregard for the impossible. That program encouraged me to pursue a crazy idea at the time: I wanted to build a personal rapid transit system on campus to replace the buses. It was a futuristic way of solving our transportation problem. I still think a lot about transportation—you never lose a dream, it just incubates as a

hobby. Many things that people labor hard to do now, like cooking, cleaning, and driving will require much less human time in the future. That is, if we "have a healthy disregard for the impossible" and actually build new solutions. (Google Press Center, May 2, 2009)

Google continues to challenge what is possible and has developed that "healthy disregard" deep into its culture. It will be fascinating to watch the continued innovations from this company.

APPLICATION TO HYPOTHETICAL ORGANIZATIONS

Large City Metro Food Bank

When the time came to work on the vision, Jeff, the LCMFB facilitator, did a brief presentation for the group on the differences between an analytical vision and aspirational vision. He split the SDG up into three teams of five people each, spreading out the board members, staff, and so on. Then he sent them off to different areas at the meeting facility, asking each team to come back with a bold, aspirational vision for LCMFB. He gave each group flip-chart paper with markers and asked them to bring back a report for the rest of the group. He gave them 40 minutes to create their visions, and encouraged them to see which team could come up with the most outrageous vision.

The teams reconvened and Jeff asked each one for a report. There was a lot of energy in the room and some good laughter at some of the more wild dreams in some of the visions. "That's great creativity," Jeff remarked. "You'll never know what's possible until you get a little wild with your dreams."

When the reports were finished, Jeff went to a fresh flip-chart pad and asked people to begin listing items that each vision had in common. When there were disagreements over the magnitude of some items, such as the size of the staff and the amount of the endowment, he asked, "Well, if you could really have it any way you wanted it, what would you want?" This helped the group clarify what they wanted.

Then the group discussed other aspects of the different vision reports that they did not have in common. They worked through these pretty easily as well with Jeff's facilitation. The aspirational vision they came up with for the ideal Large City Metro Food Bank looked like this:

- A headquarters for LCMFB that would include five times the square footage of our current building with food storage space, our own pantry, a training room, a full kitchen, quality technology and office furnishings. And it would be "green."
- Triple the number of volunteers we have now
- A staff of 70 who are paid competitively and receive professional development opportunities
- A board of directors who are extremely well connected within the community and have access to considerable funding
- An annual fund of $30 million
- Triple the number of delivery trucks we now have
- A comprehensive marketing program
- An extensive planned giving program
- Triple the number of food donations per year
- Community and nonprofit leaders think of us as the exemplary nonprofit in the region
- A new division of SNAP (Supplemental Nutrition Assistance Program; formerly food stamps) counselors

Big River Regional Housing Services

Tom decided the group needed a change of pace when it came time for him to facilitate the vision discussion. Once he finished his presentation on vision, he said, "I am going to have you use a different part of your brain for a while now," and he handed out flip-chart paper and markers to each person. "I'd like each of you to take about 20 to 25 minutes and work on your own to create your pictorial representation of what Big River Regional Housing Services would look like if you could have it any way you wanted it. Just find some private space here somewhere to get creative, and remember—no constraints."

When the group reassembled, Tom had each person hang their pictures around the room and gave everyone the chance to walk around to check out the creativity. He then gave each one a chance to explain their picture and their vision. Some, of course, were more artistic than others, but all of them included some very thoughtful ideas of what the ideal BRRHS would look like.

"I had no idea that this was such an artistic group," said Pat, "and I am really inspired by the creative ideas you have going on here. Whoever your next CEO ends up being they will be fortunate to work with such a passionate and committed group of people."

"Thanks Pat," said Kendra. "We really do have a great crew here. Where do we go from here, Tom?"

Tom went to the flip chart and said, "Well, why don't you all look at the pictures and describe for me some of the aspects of the visions that you think many of them have in common as well as some of the more unique things people mentioned that you think we should make a part of our aspirational vision for BRRHS."

Tom facilitated the group through the discussion and they came to consensus on the following list of items for their vision:

- A new main administration building that is four times the square footage of the current facility with up to date technology and furnishings. Two new satellite offices are established in other counties. New and current satellite offices also have up to date technology and furnishings. All facilities are "green."

- A staff of 200 who are paid competitively within the nonprofit and government environments and who each have professional development plans that the organization supports

- A board of directors of 25 people who are well connected within the region, and an executive committee of seven. All board members are active donors, organization promoters, and annual fund solicitors

- An annual fund of $5 million

- Corporate and foundation funding of $7 million per year

- Collaborations

- Government funding of $4 million per year

- Residents feel proud to be living in our facilities and have a good quality of life

- We are widely recognized for making a significant impact on the quality of life in the region, including the economic vitality of counties we serve
- Reserves of $10 million (quasi-endowment)

Merrill County Literacy Council

As Mark finished facilitating the discussion on mission, he then said, "I think that wraps up mission, and we will move on to vision next." Before he could say another word, Ellen jumped in. "Great," she said. "I was working on this last night and I have some ideas. First, Colleen needs a new computer. I know they are expensive, but we have to be visionary and find a way to get her one. Next, when is the last time that any of you have seen our brochure? It is sorely in need of an update. And finally, of course, we have to find a way to keep that budget balanced. There, that should get us started."

"Thanks, Ellen," said Mark, "that's great. But before we get started, I want to give you all a quick briefing on different ways to go about visioning. We're going to talk about the difference between analytical visions and aspirational visions."

When Mark finished his briefing, Ellen said, "Okay, I get it and I can definitely dream bigger."

"Thanks, Ellen," replied Mark. "Now what I would like each person to do is to just take 10 minutes of quiet time here at your tables and write down your dreams for what the ideal Merrill County Literacy Council would be like if you could have it any way you wanted it. What do we want MCLC to look like so we can close that mission gap we identified as effectively as possible? Just take some time on your own to write as much of a description as you can, and remember—no constraints."

After just a few minutes, Alice could no longer contain herself. "I am having a brain hurricane here all by myself," she said. "Never mind the brainstorming!"

"I'm glad you have the creative juices flowing, Alice," said Mark, in his supportive facilitator voice. "Now let's take some more quiet time, and I'll again encourage everyone to get as creative as you can."

When time was up, Mark stood at the flip chart and went around the room asking each person to share one item from their list and he wrote each one down. He kept going around the room until everything that everyone had on their lists had been listed. When similar items were mentioned, he asked the group to work out how they wanted to state it.

After the lists were exhausted, the group looked over what was on the flip-chart pages. "That looks like a pretty amazing organization to me," said Colleen. "That organization is going to make an impact for sure."

"It is a great list," said Mark. "Now which ones do you want to make sure to keep on our final version of our vision for MCLC?"

The group discussed the list and came to consensus on the following vision of the ideal Merrill County Literacy Council:

- Twenty-four total full time staff (five times current size)—all highly qualified and fully engaged, adding more middle managers, counselors, volunteer managers, and child care managers

- Total compensation for all staff is competitive with similar jobs in government and education, including benefits (insurance, retirement, etc.)

- Every employee has a professional development plan that is supported by the organization

- Fully engaged board with strong community connections

- Five hundred certified literacy teaching and tutoring volunteers (25 times the current number)

- $3 million per year in reliable unrestricted grants

- Five times our current office space with mid-quality furniture and up-to-date equipment and technology for all staff

- Free access to as many quality classrooms as needed at any time

- Free transportation for all volunteers and students to classrooms

- Endowment of $15 million

- Two hundred child care volunteers (30 times current number)

CHAPTER 5

Strategic Stretch Goals

I n this step of the process, the strategy development group (SDG) sets five strategic stretch goals that are designed to catapult the organization toward its vision. The goals further sharpen the organization's focus for the strategy development process and spur creativity. Working toward the accomplishment of the goals begins to bring the vision into reality. In this way, the goals are strategic—their completion point is at the end of the strategy time frame being used (three to five years out). They are outcome-based goals. And the goals are SMART: specific, measurable, almost impossible, relevant, and time bound. One or more of the goals should list intended changes in the mission accomplishment measures for the strategy time frame.

WHAT WE KNOW ABOUT GOALS

Goal setting is one of the most researched topics in organizational studies. Many years of research and more than 1,000 studies have produced findings that provide very helpful information for practical application. Two of the leading goal-setting researchers are Edwin Locke and Gary Latham. They provide an extensive summary of this research in their book *A Theory of Goal Setting and Task Performance* (1990) and have authored numerous articles before and after that book. What is reviewed here are the highlights of the goal-setting studies that are of the most applicable use for practitioners. Unless otherwise noted, the following summary is based on Locke and Latham (1990).

Research has shown that: "specific, high (hard) goals lead to a higher level of task performance than do easy goals or vague, abstract goals such as the exhortation to "do one's best." (Locke & Latham, 2006, p. 265) Specificity eliminates ambiguity, but—not surprisingly—specific and easy goals may produce low performance (for example, "lowering the bar"). So it is the combination of specific and difficult goals that increases performance. And when it comes to difficulty, Locke and Latham explain: "So long as a person is committed to the goal, has the requisite ability to attain it, and does not have conflicting goals, there is a positive linear relationship between goal difficulty and task performance" (2006, p. 265).

Goals direct attention toward relevant activities and help people understand what to focus the intensity of their effort on. Goals also have an effect on persistence, as people tend to persist until a goal is met. For complex tasks, goals also stimulate the development of creative thinking if it is needed to achieve the goal. With these ideas in mind, it is also important that a reporting and feedback mechanism exists so that people know how well they are doing on the goal. Feedback tells them if they need to intensify efforts, persist more, and/or get more creative.

People must be convinced that a goal is relevant and important, and that they have the capability of achieving it—or at least making substantial progress. Training can help build confidence that a goal is achievable. With respect to a goal's relevance and importance, research shows that—surprisingly—participation in setting one's own goals does not necessarily increase performance when compared to being asked by a supervisor to work on a goal that they think makes sense.

While goal difficulty generally increases performance, this may not be the case if people are confronted with a new complex task that is difficult. It may even be harmful. Seijits & Latham (2005) provide the example of a novice golfer gets so overly concerned with shooting a low score that he fails to take the time necessary to actually learn the game first—before worrying about what score he ultimately shoots. In these cases, they suggest that learning goals may be more appropriate early on, rather than performance goals. In the case of the golfer, for example, perhaps his early goals should focus on understanding the situations during a game in which he will use the different clubs or getting comfortable hitting with just one club before using the others.

We know much, much more than this about goals, but these are the most important elements to keep in mind as we look at establishing strategic stretch goals.

Outcome-Based SMART Goals

Outcomes versus Activities

The strategic stretch goals should be outcome-based goals, not activity-based goals. They should articulate results that the SDG wants the organization to produce during the strategy time frame that will indicate they are making significant progress toward the vision.

Unfortunately, outcome-based goals are all too rare in organizations. It seems much easier to list the activities that an individual or team is going to work on rather than the specific outcomes that the activities are intended to produce. One of the reasons that we lack outcomes is that our language around performance lacks rigor. When a supervisor meets with their direct reports, for example, the question is typically something like "What are you working on during the upcoming quarter?" instead of "What outcomes will you produce during the upcoming quarter?"

This lack of rigor makes it more difficult for people to be held accountable. Completing a task is easier than completing a task that produces an agreed-upon outcome. This lack of rigor exists at the individual level, at the team level, and at the organizational level. The SDG needs to be rigorous about setting strategic stretch goals that are outcome based.

Certainly, tasks and to-do lists need to be created once an outcome goal is established, but the focus must stay on the outcomes being produced instead of the activities being completed.

The SDG will notice that some outcome-based goals are, indeed, outcomes—but then also are the means toward producing other important outcomes. For example, consider the following strategic stretch goal:

> *To increase the annual fund to $500,000 received per year (+500%) by June 30, 2015.*

This is an outcome-based goal. It does not say that 100,000 fundraising letters will be mailed out that year or that 10,000 phonathon calls will be made. It is an outcome—money will be received.

But it is also a means to other goals of the organization, such as expanding programs or hiring new staff or upgrading technology. This is true, but in the grand scheme of things, all goals are means to the outcome of the mission accomplishment measures. Therefore, the SDG should not be concerned when they notice that some of their outcome-based goals are also means for other goals. As long as the SDG believes that the goals they set are outcomes and strategic, because they are going to catapult the organization toward the vision, then the goals are acceptable.

Two excellent resources for more information on creating outcomes for goals are *Make Success Measurable* (Smith, 1999) and *First Break All the Rules* (Buckingham & Coffman, 1999).

SMART Goals

There are many versions of what the letters stand for in the SMART goal acronym, and some have suggested more than 100 variations exist. Drawing upon the goal research mentioned above, following is the SMART formula used in this book.

S. The *S* is for specific. As revealed in the research, vague goals do not provide the benefits that specific goals provide—directing attention, encouraging persistence, focusing intensity of effort, or generating creativity. Of course, remember that specific low goals are not helpful as they lower the bar of performance. The *S* in SMART has to be used along with the *A* below.

M. The *M* is for measurable. A reliable way to judge the extent to which the goal is being met must be established. Opinions and subjective criteria are not helpful here. As discussed in Chapter 3, a reliable measure is one upon which different objective observers would agree. If the goal is not measurable, then progress cannot be tracked, feedback cannot be provided, and one will never know if the goal has been accomplished.

A. The *A* in SMART is for almost impossible stretch. This is related to the research finding that difficult goals lead to higher performance. This is what makes the goal a *stretch*. However, using an "almost impossible stretch" approach to goals requires special attention for it to work correctly. The next section will deal specifically with this aspect of a SMART goal.

R. The *R* is for relevant. The SDG needs to set goals that are relevant for taking the organization toward the vision—this is what makes them strategic. In setting these goals they will want to identify accomplishments, which, if achieved during the time period, would catapult the organization toward the vision.

T. The *T* is for time bound. A specific date by which the goal is going to be achieved must be listed. This requirement further amplifies the research finding of the need for a goal to be specific.

Based on the summary of the goal research discussed above, the *S, M, R,* and *T* aspects of SMART seem very straightforward. It is the *A* where confusion often exists. Some SMART versions will use the word *achievable*, but this opens the door for setting a low goal—"one we are sure is achievable"—and we know that this will lower performance. Another version is "aggressive, yet achievable" (Smith, 1999), and these goals can be thought of as somewhat of a stretch. And this is definitely an improvement over simply "achievable." But better yet, is "almost impossible." That is a real *stretch*. In the next section, we will see why.

ALMOST IMPOSSIBLE

Different methods of using stretch goals are used in organizations and in this section I am recommending my own special version. As mentioned above, "aggressive, yet achievable" goals are also called stretch goals by some. The almost impossible stretch version of stretch goals is one that I have been evolving over nearly the past 20 years as a practitioner and as a consultant. My recommendations for using these almost impossible stretch goals are based on those experiences.

Using the almost impossible stretch approach to SMART goals is based on using the aspirational mind-set discussed in the previous chapter. Just as when creating a vision, the SDG should use a healthy disregard for the impossible when setting goals. The purpose for using almost impossible stretch goals and the aspirational mind-set is to spur creativity within the organization.

When I teach this almost impossible stretch goal approach to others, I will often ask them to write down a goal they are currently working on. Once they do this, then I will ask:

"If I can show you a *new way* to go about accomplishing that goal that will give you twice the results in one-third the time with less stress and without costing any more money or making anyone work more hours, then would you be interested?"

Yes, of course.

I learned to introduce the idea of the almost impossible stretch this way because when a lot of people first hear the idea of a stretch, they think, "You are trying to turn my 60-hour work week into an 80-hour work week" and "I am already stressed out enough—no more!"

Introducing the concept in this way helps to point out that the idea of setting an almost impossible stretch is to generate new creative ways of doing things. But only by setting the goal at that almost impossible stretch level will you be able to generate the new creative ways of accomplishing the goal.

The almost impossible stretch allows individuals, teams, and organizations to utilize what Peter Senge calls "creative tension" (1990, p. 142). When a goal is established that is far distant from current reality, this creates a natural tension in the mind, which must be resolved. As long as a person can maintain a commitment to the goal, this will naturally trigger creative energy within them to invent a way to resolve the tension. In this way, setting an almost impossible stretch is a trigger for personal creativity or group creativity.

Creativity and innovation are vital for the success of all organizations today, and the almost impossible stretch is a vehicle for triggering that creativity. This is why Hamel and Prahalad, the Strategic Intent authors mentioned in the previous chapter, say, "Creating stretch, a misfit between resources and aspirations, is the single most important task senior management faces" (1993, p. 77).

Just as most visions are created using an analytical mind-set, most goals are created using that same mind-set. The analytical approach to setting goals includes:

- Analyzing past results and process used
- Analyzing changes in environment
- Determining process improvements and resources available
- Forecasting performance

Chances are that you are an expert at this process, as we learn it from the time we are young. "How did it go?" "What can you do differently?" "How much better do you think you can do?" Note that the analysis and thinking are done by looking at the past.

By contrast, the aspirational approach includes:

- Committing to breakthrough performance
- Setting a goal at the furthest distance of your imagination
- Searching the environment for opportunity
- Creating a new process

The aspirational approach is the opposite of the analytical approach as it sets the goal before the process to accomplish it is established. Also, all of the thinking is done from the future. By making a commitment to breakthrough performance, one stands in the future and imagines the goal being accomplished. Next, the environment is scanned for opportunities to help accomplish the goal. And then, creative tension energy is released to invent a new process to accomplish the goal.

Standing in the future and working backwards to the present gives a different and more advantageous perspective from which to generate new solutions to accomplish the goal. Rock climbers will explain that they often picture themselves at the top of the rock at the end of their climb and then map their way down to figure the best way to make the ascent. Children know this when they are given a maze to solve. They go to the end and find their way out, rather than having to find their way in.

People will often exhort others to "think outside of the box." I suggest that the analytical mind-set *is* "the box." Positioning oneself in the present day and analyzing the past is sitting in the box. Positioning oneself in the future, with a commitment to a breakthrough, is getting out of the box.

Again, there is nothing wrong with the analytical approach. However, it will produce only incremental improvements. The opportunity for producing breakthrough results exists with the aspirational mind-set and almost impossible stretch goals.

After all the analysis is done, an analytically generated goal is presented as this:

This is a forecast of the result we should be able to produce assuming we work hard at it.

Once an almost impossible stretch goal is generated, using the aspirational mind-set, it is presented as:

This is the very best result we can imagine possible (1 percent chance), and we have no idea how to make it happen.

Some will say that setting almost impossible stretch goals is unreasonable. George Bernard Shaw's famous quote comes to mind:

The reasonable man adapts himself to the world; the unreasonable one persists in adapting the world to himself. Therefore, all progress depends on the unreasonable man.

Setting the Almost Impossible Stretch Goals

To set a SMART goal that is an almost impossible stretch, the SDG focuses on its mission gap and its vision. It then answers the question:

"What five outcome-based, strategic stretch goals can we set that will catapult us toward our vision and help us significantly close our mission gap? Make sure that the goals are SMART: specific, measurable, almost impossible, relevant, and time bound. These goals are strategic—their completion point is at the end of the strategy time frame being used (three to five years out)."

One or more of the goals should list intended changes in the mission accomplishment measures for the strategy time frame. For example, if the organization wants to end homelessness and it is using data from the county government to tell it what the homeless population is as its mission accomplishment measure, then one of the goals should be to see a reduction in that measure.

Also, keep in mind the earlier definition of an almost impossible stretch, the SDG will want to be able to look at the goal and say:

This is the very best result we can imagine possible (1 percent chance), and we have no idea how to make it happen.

Why do I recommend that you set the goals so very far out at this 1 percent possible threshold? First, the goal research tells us that we get higher performance when we make a goal more difficult. So we want to take advantage of that dynamic of a goal to move as close to the vision as we can. Next, however, the research also tells us that you have to be able to imagine the possibility—even remotely—that the goal can either be achieved or you can come very close. I have experienced this in the work I have done with people on an almost impossible stretch. Once they are convinced that the goal is 100 percent impossible, they typically give up.

As mentioned earlier, however, we also have to keep in mind that an almost impossible stretch will likely require individuals—perhaps the entire organization—to learn new skills and invent new processes in order to achieve the goal. This means that the first steps toward the almost impossible stretch may be to create learning goals that can lead toward the ultimate accomplishment of the goal. This will be discussed further in the upcoming section on the organization culture needed to make the almost impossible stretch successful.

Following are other important guidelines to keep in mind as you pursue the almost impossible stretch. A theme that you will see in these guidelines is that the almost impossible stretch is most effective when people have the freedom to creatively play with ideas on how to accomplish the goals. When people have freedom like they are playing a game, they can be more creative.

You Use Them   You use the almost impossible stretch goals, they don't use you. Traditional, analytically based goals use you. You are supposed to be able to accomplish them, and if you don't, it means you are not doing your job right. They dominate you and stress you out. What if you fail? However, *you* use almost impossible stretch goals as a method to trigger your own creativity. They give you something to shoot for and to have fun trying to see if you can invent a new way to make it happen.

Focus on Progress   Fully achieving the almost impossible stretch is not the main focus of your attention. Of course, you want to accomplish it. But you focus more on being creative, making progress, and learning. In the long run, this will produce more innovation and success.

"Safe-Fail" Culture   You need to create a "safe-fail" culture in the organization so people are free to invent, innovate, and play with new ideas. This is very important and will be discussed in more detail in the upcoming section on culture.

You Make the Rules   You have to set boundaries for your actions. Obviously, you will not do anything unethical to accomplish the almost impossible stretch. But what else? You can set boundaries on how much staff time you will devote to the effort, that you will provide only so much funding, and that you will only spend so many hours per week working on it. These are the rules that you set for the game that you are playing. The idea is not to manipulate people into working 80 hours per week; it is to innovate new processes.

Be Willing to Fail   Since the reasonable prospect of failing at the almost impossible stretch is very high—99 percent—you need to consider the real-world implications of this. Any time you set an almost impossible stretch, ask yourself "Am I willing to live with the worst probable outcome?" If not, don't set it that high. With this in mind, an organization will not want to set an almost impossible stretch for every domain of their operation. Budgets, for example, may want to remain conservative. However, once the conservative budget is set then perhaps a team can attempt to create ways to save even more on expenses or bring in even more revenue. In this way, the conservative budget provides a safety net for innovation.

Most People Have the Old Mind-Set!   This is *very important*: The vast majority of people operate in the traditional, analytical mind-set. When they hear you talking about a goal, they will think you have figured out how to accomplish it and that if you work appropriately hard at it you will make it happen. In adopting the almost impossible stretch approach, one needs to take care with whom they communicate their goals and how.

It Is Easy to Fall Back into the Old Mind-Set   It is very easy to fall back into the traditional, analytical mind-set and get yourself stressed when you are not making progress on an almost impossible stretch. Remind yourself and others that this is almost impossible! Maybe it is impossible! We are the people who are going to try to go for it.

No Guarantees for Quality Creativity   The almost impossible stretch approach will trigger creative energy. However, there is no guarantee that your new creative ideas will be good ones! Try out the new ideas. If they don't work, try to learn why and make a change—or try something else. The idea is to learn quickly what works better and what does not. As management guru Tom Peters says:

. . . there's no substitute for getting smarter faster. And the way you get smarter faster is to screw around vigorously. Try stuff. See what works. See what fails miserably. Learn. Rinse. Repeat." (Peters, 2001)

Quick Illustration: It Can Be Productive to Play   Years ago, in the days before PowerPoint, I was supposed to give a talk at a conference and the hotel had not set up my overhead projector or screen. There was a speaker on before me, there was no break between the two of us, and I already had limited time for the presentation. When the overhead projector guy showed up at the door at the back of the room with me, we realized that he would have to hustle in while I was being introduced and I would get started as soon as he was done.

Looking at my watch, I said to the young man, "What is the absolute fastest you can get this equipment set up?" He pondered the challenge and resolutely said, "Nine minutes." I said, "Okay, why don't you go for it in four minutes." He looked at me with a shocked gaze. "Hey," I said, "I won't be mad, just go for it. Why not? Look, I'll time you." "Okay!" he said with gusto.

The door opens and we both walk in. He begins connecting wires and putting up a screen and positioning the projector, all while I am being introduced and saying hello. I keep glancing at him with an eye on my watch. He gets done and looks up at me. I say, "Three minutes and forty-five seconds." He gives a fist pump and I ask the group to thank him for helping us out this morning—so he gets a round of applause.

Yes, I got my equipment up quickly so I could do my talk, and yes, he ended up performing in less than half of the time he expected. But also, he actually had some fun and joy in his job that morning. I am not sure how often that happens when people set up audiovisual equipment.

Quick Illustration: You Make the Rules of the Game   A colleague of mine was working on a stretch goal, and it was looking like he would not make it as the deadline approached. We had a coaching session and, together, brainstormed many new ideas of things he could do to give it a good last effort to make the goal.

I noticed an intensity about him as we finished up the meeting, and I said, "So, what are your next 10 days going to look like—between now and the deadline?" "I am totally focused on this," he said, "and I'll be working on it all during Thanksgiving when I am visiting my family." I said. "Well, you can do what you want to do. You are the one who set the goal, and you are the one who gets to make the rules about how you are going to go for it. But how about a game where you use the new ideas we came up with and you still try to make the goal, but you only let yourself work before and after Thanksgiving? Then you could relax and enjoy the time with your family." He smiled and nodded. "Yes, yes, I really like that game much better."

No, he didn't make the goal but he got very close. And he very much enjoyed the Thanksgiving time with his family.

Quick Illustration: The Real Consequences of Failure You must be willing to fail if you are going to take on an almost impossible stretch, and often we exaggerate the real consequences of failure. I was finishing my doctoral dissertation while working full time. It was February, and I had really been hoping to make the June commencement at Ohio State, which is held at the football stadium. But as I looked over what was left to be done, and what I had going on at work, and my other responsibilities, I realized there was no way. I would just graduate in the smaller winter commencement in December that is held inside at the basketball arena.

But then I realized I was in the analytical mind-set. I was making a forecast based on my analysis. What I really wanted was to graduate in June. So I decided to go for it and to try to figure out a way that I could responsibly get everything done that needed to get done in my life and still finish in time for June. The only downside was that I had to pay about $200 to register for a course at the beginning of the term during which I was going to graduate. If I didn't make it, I would have to pay this again.

Not long after I decided this, my mother came for a visit. After a while, she asked when I thought I would graduate. I said, "I am going to go for it and try for the June graduation!" She realized how little time that left me and, with a worried look on her face, said, "But what if you don't make it?" "Well," I said. "It will be okay. I actually have up to four more years to finish—so I'll just graduate at a later time if I don't get everything done." She didn't seem totally satisfied with my answer, but I think that's because people who care about us get worried that we will be disappointed if we try and fail. But the real consequences are often really not that bad, and the payoff for trying an almost impossible stretch can be great. And, yes, I made it, and it was a fabulous June day in the Horseshoe.

The Stretch Culture

An organization that is going to use the almost impossible stretch approach needs to create a culture that will support it. If the organization is used to an operation that runs on analytical goals, then people will need to be trained in the new approach, as it is radically different. It will take continual work to create and sustain the new culture, but the long-term results will be well worth the effort.

The culture needs to reward and provide resources for innovation and experimentation. When new complex tasks are required that are part of an almost impossible stretch, people need to be given time and resources to learn.

Most importantly, as briefly mentioned earlier, the organization needs to establish a safe-fail environment. Creating a safe-fail environment does not mean that basic errors in operations or ineptitude are tolerated. It means that failing when trying new ideas is accepted as a learning opportunity. Research has been done that considered elements that organizations need to establish to make stretch goals work effectively and has identified the value of "safefailing," which encourages "employees to try new ideas and work toward constant improvement and processes" (Thompson, Hochwater, & Mathys, 1997, p. 56).

Employees will need to trust the leadership in the organization that innovative attempts at trying new processes will be supported and not punished. As has been discussed, failure is not tolerated in the traditional analytical mind-set that exists in most organizations. In these organizations, a goal is a forecast of what should be accomplished if the individual or team works hard on it. If there is failure, it means that either the analysis that led to the forecast was done incorrectly or that someone did not work hard enough at accomplishing the goal. In short, in the traditional, analytical mind-set, failure means that someone is either stupid or lazy. Failure does not have a good name.

Failure in the aspirational mind-set needs to be embraced if the organization wants to fully seize the value of the creative energy that an almost impossible stretch can produce. As Peter Senge says:

> Mastery of creative tension transforms the way one views "failure." Failure is, simply, a shortfall, evidence of the gap between vision and current

reality. Failure is an opportunity for learning . . . Failures are not about our unworthiness or powerlessness. (1990, p. 154)

In the aspirational mind-set, failure certainly includes some disappointment, because the almost impossible stretch would not have been set if it was not desirable. But more of the focus is on an appreciation for what was accomplished, an understanding of what was learned, and an acknowledgment of the fact that hard work was done toward a meaningful goal.

This issue of failure will certainly come up during the deliberations of the SDG. Some people will have more tolerance for setting the goal at more difficult levels than others. This tension is normal in a group. The SDG, though, should work through these differences and come to consensus on the level of stretch they collectively think and feel is at their threshold of impossibility.

Implementing the Almost Impossible Stretch

Following is an example of how an almost impossible stretch goal might be implemented within an organization that has a culture that supports the aspirational mind-set. We will use an example of a goal mentioned earlier and show how it could be implemented as recommended. The example is that an SDG of an organization sets a strategic stretch goal of:

> To increase the annual fund to $500,000 received per year (+500 percent) by June 30, 2015 (five years from now).

This seems to fit the criteria. It is outcome based. It seems like a huge stretch, and it fits the other SMART criteria. Once it comes time to implement activity to produce this outcome, the organization is going to need to invent a new way of going about it than they have used before. They cannot produce a 500 percent increase in five years with incremental improvements.

Next, as a part of the strategy development process, the SDG identifies an underutilized strength—the board, and how they can be used to seize an opportunity—raising more money through personal solicitations in the community.

In this situation, since the board has not done this before, the organization would be wise to begin with some learning goals. For example, it could create a task force that might work with a consultant to develop a training program for the board and staff on how to implement these new activities.

Once the consultant provides the training, the initial goals of the board members should focus more on learning and less on a performance measure like trying to double the annual fund in the next year. For example, once they are trained, the board members could be sent off with the names and contact information of five previous donors with three assignments:

1. Contact each person to set up a personal meeting.
2. Ask each person for a gift larger than the one they gave the year before.
3. Send a personal thank you note after the visit.

The staff collects weekly updates from the board and sends out a report card that lists the following data for each board member:

- Number of appointments each board member has set
- Number of people they have asked for a gift larger than last year
- Number of people they asked who gave something
- Number of people they asked who gave more than the year before
- Number of people they sent thank you notes to

Since learning is more important at this stage of the process, a number of factors are put in place to encourage development. First, they are making calls on people who gave the prior year—so they are visiting with friends of the organization. They should expect that most people would be willing to make an appointment and the report card (feedback mechanism) gives them credit for that. Next, the report card gives them credit just for asking for more than the person gave the year before. They get a positive report for getting any kind of gift and an additional positive report for getting a larger gift than the year before. They can accomplish three of five items on their report card for each prospect even if they receive no gift at all.

This type of training experience will develop the board members into more confident solicitors. Once the process is completed, they can meet for a review of what they did that worked and what they could have done better. This is just one example of how people can be developed. For example, they might also be sent in pairs early on to have a partner who gives them reassurance.

This is just the first step. Next, the board could go out and ask some donors to join the volunteer development committee, and those who agree would also be trained. As the group grows in size and confidence they can begin shifting to more difficult tasks, such as contacting people who have never given before and asking for much larger gifts. And the focus can begin changing from learning to performance. In time, the only report cards sent out would involve dollars raised.

This is an example of applying a learning orientation early on with an almost impossible stretch. Innovation and learning need to come first, and then a shift of focus to performance alone can be established. But even early on in the learning phase, everyone understands that ultimately their efforts are designed to produce an almost impossible stretch accomplishment.

REAL-WORLD APPLICATIONS OF STRETCH GOALS

Man on the Moon

One of the most famous almost impossible stretch goals that has been accomplished in the last 50 years was the Apollo moon landing and safe return of those astronauts. On May 25, 1961, President John F. Kennedy, in a speech to a joint session of Congress entitled "Urgent National Needs," proposed:

> I believe that this nation should commit itself to achieving the goal, before this decade is out, of landing a man on the moon and returning him safely to the earth. No single space project in this period will be more impressive to mankind, or more important for the long-range exploration of space; and none will be so difficult or expensive to accomplish.

Perhaps five years earlier a president would have been mocked for such a declaration. But in 1957, the USSR launched the *Sputnik* rocket that shook the ego—and security concerns—of the United States. Then, earlier in 1961, the USSR succeeded in sending a man into space, who orbited the earth. The United States was able to send Alan Shepard into space after the USSR, but for only a brief period of time (five minutes of weightlessness).

Space travel was no longer impossible, and it was capturing the imagination of the human race. But could mankind really get to the moon and back by the end of the decade? How would that be done?

The science and technology did not exist in 1961 to make the moon shot at that time. And many scientists thought that it was impossible to create this technology by the end of the decade. But enough scientists existed who did not reject the idea as totally impossible, and they set to work to invent everything necessary to make it happen. And, of course, on July 20, 1969, the United States reached the moon and returned the *Apollo* crew safely home a few days later. An almost impossible stretch was accomplished.

Postscript: First the moon, now cancer. In 1970, flush with confidence over the success of the moon landing, the U.S. Congress decided to work the magic of the stretch goal for the benefit of medicine. It passed a resolution to "cure cancer by 1976 as a fitting celebration for the bicentennial." And one year later, it passed The National Cancer Act of 1971. This act strengthened the National Cancer Institute and took many important actions to help fight cancer. Yet, despite hard work by many intelligent people and billions of dollars in research funding, we are still looking for a cure for cancer or, more likely, cures for different cancers.

What happened? It was an almost impossible SMART stretch goal. Why didn't it work? Why isn't cancer cured yet? Another way to look at this is that the almost impossible stretch has worked very well, even though it still has not fully achieved its intention. Even though cancer is not fully cured yet, many new treatments have been discovered that have, in fact, cured many people of their particular type of cancer. More has been learned about lifestyles, which, if followed, can lead to a reduction in cancer occurrences in people. And more progress on new cancer treatments is made all the time.

But, like an aspirational vision, the setting of an almost impossible stretch does not guarantee victory—far from it. And while cures for all kinds of cancer now still seem years away (who knows?), you can make a very good case that much more progress in battling cancer has been made since this goal was set in 1970 than we would have otherwise made without it.

LeaderShape

As mentioned earlier, my second CEO position was at LeaderShape, Inc. (1992–2001), an organization that provides ethics-based leadership programs for young adults—primarily the college-age population. The flagship program of LeaderShape, Inc., is The LeaderShape Institute, an intensive six-day program designed to develop young adults to "lead with integrity and a healthy disregard for the impossible."

The organization already had an aspirational mind-set when I arrived, and we specifically included aspirational visioning and almost impossible stretch goals in our curriculum. With this in mind, we thought we should practice those concepts in running the organization as well.

My first close-up experience with The LeaderShape Institute program had come one year before I joined the staff, when I served as a volunteer facilitator for a week of the program. My experience, like that of many students and volunteers before and since, was that the program made a profound impact on participants. Many would call it life changing. People who have participated in the program end up sharing a number of aspirations. They want to help create a world in which people lead with integrity and a healthy disregard for the impossible, and they want to create ways to provide The LeaderShape Institute experience to more and more young people everywhere.

These were the aspirations that our staff, board, and volunteers shared when I started working with the organization in 1992. That year, we had 229 young adults attend the program, and we wanted to grow it much, much larger. However, at the same time, we were all very concerned about maintaining the quality of the program as we eyed growth for the future. Therefore, early on we developed a set of program delivery metrics that would serve as objective indicators for us that we were consistently implementing the program in a high-quality manner.

I encouraged the staff to set stretch goals in all areas of our operation and suggested that they use the method to create quarterly, monthly, or even weekly stretches to boost creativity. But the one place that we used stretch goals as a team was when we set our goals for the number of students that we wanted to have as participants in that year's sessions of The LeaderShape Institute. Importantly, one constraint we set for ourselves was that we also had to achieve high-level program delivery metrics to assure quality each year. We adopted a number of Total Quality Management initiatives to support us with the quality delivery commitment (for more details, see "Achieving Growth and High Quality by Strategic Intent," Sheehan, 1999).

At our annual staff retreats, we would ask ourselves three questions:

1. How far can we stretch our goal so that we think we have the smallest possibility of achieving it?

2. Are we willing to live with the worst probable outcome if we fail to make the goal? If not, we would lower the goal.

3. Are we confident that we can maintain our quality standards? If not, we would lower the goal.

During my nine years as CEO at LeaderShape, we set goals with an almost impossible stretch, and we failed to achieve the number of participants for our goal each year. Figure 5.1 shows the results of the growth of the number of participants starting in the year the program was founded, 1986, and through the years that I was CEO, 1992 to 2001.

How did we achieve growth from 229 participants in 1992 to 2,230 in 2001? The short answer is that we did it through the creativity and dedicated efforts of many staff, board members, campus partners, volunteers, donors, and funders who are committed to the mission and to providing high-quality, ethics-based leadership development experiences to young adults. Beyond that, every year had its own story. We worked hard to learn each year from the new ideas we tried that did not work. And we continually applied that learning to the next year.

Did we want to make the goal each year? Of course! We wanted as many young people as possible to the experience. But while we always wanted more participants, we focused on our accomplishments, on learning that we could apply for the future, and on making sure that we maintained our high standards of quality. In fact, our commitment to quality garnered us a designation by the W. K. Kellogg Foundation as an Exemplary Program in 1999.

LeaderShape today continues to expand, and I have been reinvolved as a volunteer after leaving staff. More than 34,000 young people have attended the program since its inception, and it has begun expanding globally (e.g., Qatar, Canada, South Africa). For more information, check out the site

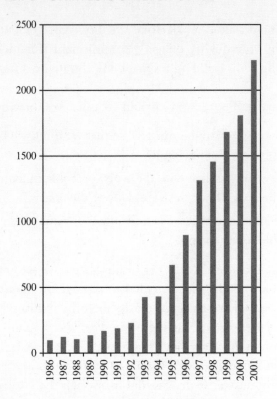

FIGURE 5.1   Number of Participants (1986–2001)

www.LeaderShape.org and figure out a way for some of your favorite young adults to attend.

General Electric

The first public presentation I made about setting stretch goals, outside of a LeaderShape program, was at the annual national conference of the Association of Fundraising Professionals (then National Society of Fund Raising Executives) in Boston on March 8, 1994. Stretch goals were still a relatively new idea, and I remember thinking during that time that I wished I had some good public examples to share with the participants.

On the plane ride home that evening I looked at my copy of the *Wall Street Journal* to find a page one story entitled "GE Chairman's Annual Letter Notes Strides by 'Stretch' of the Imagination." It was all about how

CEO Jack Welch had instituted the use of stretch goals into the company. The article included excerpts from Welch's annual letter to shareholders and other quotes from him, including:

> Stretch is a concept that would have produced smirks, if not laughter, in the GE of three or four years ago, because it essentially means using dreams to set business targets—with no real idea of how to get there . . . if you do know how to get there then it is not a stretch target.
>
> In a company that now rewards progress toward stretch goals, rather than punishing shortfalls, the setting of these goals, and quantum leaps toward them, are daily events.
>
> And the goals "are making seemingly impossible goals exciting, bringing out the best from our teams."

Steven Kerr, who served as chief learning officer and Vice President of Leadership Development for General Electric from 1994 to 2001, recounts how enthusiastic Welch was about the stretch approach (Kerr & Landauer, 2004). Welch would often tell the story of the development of the bullet train in Japan. The engineers were not asked to make an existing train go faster, which would have resulted in incremental improvements. They were given a performance level that required them to invent a totally different way for a train to operate. They would not have created the bullet train idea if they had been operating from a traditional analytical mind-set.

One of the challenges that GE faced in implementing the aspirational mind-set of the almost impossible stretch is that it had a very high-performance culture that did not tolerate failure. But GE quickly learned that punishing people for missing stretch targets did not work. This created a significant amount of turmoil, but the organization adopted different ways of evaluating performance for individuals or teams who were working on stretch targets. Instead of looking strictly at whether a goal was achieved or not, they began looking at aspects such as improvement over past performance and meaningful progress toward the goal.

Evidence of this change in mind-set is demonstrated in Welch's 1995 shareholder letter where he constructively discussed the failure of the company to reach stretch targets:

> As strong as the year was, we did not achieve two of what we call "stretch" performance targets: operating margins and inventory

returns . . . But in stretching for these impossible targets, we learned to do things faster than we would have going after "doable" goals, and we have enough confidence now to set new stretch targets. (Welch, 1996)

While there were many different variables that made General Electric a high-performing company during this time frame, the application of the aspirational mind-set and use of the almost impossible stretch is clearly one aspect of their success.

APPLICATION TO HYPOTHETICAL ORGANIZATIONS

Large City Metro Food Bank

Jeff completed a presentation on strategic stretch goals, and then directed the group's attention to the flip-chart pages that had the vision description listed. "You all came up with a fabulous vision for your ideal organization," he said. "Now we want to come up with five outcome-based strategic stretch goals that are almost impossible."

"Why don't we just adopt the vision as our stretch goals and break for an early lunch," said Tim.

"I like your style, Tim," said Jeff, "and your comment reminds me of an old Cheech & Chong bit—but we won't go there."

"You know," said Bob, "Tim was kidding, but when you think about it I wonder how crazy it really would be to get all of that done in the next five years. I mean is it really so impossible to think of tripling our capacity in that amount of time?"

"Yes," laughed Al.

Jeff smiled. "You all get to choose what you think is almost impossible. And just remember how many things people once thought were impossible have happened in our lifetimes. Why don't you pick something related to your vision list and talk about it as a strategic stretch goal. See what you think."

"Okay, the building," said Andy, an executive committee member. "We need it badly and we can't distribute much more food from our current facilities. Does anyone have any idea how much money we would need to raise to build that kind of facility?"

APPLICATION TO HYPOTHETICAL ORGANIZATIONS

"We have discussed this a number of times during the past couple of years, so yes," said Tim. "I have some ideas. Based on preliminary information from a number of sources, we are probably looking at the need to raise $22 million. And that would be for everything—furnishings, technology, everything."

"Think about it," said Bob. "We're already raising about $10 million per year from various sources. How can we say that another $22 million over three to five years is impossible? I mean, I don't know how we would do it, but I can't say it would be impossible. And it is strategic—we need that building to make the rest of our vision begin to come into reality, and close our meal gap."

"You know," said Andy, "as you say that, the idea that anyone in the United States of America, and especially in this community, should have to go a day without the basic meals that they need . . . I mean, it should just be unacceptable. I don't mean to be the one that is talking crazy now, but maybe we should tell the community that it is our goal to close that meal gap within the next five years and that we need everyone to step up to do whatever it takes to make that happen."

"Why not make that one of our strategic stretch goals?" said Hugh. "My hypothesis is that it will rally a lot of people. And what's the worst thing that could happen if we fail? We just keep going until we do get there."

Remarkably, by the end of the session, the SDG created a set of strategic stretch goals that would triple their capacity and could close the meal gap within five years. They saw no significant downside to falling short of the goal and someone mentioned something about the notion of a "noble failure" if that's what it came to. They selected the following strategic stretch goals that would actually have them fulfill their vision within the next five years:

1. Raise $22 million for a new building and move in by June 30, 2013.
2. In addition to the building fund, raise $128 million in gifts from individuals, corporations, foundations, and in qualified planned gifts by June 30, 2015 (cumulatively).
3. Triple the amount of food donated annually by June 30, 2015.
4. Triple the number of volunteers utilized annually by June 30, 2015.
5. Close our community meal gap by June 30, 2015.

Big River Regional Housing Services

"Now that you have an idea about what we mean when we say a strategic stretch goal, I would like each of you to spend some time looking at the vision you created and think about one goal that will really catapult you in that direction," said Tom. "I'll give you a few minutes to think about it."

Once everyone had a goal written down, Tom went around the room and wrote each one down on the flip chart.

"We have so far to go," said Lauren. "I mean we really do have—like you said, Tom—a mission gap that is more like a chasm. It is hard to know where to begin."

"Right," said Erin, "but let's get pragmatic. I guess we need to start with cha-ching, finding ways to bring in a lot more money. A number of us mentioned that. How about a stretch goal for the annual fundraising from individuals and another one for corporations, foundations, government grants?"

"That sounds right," said Troy. "But how much is almost impossible for each of those?"

"Our individual giving is so small," said Elaine. "How about we go for $150,000 for individuals and $500,000 for corporate, foundations, and government grants?"

"Why not," said Kendra. "I don't think we have any idea what we can do since we really have never tried. What about our mission accomplishment measure? How much should we try to improve there?"

"How about 5 percent," said Joyce, one of the residents.

"Five percent?" said Kendra. "But that seems so small."

"But its 4,000 households," said Lauren. "That is gigantic. That is more than gigantic. We are going to have to get many other entities on this bandwagon with us if we are going to even get anywhere near that."

"Right," said Troy. "But you know, just as we're talking about it I am starting to get some ideas of some different things we can do. I say we go for it."

The discussions went around and around for quite a while about what was really possible and almost impossible and totally ridiculous. By the end of the session, though, the SDG agreed on the following strategic stretch goals:

1. Increase annual fund donations from individuals to $150,000 per year by June 30, 2015.

2. Increase corporate, foundation, and government grants to $500,000 per year by June 30, 2015.

3. Increase reserves by $200,000 by June 30, 2015.

4. Acquire or build 1,000 multifamily or senior affordable housing units by June 30, 2015.

5. Demonstrate at least a 5 percent improvement (compared to baseline) on all indicators tracked for our region's Success Measures® by June 30, 2015.

Merrill County Literacy Council

Mark completed a presentation on the guidelines for setting strategic stretch goals and then wrote the mission accomplishment measure on the flip chart:

> *The percentage of adults in Merrill County, age 16 and older, who are literate as measured by the NAAL annual survey.*

"It is suggested that one of the five strategic stretch goals you set is for a change in the mission accomplishment measure," said Mark. "So why don't we start with this one. We currently have 80 percent of the adult population literate and we want it to be 100 percent. What would be an almost impossible stretch for five years from now?"

"How about 90 percent?" said Janelle.

"What!?" said Anne, a volunteer tutor. "Okay, I want everyone literate, too, but that would be 10,000 more people through our programs in five years—and five years is not that far away. I simply cannot even imagine that."

"I appreciate the desire for that kind of a breakthrough," said Alice, the HR director from the hospital, "but that would be more than remarkable. How about half that?"

"Okay, at least we are operating in some kind of reality, but how are we going to do that?" wondered Anne. "I just can't see how."

"Well," said Donta', "I don't either, but who knows? Maybe we can come up with something. It would be really incredible if we could make that kind of progress—even close."

"We certainly would have to rethink how we do things," said Colleen. "We would have to be talking about way more resources than we have now—money, volunteers, staff, classrooms, transportation. Ai yi yi."

"Sounds like a noble adventure to me," said Ellen. "What does everyone else think? Are we willing to fail at this? What's the downside?"

"Good point, Ellen," said Alice. "I say we go for it. Let's go for 85 percent in five years!"

"Does that work for everyone?" asked Mark. Heads nodded and the group had their first strategic stretch goal.

"Now, with the mission gap and your vision in mind, I am going to divide you up into three groups of five each and give you about 45 minutes to work together to come up with three more strategic stretch goals for MCLC for the next five years," directed Mark. "Remember that they need to fit the SMART criteria and we want them to give us a quantum leap toward the vision so we can close that mission gap most effectively. Please use whatever space you want to here to meet in your small group and bring back your goals on a piece of flip-chart paper."

The group returned after 45 minutes and hung their goals on the wall of the meeting room. "Of the nine goals you all came up with in total, I definitely see some overlap among them. And then we have a few that nobody else thought of," said Mark. "Let's work through the ones where we have some overlap first."

There was agreement that goals for fundraising and volunteer recruitment were needed, and the group came to consensus on the numbers for each. The final two goals were more difficult to narrow down, but the group finally decided that they needed multiple goals in the area of funding.

"If we are really going to get this mission gap closed," said Ellen, "then we are going to need to be well funded. If we can get this funding in place in the next five years, as well as reduce illiteracy by 5 percent and recruit all those volunteers, it will be astonishing. But if we even get close, then we will really be setting ourselves up for some even bigger breakthroughs in years 5 to 10 from now."

"Right," said Colleen, "and it's not like we are not going to work toward some of those other goals we discussed, like increasing the staff; they are just not making our top five."

And with that the SDG agreed to their final list of strategic stretch goals for MCLC:

1. Unrestricted grants from all sources will increase by 300 percent to $2 million by June 30, 2015.

2. The number of certified literacy teaching volunteers will increase by 500+ percent to 100 by June 30, 2015.

3. Financial reserves will be increased by $400,000 by June 30, 2015.

4. An endowment fundraising campaign for $5 million will be initiated and a lead gift of $500,000 will be pledged by June 30, 2015.

5. The literacy rate in Merrill County, as reported by county officials, will be 85 percent by June 30, 2015.

CHAPTER 6

Organization Assessment

A clear strategic understanding of the organization's current reality is essential in order to craft a strategy that breaks through from that current reality toward the strategic stretch goals and vision. The strategy development group (SDG) identifies the organization's strengths, weaknesses, opportunities, and threats (SWOTs) in the context of the organization's commitment to achieve the strategic stretch goals, pursue the vision, and close the mission gap.

PLANNING YOUR ASSESSMENT

At this stage in the process, the SDG has created the future it wants for the organization by identifying the mission gap, creating its vision, and setting the strategic stretch goals. The question in Chapter 7 on strategy development will be "how do we get from here—where we are today—to our desired future?" The answer will be captured in the strategy the group develops. But in order to craft the strategy, the organization first needs to clearly and completely understand its current situation.

The end result of whatever assessment process an organization decides to utilize is that by the end of this step of the process the SDG will select what it believes to be the most important SWOTs of the organization. They will then also identify important interactions between those SWOTs. These understandings of the organization's current situation will be very important during strategy development.

During the design portion of the strategy development process, the organization needs to make important decisions about the type and volume of information it will assemble for the SDG to consider as it chooses the SWOTs. Options organizations typically follow for collecting assessment information run a wide spectrum from doing almost nothing to very elaborate processes. In fact, there are many organizations that simply have their SDG do a SWOT analysis without any additional input. This should be avoided if at all possible for two reasons. First, as discussed in Chapter 2, collecting organization assessment data is an ideal way to meaningfully involve stakeholders in the process. Second, providing the SDG with more input into their decision-making process should produce a higher quality list of SWOTs. Either the SDG will choose different SWOTs as a result of this input, or their understanding of the SWOTs will be deepened as a result of the additional input.

My experience with SDGs is that they typically overstate strengths, understate weaknesses, and often miss many opportunities and threats. These errors can result in the development of a very poor strategy, regardless of how important the organization's mission may be or how compelling its vision might be. If the organization doesn't clearly understand its current situation, then it cannot effectively navigate into the future. Therefore, designing an organization assessment process that provides quality information to the SDG is very important. It is ideal to create enough opportunities in the information collection process for different perspectives on the organization and its environment to emerge.

For example, an organization for which I was doing some consulting once distributed an organization self-assessment tool to its staff and key stakeholders as a part of their ongoing review of operations. When the CEO reviewed the results with his senior managers, they noticed that a major theme throughout the report was a low rating in anything connected to performance metrics. When he asked the managers what they made of the report, one person suggested, "It seems like people want us to set specific goals." The CEO was actually quite surprised. He had been rather laissez faire about goals and thought people liked that. He figured everyone would do their best and things would take care of themselves. For the most part, he was right—the organization was performing well from all outside indicators. But others in the organization realized that performance could be improved if they set specific goals for their work. This was a simple improvement to make once the weakness was recognized. But without the additional perspectives provided through the assessment, he might never have realized this.

The challenge for an organization is in selecting how much information to collect, how much it will cost, and how long it will take. The simplest way to reach out for input is the distribution of a simple survey. As mentioned in Chapter 2, some of the questions that could be included in a survey are:

- Does our current mission statement properly reflect our purpose and activities? Should it be changed or improved in any ways?

- We are going to explore various methods for assessing our effectiveness. Do you have any suggested criteria that we should keep in mind?

- We are going to create a vision for what our organization would look like ideally, so we are situated to accomplish our mission most effectively. What would you want to include in that kind of vision for the future?

- What ideas do you have for how we could accomplish our mission more effectively?

- What do you think are our organization's strengths and weaknesses? What opportunities do you think we should be aware of in the coming years? What threats or challenges may we want to keep in mind during the coming years?

- What thoughts do you have on what our most important goals should be for the next three to five years?

- What ideas do you have on how we can most effectively go about achieving those goals?

If the organization decides to host town hall–type meetings, then these questions could be used to guide those meetings. More in-depth information, using these same types of questions, could be collected through focus groups and interviews.

If time and budget allow, it is very helpful to do a more extensive assessment of the organization's internal operations and its external environment. The following sections review various options for collecting this information.

EXTERNAL ASSESSMENTS

Changes occurring in the relevant external environment in which the organization operates are important to monitor both during strategy development and implementation. For this reason, many organizations collect and review this type of information on a regular basis. This data is often maintained as part of the organization's overall information system.

Much of this data is available for collection from other sources, particularly from government agencies or other public records. Foundations and other funders may also be sources as they follow various trends regarding issues of importance to them. In recent years, colleges and universities have become a better source for this type of data, especially as various centers on nonprofit management and philanthropy have been established. Local nonprofits which are a part of a national association may have access to data they may collect.

There are times when an organization may find the need to collect its own data from the external environment. This may be especially true for organizations that operate on a national basis and want to understand trends that are relevant for its programs and operations, such as attitudes or patterns of behavior. In order to collect these types of data in a reliable and valid manner, outside consultants are typically used.

Some of the forces and trends that are often of interest to organizations include those in the political, economic, social, technological, environmental, and legal categories (Bryson, 2004).

INTERNAL ASSESSMENTS

During the strategy development process, the purpose of conducting an organization assessment is to gain an accurate understanding of the current operations so the SDG may craft a strategy toward the vision and strategic stretch goals. Of course, a regular monitoring of an organization's operations by the board of directors and senior management is simply a wise ongoing activity.

Some organizations will retain evaluation consultants to provide an objective review of their operations. This can be especially helpful in making sure that a voice is given to weaknesses that may be otherwise overlooked and to temper an overly optimistic assessment of strengths.

Whether an organization retains the services of an external consultant or conducts an assessment on their own, an assessment is most effectively done in a systematic fashion. In recent years, more attention has been devoted toward research on nonprofit organizations. This has led to the development of more sophisticated instruments for assessing the performance of nonprofits. Many national nonprofit organizations have developed these instruments for use by their local entities, and some of these organizations also provide external consultants to review the assessments with organizations. Academics have also developed some of these instruments for use in their research.

In my opinion, one of the best organization assessment instruments that is publicly available for all nonprofits to utilize was developed for Venture Philanthropy Partners by the consulting firm McKinsey & Company in 2001. More detail on that instrument is provided in an upcoming section. I am very pleased that Venture Philanthropy Partners and McKinsey have allowed for the inclusion of their entire Capacity Assessment Grid in Appendix A of this book.

Another widely used assessment tool was developed by Peter Drucker and the Drucker Foundation (1993). It is organized around Drucker's *Five Most Important Questions*, which are:

- What Is Our Mission?
- Who Is Our Customer?
- What Does the Customer Value?
- What Are Our Results?
- What Is Our Plan?

Centered around these questions, the self-assessment tool—and an associated process guide (1999)—is really more than just an assessment, it provides a way of thinking about nonprofit organizations and their purpose. It is now commercially available through the Leader to Leader Institute and is used by many nonprofits to guide their planning and performance.

In preparation for writing this book, I have reviewed a number of other nonprofit organization assessment instruments that are publicly available. In addition, fellow researchers from the Association of Research on Non-profit Organizations and Voluntary Action have shared instruments with me that they use in their research. And a number of national nonprofit associations have shared their instruments with me as well.

After reviewing all of these instruments, I have found that most of them ssess the following seven categories of operational activity in one way or another:

- Strategy and Planning
- Human Resources
- Board and Volunteers
- Funding
- Programs and Services
- Infrastructure
- General Administration

What follows is a summary of some of the themes of high proficiency that are mentioned in each of these categories in the instruments reviewed, as well as some insights from other research on organization performance. These are provided as information for the SDG, and others who assess the organization's operations, to consider as they identify strengths, weaknesses, opportunities, and threats. Depending on how well the SDG thinks they are doing in the category—according to the summary information provided—they may list aspects of the category as a strength or weakness.

Strategy and Planning

High levels of proficiency in this category include having a strategic plan that is connected to annual operating plans. The assumptions underlying the plan are reviewed on a regular basis to make sure that the strategy is still relevant. The strategy should be based on the mission and vision of the organization and include goals.

The process of developing the strategy should include the board of directors and staff, as well as relevant stakeholders. The plan should identify resources that are needed for implementation.

Marketing efforts are integrated with mission, vision, and strategy. The value proposition is clearly articulated as a function of the mission and vision, and the impact the organization is committed to making. Branding activities are a natural extension of the mission and vision.

Annual plans are based upon the strategic plan. They should include specific goals for the year as well as milestones so that progress may be tracked during the course of the year. Staff who direct major areas of the organization's activities share their annual plans to assure integration. The annual plans drive the budget. Annual plans are reviewed by the board of directors with updates provided on a regular basis.

Common mistakes include not involving stakeholders, not assuring that strategic plans continue to be relevant on an annual basis, not connecting the annual plans to the strategic plan, and not connecting budget to the annual plan.

Human Resources

High proficiency includes creating a staff structure that supports the strategic plan and the annual plans. Lines of accountability are clear, and the results/outcomes that every person is responsible for are specified in job descriptions and an annual individual work plan. Outcomes for which individuals are accountable connect to the goals of the annual plan.

Staff should have demonstrated that they have the talent and skills required for high performance in their role. Each staff member should have a professional development plan that is designed to enhance performance as well as support the individual's career development. Each individual's performance and development plan should be monitored regularly by a supervisor. Merit compensation should be connected to results that are produced by the individual.

Documented human resources policies that are in compliance with all governmental regulations should exist and be well known to the staff.

Compensation and benefits should as competitive as possible with similar nonprofit or government jobs in the organization's region. Jobs should be designed so that a person working a reasonable schedule can perform well in the position.

Emergency succession plans exist for key staff positions and cross-training is done to assure uninterrupted operations if staff miss significant time at work. The organization has effective methods for recruiting and retaining staff. People are valued as an essential asset.

Personal and organizational integrity is highly valued and individuals work together in a trusting environment. Teams are high performing and engage in constructive conflict. Meetings are run in an efficient and productive manner.

The CEO is effective, yet the organization is not overly reliant on the CIO. Shared leadership exists and the senior management team could smoothly welcome a new CEO when a transition occurs.

Problems that occur when these functions are not carried out effectively include high turnover, high absenteeism, burnout, and/or lack of coordination among individuals or teams.

Board and Volunteers

Volunteers are managed well and the board is engaged in highly proficient organizations. Volunteers are utilized in situations where their skills fit the program or operational need. Training is provided for them and staff are available to coordinate their efforts.

The board is actively engaged in strategic planning and in monitoring progress on a regular basis. This includes sound fiscal management as well as program effectiveness oversight. Board members connect with stakeholders and supporters in the community to promote the objectives of the plan and the organization.

The board regularly reviews its membership and size to ensure that it has the talents, skills, and attributes the organization needs to advance the organization's mission and vision. Term limits for members and officers exist. Active recruitment of new board members is routine and an effective orientation is provided for new board members.

Fundraising efforts are led by the board, both by giving and soliciting the support from other donors and funders to support the organization.

The staff and board have a respectful relationship with an appreciation of the different roles that each carries out for the organization.

The board regularly evaluates its own operations and has a systematic procedure for evaluating the CEO's performance and compensation.

Organizations which do not carry out this functional area well have difficulty attracting and retaining volunteers, volunteer efforts are ineffective, recruiting new board members is difficult, community relations suffer, strategy is lacking, and fundraising results are poor.

Funding

Organizations that demonstrate high competence in the funding area have diverse streams of revenue and consistently produce annual surpluses. A reserve fund and endowment fund have been established and are added to regularly. New programs and services are not added until funding support has been demonstrated. Cash flow is actively managed and monitored.

The organization has a comprehensive fundraising program in which the board of directors is intimately involved. This includes an annual fund fundraising program, corporate support, foundation and government grants, major gifts, planned gifts, endowment gifts, and—when appropriate—campaigns. An integrated marketing and fundraising plan exists. The organization proactively seeks new sources of funding for strategic priorities.

Fees for services are evaluated regularly to keep them at appropriate levels as compared with other similar services and the organization's ability to subsidize those services.

Active oversight of the investments of the organization's reserves and endowment is provided either directly by the board of directors or by a committee of experts who report to the board.

Difficulties experienced by organizations that do not perform well in this category include regular deficit spending, poor fundraising results, and an inability to fund new programs.

Programs and Services

Highly proficient organizations rigorously evaluate program/service outcomes and establish procedures to ensure consistent, high-quality delivery. Innovation in the design and delivery of programs/services is regularly considered. Other organizations benchmark their programs/services against those of highly effective organizations.

Expanding the impact of programs/services is explored, as consistent with strategic priorities. This includes the development of new programs/services as well as scaling up those that currently exist.

Stakeholders and beneficiaries of programs/services are involved in evaluation as well as innovation efforts, to ensure relevance.

Problems experienced by organizations that do not perform well in this category include inconsistent program/service quality, limited program impact, and irrelevance of programs/services.

Infrastructure

Organizations with high competency in infrastructure extensively utilize technology to improve efficiency and effectiveness of the overall operation. This begins with a networked computer system with updated software applications that provides access to reliable internal and external communications for all staff.

Information systems and databases exist which can seamlessly provide updated reports for staff on program/service activities. These systems also regularly track important trends in the external environment that need to be monitored by the organization. Documentation of important information is tracked in a knowledge management system.

A quality telephone system exists with voice mail and clear instructions for callers to reach the individuals they need to talk with. Mobile devices for phone and email are provided for staff.

An up-to-date, interactive web site exists which promotes the mission and vision of the organization. It promotes the various programs, services, and activities of the organization and actively supports all strategic priorities.

Adequate office space and facilities that are needed are available with updated equipment that is required for office work as well as programs/services. Facilities are inspected regularly and maintained for continued productive use.

All information systems and databases are backed up regularly.

Problems experienced by organizations that are not proficient in infrastructure activities include breakdowns in communications, general inefficiencies, lack of information needed for staff to do their jobs, and ineffective external communications.

General Administration

This broad category captures the organization's proficiency in integrating and coordinating its various activities. This includes the documentation of standard operating procedures that are explained in staff orientation and used by staff in their various roles.

Financial management systems and practices are regularly reviewed by external auditors and assured to be in compliance. Appropriate internal financial controls, including separation of duties, are in place and practiced. The organization is in compliance with all laws and government regulations (for example, tax filings, Sarbanes–Oxley). Costs are accurately assigned to different categories of programs/services so comprehensive monitoring of expenses can be done. The board has approved a formal investment policy.

Legal issues are regularly monitored, as are risk management procedures. Appropriate insurance is purchased and reviewed annually with the board of directors.

Other important issues include:

- A statement of ethical values and practices is well known and committed to by all staff and board members.
- A regularly updated crisis management plan is well known by all staff and board members.
- Public relations, communications, community relations, and media relations activities are all conducted consistently with the mission, vision, and ethical values.

Organizations that do not conduct their general administration activities effectively may have legal problems, breakdowns in quality due to lack of standard operating procedures, breaches of ethical conduct, and poor community relations.

THE VENTURE PHILANTHROPY PARTNERS CAPACITY FRAMEWORK

Venture Philanthropy Partners is a philanthropic organization founded in 2000 by a group of donors/investors, with a goal of providing funds/investments to nonprofits in the metropolitan Washington, D.C., area that have missions to improve the lives of low-income children. Their idea has been to invest in the capacity of these organizations, so they could become sustainable high-performing organizations.

As a way to help them learn how to leverage their contributions/investments most effectively, VPP retained the services of the McKinsey &

Company consulting firm to provide them with a road map of what effective capacity building for nonprofits would look like. The result of that research is a report, published in 2001, entitled *Effective Capacity Building in Nonprofit Organizations*. The full report is available at no charge at the Venture Philanthropy Partners web site (www.vppartners.org). Check the section on Learning, and then Reports.

The research includes case studies of a variety of nonprofit organizations that had recently taken on capacity building efforts. One result of the report was the development of a Capacity Framework, which captures seven essential elements of a nonprofit organization's operations that are crucial to developing organization capacity. According to the McKinsey team that developed the Framework, those elements are:

- *Aspirations.* An organization's mission, vision, and overarching goals, which collectively articulate its common sense of purpose and direction.
- *Strategy.* The coherent set of actions and programs aimed at fulfilling the organization's overarching goals.
- *Organizational skills.* The sum of the organization's capabilities, including such things (among others) as performance measurement, planning, resource management, and external relationship building.
- *Human resources.* The collective capabilities, experiences, potential and commitment of the organization's board, management team, staff, and volunteers.
- *Systems and infrastructure.* The organization's planning, decision making, knowledge management, and administrative systems, as well as the physical and technological assets that support the organization.
- *Organizational structure.* The combination of governance, organizational design, interfunctional coordination, and individual job descriptions that shapes the organization's legal and management structure.
- *Culture.* The connective tissue that binds together the organization, including shared values and practices, behavior norms, and most important, the organization's orientation towards performance.

Graphically, the Framework is captured in the pyramid diagram in Figure 6.1, which shows the three higher-level elements of aspirations, strategy, and

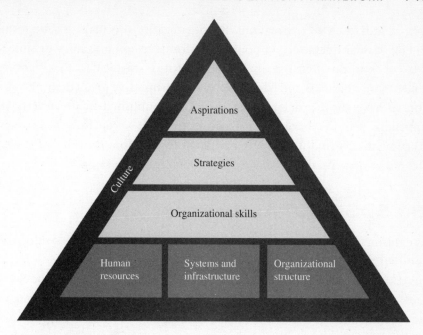

FIGURE 6.1   **VPP Pyramid**

Source: All rights reserved and used with permission. This figure was taken from the report "Effective Capacity Building in Nonprofit Organizations" (2001), Venture Philanthropy Partners (VVP), which was prepared for VVP by McKinsey & Company.

organizational skills, followed by the foundational elements of human resources, systems and infrastructure, and organizational structure. Culture then connects all the elements together.

Based on the Capacity Framework, the McKinsey team also developed an extensive Capacity Assessment Grid, which is included in the report, at the web site referenced above. Again, this is available with no charge. VPP and McKinsey are providing this as a service to the nonprofit community.

During the past eight years, I have used the VPP-McKinsey Capacity Assessment Grid in numerous courses I have taught for nonprofit executives and in consulting I have done with nonprofit organizations. Given the diversity of the nonprofit sector, it is very difficult to design any kind of assessment instrument that fits exactly right for all organizations. But this assessment instrument is very thorough and comes as close to any I have seen at providing an opportunity for organizations to make a thoughtful review of their operations in preparation for developing strategy or simply as a checkup on their organizational health. I am pleased that Venture Philanthropy Partners and McKinsey & Company have given their permission to have the Capacity Assessment Grid published in its entirety in Appendix A of this book. Organizations that choose to use it as a survey instrument may find it easier to download the version from the VPP web site, rather than attempt to make photocopies from the book.

The SDG SWOT Analysis

As explained in Chapter 2, the SDG receives all of the assessment information that the organization decides to collect prior to its first meeting and this data is reviewed at that initial meeting. These reports inform the decisions that the SDG makes in the early parts of the strategy development process, but the SDG does not make its final decisions on what it thinks the key SWOTs are until this point in the process—after vision and strategic stretch goals have been set.

This sequencing is much different than what is done in most strategic planning models. Most approaches, which are more analytically based, suggest that SWOTs be determined early in the planning process. The SWOTs then are considered to be constraints that are factored in as the organization attempts to forecast the kind of future that may be possible.

In the approach I am advocating, the future—both the vision and strategic stretch goals—is first envisioned from an aspirational mind-set, without worrying so much about the reality of the organization's current situation. Now—in this stage in the process—is the time to look clearly at that reality, but from a different perspective. The SDG has already established a commitment to achieve the vision and the strategic stretch goals, and they will now consider the organization's current situation from that viewpoint. Looking at the organization from the new future they have created, the SDG will see different SWOTs than they would have seen if they had looked at them in the present day.

The SDG SWOT analysis includes two parts, identification of the SWOTs and then identification of the SWOT interactions. In identifying the SWOTs, the SDG needs to come to consensus on their answers to these questions:

1. Given our vision and commitment to achieve the strategic stretch goals, what are the five most important strengths of our organization?

2. Given our vision and commitment to achieve the strategic stretch goals, what are the five most concerning weaknesses of our organization?

3. Given our vision and commitment to achieve the strategic stretch goals, what are the five most important opportunities our organization may take advantage of in the future?

4. Given our vision and commitment to achieve the strategic stretch goals, what are the five most important threats our organization needs to be mindful of in the future?

There are a variety of group process techniques that the SDG can use to help it come to consensus on these SWOTs. The important aspect of making the decision on the top five in each category is that there is an opportunity for some good discussion and healthy disagreement over the SWOTs so they become well understood by the group. This clear understanding is invaluable for the SDG during the strategy development process, which will be discussed in the next chapter.

While traditionally people tend to think of strengths and weaknesses as internal aspects of the organization and of opportunities and threats as existing in the external environment, this distinction is not worth too much discussion. Is the possibility of the 62-year-old CEO's retirement during the next five years a threat or weakness? The SDG can choose whatever category works for them.

Once the SWOTs have been chosen, the SDG then needs to look at its lists and identify any possible interactions between each item on the SWOT list. This will be used along with the SWOTs to craft strategy in the next step of the process. The importance of identifying these interactions is a key concept in systems thinking, as has been discussed in Chapters 1 and 4. The interaction of two or more of the SWOTs can present opportunities or challenges. For example, Kearns (1992) discusses the fact that when a weakness interacts with a threat, this can pose a strategic issue that he says calls for "damage control" (p. 15). Indeed, as will be discussed in the next chapter, if any interactions between threats and weaknesses are identified that have the potential to debilitate the organization; this becomes the top priority of the new strategy. Of course, more positive interactions can also arise, such as when strength meets opportunity. These circumstances provide significant leverage and are high priorities for strategic action.

The SDG will want to review the SWOTs and identify possible interactions between:

- Weaknesses and threats
- Strengths and threats
- Weaknesses and opportunities
- Strengths and weaknesses
- Opportunities and threats
- Strengths and opportunities

If more than five possible interactions are identified within each of these categories, then the SDG needs to come to consensus on the most important five interactions.

Some interactions are immediately identifiable while others may be more difficult to discern. This is a situation in which members of the SDG who have the talent of organizational wisdom, as mentioned in Chapter 2, are particularly valuable.

APPLICATION TO HYPOTHETICAL ORGANIZATIONS

Large City Metro Food Bank

LCMFB conducted extensive assessment activities with stakeholders including interviews, town halls, and focus groups. They also used the Venture Philanthropy Partners Capacity Assessment Grid (Appendix A) as a survey tool with their various stakeholder groups. All of this data was provided to the SDG prior to their first meeting and then reviewed there.

The SDG had the SWOTs in mind as they did their work in the earlier stages of the process. After the second day of their deliberations, once the vision and strategic stretch goals were established, the four SWOT questions were sent to them to complete and send back to their consultants.

The results were tabulated and sent back to the SDG for their review, prior to their final two-day retreat.

Jeff explained what the group was about to do to complete this part of the process and asked them to have their SWOT report available for review. "You each had a chance to select what you think are the organization's five most important strengths, weaknesses, opportunities, and threats. And you have had a chance to see what others wrote down. Now I would like you to take 10 minutes to review that report again and choose the five most important SWOTs—five per area—and we will discuss them. Your ideas may have changed now that you see what others have written. If you finish that quickly, then you can begin looking at some of the interactions between what you think are the most important SWOTs."

When the group was done, Jeff split them up into three groups of five people each and asked each group to come to consensus on their top three SWOTs—three for each area—and to bring those back to the large group prepared to argue that their answers were the best ones.

Each group made their presentation, including impassioned explanations for why their answers were the *right* ones. There was a good amount of overlap and some areas of disagreement. Jeff worked through each SWOT with the group to come to consensus on their list of five for each SWOT:

Strengths

- New, high-profile board members
- Quality and dedicated staff
- Financial reserves
- Competitive staff compensation
- Enthusiastic and committed volunteers

Weaknesses

- Senior staff nearing traditional retirement age
- Too few development staff
- Facilities not large enough to meet needs
- No real marketing program
- Board has not been active in personal fundraising solicitation

Opportunities

- Surveys show high interest among public in mission.
- Retired volunteers are planned giving prospects.
- Retirees in community are living longer and healthier, and are interested in volunteer activity.
- Foundations exist that support building campaigns.
- The Large City Metro Community Foundation has established basic human needs as a funding priority.

Threats

- Competition for donations is increasing.
- Corporations are cutting back on charitable contributions.
- Rumored corporate mergers may reduce funding.
- Foundation giving is decreasing due to lower endowment income.
- Once the economy recovers, interest in hunger issues may ease.

"Now we want to identify interactions between the various SWOTs, starting with weaknesses and threats," said Jeff. "As you look at those lists, do you see any connections?"

"The fact that the competition for donations is increasing and we do not have as many development staff as we would like is one," said Evin, the director of a food pantry. "And the same threat is connected to the fact that the board has not been active in fundraising."

"That's the exact kind of connection we are looking for, Evin," said Jeff. "Thank you for that. Others?"

"The fact that we don't have much of a marketing program is a concern on its own," said Steve, the director of Large City Human Services, "but that will be exacerbated once the economy recovers and the fantasy that most everyone is working again is back in people's heads."

"Right on the money, Steve," said Jeff. "Anything else there? Or if not, let's keep going down the list. How about interactions between strengths and threats?"

The SDG continued working through the interactions and produced the following list:

Weaknesses and Threats

- Too few development staff, and Competition for donations is increasing

- The board has not been active in personal fundraising solicitation, and Competition for donations is increasing

- No real marketing program, and Once the economy recovers, interest in hunger issues may ease

Strengths and Threats

- Financial reserves, and Competition for donations is increasing.

- Financial reserves, and Corporations are cutting back on charitable contributions.

- Financial reserves, and Rumored corporate mergers may reduce funding.

- Financial reserves, and Foundation giving is decreasing due to lower endowment income.

Weaknesses and Opportunities

- Too few development staff, and Retired volunteers are planned giving prospects

- No real marketing program, and Surveys show high interest among public in mission

- Too few development staff, and Foundations exist that support building campaigns

- The board has not been active in personal fundraising solicitation, and Surveys show high interest among public in mission

Strengths and Weaknesses

- Competitive staff compensation, and Senior staff nearing traditional retirement age

- New, high-profile board members, and Board has not been active in personal fundraising solicitation

- Quality and dedicated staff, and Senior staff nearing traditional retirement age

Opportunities and Threats

- Surveys show high interest among public in mission, and Once economy recovers, interest in hunger issues may ease.
- Retired volunteers are planned giving prospects, and Competition for donations is increasing.
- The Large City Metro Community Foundation has established basic human needs as a funding priority, and Foundation giving is decreasing due to lower endowment income.

Strengths and Opportunities

- None

Big River Regional Housing Services

Tom and Pat recommended an assessment tool to BRRHS that other housing services groups across the country have been using. This was distributed to the staff and board for their input. The results were provided to the SDG at the beginning of their first day of meetings.

At the end of the second day of meetings, after the vision and strategic stretch goals had been established, the SDG had some time to begin working on their SWOTS. Tom broke them up into three smaller groups and asked them to come back quickly with a list of the top seven SWOTs—seven for each area. Each group gave a brief report, and their responses were typed up and then sent out for them to think about prior to the final day of meetings.

When it came time to discuss these on day 3, Tom asked the SDG to get back into those same small groups and now come up with a list of five SWOTs each.

When the groups came back to give their reports, some alignment had occurred between the time they finished day 2 and started day 3. After some group processing, the SDG came to consensus on the following SWOTs:

Strengths

- Financial reserves
- Strong reputation in community
- Quality, hard-working staff
- Engaged residents who care about properties
- Dedicated board

Weaknesses

- Board does not have fundraising experience.
- Staff does not have fundraising experience.
- Compensation packages for staff are very low.
- Office facilities need repair, and technology needs upgrading.
- Senior managers are nearing traditional retirement age.

Opportunities

- The national market for CEOs includes people who have fundraising and community development experience.
- Property values are lower; good time to purchase land or buildings.
- Many individuals within our area are potential donors; have never been asked.
- Potential new board members exist who would be committed to our mission.
- Many companies and foundations have never been asked to contribute.

Threats

- Recent bank mergers may threaten contributions.
- Government or other nonprofits could hire away staff with better compensation.
- State budget crisis could lower grants for years.
- Economic slowdown could cause residents to lose jobs, move, or fall behind on payments.

- Economic slowdown will further increase need for safe, decent, affordable housing.

"Thanks for your good work on that," said Tom. "Now if you recall, we are going to look at the interactions between these various SWOTs, starting with weaknesses and threats. Essentially, what we want to do is to identify connections between one SWOT and another that could exacerbate, moderate, or complement them. What do you see?"

"The one that jumps right out at me," said Gale, "is our low pay and the idea that someone else could steal our staff. I had no appreciation for the fact that our pay was so low relative to the market."

"The other ones that I see," said Troy, "are the weaknesses around fundraising and the bank mergers. The fallout from the bank mergers is going to be real, and we do not have a fundraising capacity to respond."

"Good one, Troy," said Kendra. "We do not have the fundraising capacity—yet."

"You all really get this," said Tom. "Let's keep working through the list of SWOTs and I'll write down all of the interactions you identify."

The final list of interactions for the SWOTs report was:

Weaknesses and Threats

- Compensation packages for staff are very low, and Government or other nonprofits could hire away staff with better compensation.
- Board does not have fundraising experience, and Recent bank mergers may threaten contributions.
- Staff does not have fundraising experience, and Recent bank mergers may threaten contributions.

Strengths and Threats

- Financial reserves, and Recent bank mergers may threaten contributions.
- Financial reserves, and State budget crisis could lower grants for years.

Weaknesses and Opportunities

- Staff does not have fundraising experience, and The national market for CEOs includes people who have fundraising and community development experience.

Strengths and Weaknesses

- Financial reserves, and Compensation packages for staff are very low.

Opportunities and Threats

- Many individuals within our area are potential donors; have never been asked, and Recent bank mergers may threaten contributions.
- Many individuals within our area are potential donors; have never been asked, and State budget crisis could lower grants for years.
- Many companies and foundations have never been asked to contribute, and Recent bank mergers may threaten contributions.
- Many companies and foundations have never been asked to contribute, and State budget crisis could lower grants for years.

Strengths and Opportunities

- Strong reputation in community, and Many individuals within our area are potential donors; have never been asked
- Strong reputation in community, and Potential new board members exist who would be committed to our mission
- Strong reputation in community, and Many companies and foundations have never been asked to contribute
- Financial reserves, and Property values are lower; good time to purchase land or houses

Merrill County Literacy Council

Once the strategic stretch goals were set, Mark pointed to the flip-chart paper on the meeting room wall that had the vision and the goals written on them. "Our next task," he said, "is to come to consensus on your answers to these questions about the strengths, weaknesses, opportunities, and threats that I have written on the flip chart. Notice that we want to consider each question with the vision and strategic stretch goals in mind. You were given external environment information at the beginning of our session and you were given reports on interviews and other meetings that have been held with key stakeholders who told us their impressions of our operations. So with all of that in mind, it is time to choose your

SWOTs. I am going to give you 30 minutes to think over these questions on your own and ask that you write down your answer to what you think the top five SWOTs are for MCLC. Then we'll come back and go around the room for some discussion."

Mark went around the table asking for responses to the strengths question, listing them on the flip chart. He repeated the process with weaknesses, opportunities, and threats. Once all responses had been given, he asked for discussion. After some time passed, he asked each person to vote for their top three choices, using a collection of colored dots that represented different point values. He added up the points that each item received. The top five point winners were their top five SWOTs. The results were:

Strengths

- Talented and energetic CEO
- Educational program is very effective—nationally recognized
- Dedicated and effective volunteer teachers
- Solid, hardworking staff
- Board that cares

Weaknesses

- Limited financial reserves.
- Compensation (pay and benefits) for staff is too low.
- Not enough board members have strong community connections.
- Outdated office equipment creates inefficiencies.
- Understaffed—paid staff and volunteers.

Opportunities

- Our mission is consistent with new United Way priorities.
- Chamber of Commerce has identified workforce preparation as an important issue for the future.
- Possibility of creating stronger partnerships with schools, churches, service clubs.

- Students from local colleges and universities have not been tapped as volunteer resources.

- We are addressing a serious problem with an effective solution (program), yet the seriousness of the ripples of the problem is not well understood. Once people understand, they respond.

Threats

- Increased immigration will increase illiteracy rates.
- Downturn in regional economy could hurt funding.
- General decreases in funding sources as competition for donations increases.
- Performance of county schools has been on the decline.
- Government or other nonprofits could "poach" our CEO or other staff with better compensation.

"Our final step with the SWOTs is to look at any possible interactions that may exist between the different items in the SWOTs," said Mark. "We want to look at important connections that may exist between any of them. Let's start by looking at any connections between our weaknesses and threats. Does anyone see anything?"

"Oh, yeah," said Kristen, the long-time program staffer. "Or I should say 'oh my.' Our limited financial reserves weakness could interact with the threats of the potential downturn in the economy and the competition for donations."

"You are correct, Kristen," replied Mark, "and the purpose of this part of the exercise is to identify places where you may have special vulnerabilities or special opportunities. You have identified some vulnerabilities for sure. Let's try another category—how about interactions between strengths and threats?"

"Yes," said Donta'. "The strength of our CEO could interact with the threat of someone stealing her. Basically, that threat could neutralize our strength. The same is true for the rest of the staff, another strength."

"Right on the money," said Mark. "You are getting the hang of this. Go ahead and take a few minutes to look over the lists, and then we'll compile all of the interactions."

When the group was through, they had indentified the following interactions between the SWOTs, which Mark then wrote on flip-chart paper:

Weaknesses and Threats

- Limited financial reserves, and Potential downturn in regional economy could hurt funding.
- Limited financial reserves, and General decreases in funding sources
  as competition for donations increases.
- Compensation (pay and benefits) for staff is too low, and Government or other nonprofits could "poach" our CEO or other staff
  with better compensation.

Strengths and Threats

- Talented and energetic CEO, and Government or other nonprofits
  could "poach" our CEO or other staff with better compensation.
- Solid, hardworking staff, and Government or other nonprofits could
  "poach" our CEO or other staff with better compensation.

Weaknesses and Opportunities

- Limited financial reserves, and Our mission is consistent with new
  United Way priorities.
- Understaffed—paid staff and volunteers, and Possibility of creating
  stronger partnerships with schools, churches, service clubs.
- Understaffed—paid staff and volunteers, and Students from local col-
  leges and universities have not been tapped as volunteer resources.

Strengths and Weaknesses

- Talented and energetic CEO, and Compensation (pay and benefits)
  for staff is too low.
- Solid, hardworking staff, and Compensation (pay and benefits) for
  staff is too low.

Opportunities and Threats

- Our mission is consistent with new United Way priorities, and
  Potential downturn in regional economy could hurt funding.

- Our mission is consistent with new United Way priorities, and General decreases in funding sources as competition for donations increases.

Strengths and Opportunities

- None

CHAPTER 7

Strategy Development

S trategy development is a creative process that results in a statement of the general themes—a strategy narrative that will guide the organization's performance for the coming three to five years. The strategy narrative generally explains how the organization will leverage its strengths, fortify its weaknesses, seize its opportunities, and block its threats as it pursues its strategic stretch goals, vision, and mission accomplishment.

NONPROFIT STRATEGY REVISITED

At this stage in the process, the strategy development group (SDG) prepares the organization's strategy narrative, the key themes that will guide the organization's performance during the next three to five years. As the SDG readies itself for this, it is important to keep some of the important points made in Chapter 1 about strategy in mind. Nonprofit strategy has been defined as:

> . . . an integrated and coherent explanation of how a nonprofit organization is going to accomplish its mission of making a difference for society in the future. It explains how its essential operations (funding, paid and unpaid staffing, programs/services for beneficiaries) will interact with one another, and within the organization's environment, to accomplish its mission. (Sheehan, 2009)

With the definition in mind, following are key points to remember from Chapter 1:

- The purpose of having a strategy is to guide the organization toward its desired future, which is to achieve the strategic stretch goals as it pursues its vision and closes its mission gap.

- The strategy is an integrated and coherent cause-and-effect performance story which has a beginning, middle, and end.

- The strategic actions the organization takes need to have positive effects on the other parts of the organization with which it interacts—as well as with its environment. These positive, reinforcing interactions are especially important among the functional areas of funding, staffing, and programs/services for beneficiaries. The strategic actions need to interact positively with one another—each contributing to the others in a way that is balanced and creates a virtuous positive spiral toward high performance—a cycle of sustainable performance.

- Crafting strategy is a creative act, not an analytical function. It is a process of considering the organization's current situation, such as its SWOTs, looking at the organization's desired future, and designing a set of actions which will catapult it forward. This is strategic thinking.

- In crafting the strategy, the organization will want to leverage strengths, seize opportunities, fortify weaknesses, and block threats.

- The commitment to mission accomplishment motivates the creation of the strategy.

CREATING YOUR ORGANIZATION'S STRATEGY

While I have said—a few times—that crafting strategy is a creative act, not an analytical act, this doesn't mean that the SDG can just make up any set of ideas that they think will work. There is a process the SDG should follow to give it the best opportunity to create an effective strategy—in addition to keeping the reminders above in mind.

Since the strategic stretch goals and vision are aspirational and represent an almost impossible stretch, the SDG is going to need to create a new breakthrough strategy in order to achieve them. The organization will need to take strategic actions that are significantly different, a new set of "causes," than what it has been doing in the past in order to move it forward faster and/or in a new direction—a new set of "effects." These new actions are the organization's new cause-and-effect performance story.

To aid in the process of creating strategic actions, I recommend the use of a strategy development map, an example of which is shown in Figure 7.1. I suggest that the SDG create its own strategy development map as a visual aid to support the strategy development process. This can be done with flip-chart paper taped to a meeting room wall, for example.

The top far left side of the map depicts current reality. All five of the organization's strengths, weaknesses, opportunities, and threats are listed on flip-chart paper and hung on a wall in the meeting room. Along with the SWOTs, flip-chart paper with the lists of the interactions that were identified between the SWOTs are hung. There are 20 SWOTs and could be as many as 30 interactions, so—yes—there could be lots of pieces of paper on the wall depicting the current reality.

The top very far right of the map depicts the ideal future. A piece of flip-chart paper is hung, which explains what the mission gap looks like in its ideal condition, for example, "No Homelessness in Charles County." To the immediate left of the ideal mission gap is a summary of the vision on another piece of paper.

In the middle of the wall between current reality and the ideal future is the strategy time frame: three to five years out. The strategic stretch goals are listed on a piece of flip-chart paper. If there is a natural sequencing to the list, then goals that will need to be accomplished before others should be listed in that order.

At the bottom left of the map, the SDG leaves room to list the strategic actions it is going to take. And to the right of that it will list the impact those actions have on the operational areas of funding, paid and unpaid staffing, and programs/services for beneficiaries. As explained earlier, it is important that these areas experience positive interactions as the result of the strategic actions taken by the SDG. Their interrelationships need to maintain a positive balance over time and the changes that are made to them need to be integrated with one another. For example, a complex program/service is probably going to require a certain number of well-qualified staff to run it. If the program/service gets expanded as a part of the strategy, then the funding needs to be made available to provide the right amount of quality staffing. If the organization in this example tried to

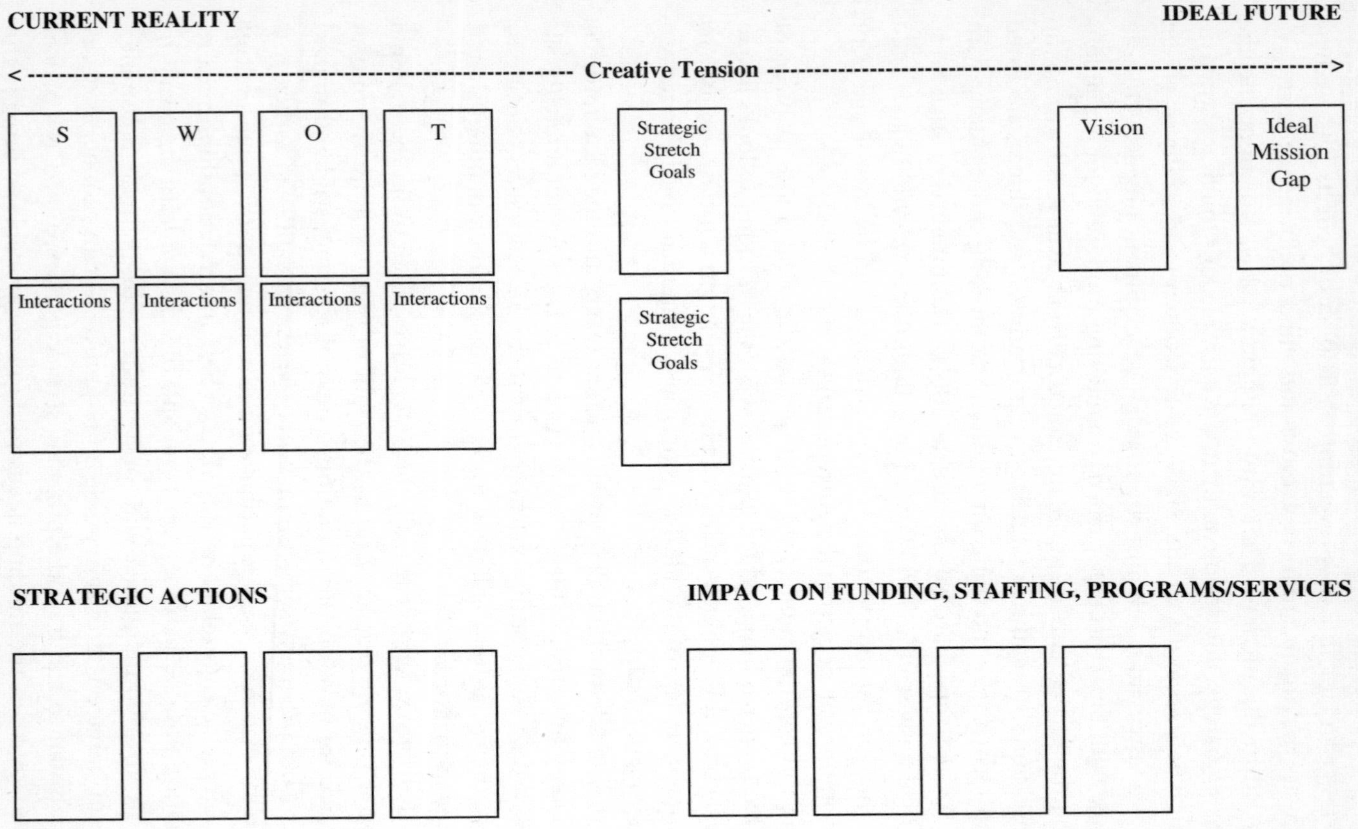

162

CURRENT REALITY

<----- Creative Tension ----->

IDEAL FUTURE

S	W	O	T
Interactions	Interactions	Interactions	Interactions

Strategic Stretch Goals

Strategic Stretch Goals

Vision

Ideal Mission Gap

STRATEGIC ACTIONS

IMPACT ON FUNDING, STAFFING, PROGRAMS/SERVICES

FIGURE 7.1   Strategy Development Map

run the program with unqualified entry level staff, that would be an example of poor fit and bad balance.

Each time the SDG selects a strategic action to take, it must note this on the map. It will write down the action it will take and also notate any changes that its action has resulted in. For example, if it decides to use a strength to fortify a weakness, then it needs to note the change on the flip-chart paper. It needs to note every ripple effect its actions may have on the map.

In a sense, the map is like a giant chessboard on which the SDG can track its actions and its ever-changing situation with every move. It is complex, and this is why it is helpful to have people on the SDG with organizational wisdom—people who understand the dynamics of organization performance.

Evaluating Threats and Weaknesses

The first actions that the SDG needs to consider are those that deal with the threats and weaknesses it has identified through the SWOT analysis. All threats should be evaluated first, and among the threats the first ones to consider are those that may have been identified as having an interaction with a weakness. As discussed in Chapter 6, a situation in which a threat and a weakness interact calls for "damage control" (Kearns, 1992, p. 15). These situations are serious and may result in a debilitation of the organization. Moving along further with the strategy development process does not make sense until these issues are addressed. The SDG needs to design a set of actions that will stabilize the organization before moving on further with the process. One place to look is at the list of strengths to see if there is a way that a strength can somehow be used to fortify a weakness or block a threat. A look at the list of strengths–weaknesses, strengths–threats interactions could identify this.

Once threats that interact with weaknesses are addressed, then the other threats need to be evaluated. Once evaluated, plans need to be taken to block the rest of the threats. Sometimes, threats need to be monitored until or if they become problematic enough to take action. If that is all that is needed, then a set of actions need to be designed which the organization will implement if the threat does escalate. If the threat does need to be addressed immediately, then places to look for ideas include the lists of interactions for strengths–threats and opportunities–threats.

Once the threats have been addressed, then the SDG can evaluate the rest of the weaknesses. They will then want to design some actions that will fortify each weakness to the point that it will not debilitate the organization or otherwise keep it from moving forward. A good place to look is at the list of strengths. Perhaps a strength or an opportunity can be used to fortify the weakness. Again, the strengths–weaknesses and weaknesses–opportunities interactions lists could identify this.

Hopefully, if a threat or weakness is of such a magnitude that it could debilitate the organization, then someone would have recognized this before the strategic development process got under way. It is likely, though, that a temporary solution was applied. When the SDG addresses these threats and weaknesses, their intention is to create a strategic response.

Looking for Leverage

Once the SDG lists actions to deal with the threats and weaknesses, this should result in the beginning of a strategy that will provide some relative stability for the organization. It can now consider moving forward without being derailed.

The SDG should now start operating from the strategic stretch goal list. It asks itself, "Given that we want to accomplish these goals, what do we see in the current reality that we can use to take new strategic actions to catapult us forward?" In this sense, they are looking for leverage. They are looking for a lever they can use to initiate progress faster and/or in a new direction.

This is the time during the process when the SDG really needs to focus on creativity and innovation. It needs to remember how important it is to close the mission gap and how helpful it will be to bring the vision into reality. It needs to let the tension of the difference between that ideal future that it wants and the current reality to ignite creativity.

As the SDG considers the first two or three strategic stretch goals and how it might create leverage toward them, a good place to look for ideas is the list of interactions for strengths–opportunities. These should present potential levers. The next place to look is the list of interactions for weaknesses–opportunities. The SDG will want to consider if there are ways to fortify a weakness so that an opportunity can be seized. The list of interactions for strengths–weaknesses may provide ideas for this. Finally, the rest of the list of opportunities should be reviewed to see if any of them can be seized in a way that can accelerate progress for one or more of the strategic stretch goals.

The next place for the SDG to look is at the list of strengths. It will have already considered interactions with opportunities. Now it can look at the remaining strengths to see if there is some way to leverage them. Perhaps the strength can even be used to create a new opportunity.

As mentioned earlier, the SDG should track its actions on the map to follow the ripple effects of its actions. For example, an ideal situation will be for a strength to be leveraged to seize an opportunity and the result of that action is the creation of a new strength, which then can be used to take a new action—perhaps to seize another opportunity. Positive ripples can continue to flow from these types of strategic actions and this is why considering the sequencing of which strategic stretch goals to address first is important.

Levers can come from a lot of different places. Consider a few examples:

- The board is a strength—they are well known and respected. They are mobilized into the community to recruit more volunteers so a program/service can be significantly expanded.

- The new CEO is a strength as they have talents for raising funds. Additional funds lift the organization out of financial difficulty, allowing it to hire more staff and increase programs/services.

- An existing program/service is a strength, as it makes a significant impact on beneficiaries—but this is not widely known. A speakers' bureau is created to make community presentations at various meetings to get the word out and attract more volunteers and donors.

- The financial reserves are a strength. They are used to develop a new innovative program/service that will make a more pronounced impact for beneficiaries and be more attractive to funders.

These are just a few examples. Leverage can come from a lot of different places within the organization. The SDG is limited only by its own creativity.

The SDG continues through its list of strategic stretch goals to plan actions that can help move each of those goals forward. Some kind of action should be listed for each goal. At this point the actions are broad explanations, not detailed action plans. As mentioned earlier, the SDG needs to remember to record the impacts of their strategic actions on funding, staffing, and programs/services for beneficiaries on the lower right portion of the strategy development map.

THE STRATEGY NARRATIVE

The strategy narrative captures the general explanation of how the organization intends to pursue the strategic stretch goals, vision, and mission gap. It is a cause-and-effect story that has a beginning, middle, and end. As suggested in Chapter 1, this is like a general explaining the overall battle plan to the troops: "First, we are going to . . . then some of you will . . . which will then allow others of us to . . . and that will give us the opening to . . . which will lead us on to victory." The actions in the example are connected with one another as a cause and effect story that describes the journey from the present to the desired future.

The importance of having this relatively simple statement of overall strategy is often overlooked by organizations in all sectors. Collins and Rukstad (2008) point this out in a *Harvard Business Review* article entitled "Can You Say What Your Strategy Is?":

> Conversely, companies that do not have a simple and clear statement of strategy are likely to fall into the sorry category of those that have failed to executive their strategy or, worse, those that never had one. In an astonishing number of organizations, executives, frontline employees, and all those in between are frustrated because no clear strategy exists for the company or its lines of business. (p. 82)
>
> Leaders of firms are mystified when what they thought was a beautifully crafted strategy is never implemented. They assume that the initiatives described in the voluminous documentation that emerges from an annual budget or a strategic planning process will ensure competitive success. They fail to appreciate the necessity of having a simple, clear, succinct strategy statement that everyone can internalize and use as a guiding light for making difficult choices. (p. 84)

The creation of your organization's strategy narrative will help ensure that you do not fall into this "sorry category" of those who cannot say what their strategy is.

The SDG should be able to put together its strategy narrative by looking at the list of strategic actions it has come up with and listed on the bottom left of the strategy development map—these are their "causes." They will also want to explain the effects of their actions/causes. This will include the impacts their actions will have on funding, staffing, and programs/services that they have listed on the bottom right of the map. It is important that this be written up and synthesized in a coherent fashion. For example, the changes in one operational area need to be consistent with changes in other operational areas. If programs/services are expanded, then funding and staffing somehow will need to be expanded, and so forth.

Once the SDG finishes the strategy narrative, their work is nearly complete. The last thing they need to do is to list the key assumptions they are making regarding the strategy. These would include assumptions about what is happening in the external environment as well as assumptions about how the strategy is going to unfold.

There are three things I look for in evaluating a strategy:

1. The strength of the levers used

2. The integration and balance among funding, staffing, and programs/services

3. Potential derailers

Following are some hypothetical examples of strategy narratives. I will comment on these aspects of each strategy.

EXAMPLE: YOUTH SERVICES ORGANIZATION

STRATEGY NARRATIVE

We need to hire a new CEO as our current CEO is retiring. We will use our reserves to increase the compensation available for the CEO position. Then we will heavily recruit for a new CEO who has a successful track record in fundraising and marketing so they can generate revenue to expand our highly regarded program services. We will arrange for a line of credit to protect our cash flow.

We will maintain our commitment to quality by fully funding all program needs and continuing to assure the competitive salaries of our current top-notch program staff.

(continued)

As net revenues increase, we will stabilize the budget and return to producing surpluses.

Finally, as net revenue continues to increase we will begin to repay reserves and begin to expand our program services. Our impact will continue to expand as our net revenue continues to increase.

KEY ASSUMPTIONS

- Funders exist who would support our programs if effectively approached.
- We can recruit the quality of a CEO needed to add net revenues in a timely way.

COMMENTARY

This is an organization with high-quality programs, and they are not reaching the number of people that they could be impacting. They believe that there is funding available from sources if they can find the right person to raise the funds. They need a new CEO and they have decided that none of the current staff have the talent they need to raise the additional funds.

Levers. They are using a strength, their financial reserves, as a lever to seize an opportunity—the talent pool for CEOs. They will hire a new CEO with the talent and skill to raise additional funds for the organization. Successfully hiring the CEO will provide them with a new strength that they can leverage to seize another opportunity—funding available from sources they are currently not accessing. The strength of the levers depends on the accuracy of their identification of the opportunities. Assuming that credible sources provided this information during their SWOT analysis, then the levers seem to be strong.

Some nonprofit executives with whom I have shared this example do not like the idea of hiring someone from the outside as CEO. They would rather promote a program person and let them learn to raise money. This is a strategy that has worked successfully for some organizations and not so successfully for others. In this case, the board decided that the current staff does not have the talent for fundraising. They need to go outside for their lever.

Integration and Balance. This is a classic case of a situation where an organization staff has been built around an excellent set of programs. When we think of the balance necessary for high performance among funding, staffing, and programs/services, this organization is strong in staffing (quality staff who are paid well) and programs/ services (high quality), but low on funding. They need to improve their funding to grow further and for that, they need to improve this capacity on their staff.

Another aspect of this strategy that people often do not like is spending reserves to hire an outside CEO whom they will pay more than the retiring CEO. Unfortunately, the compensation issue is an all-too-common occurrence, as many nonprofit staff (CEOs and others) are not paid competitively and their organizations need to pay more to replace them. The decision that this board makes is interesting in that they will maintain funding for compensation for their top-notch staff and for funding of the quality programs. If they wanted to pay the new CEO more and maintain a balanced budget, they could have cut other staffing or cut program expenses. But they don't want to throw the organization out of balance by doing that. Instead, they decided to spend reserves for the short term to afford the new, more highly paid CEO.

As the organization looks to the future, its strategy maintains a balance and an integrated positive reinforcing cycle by making sure that programs are not added until surpluses are produced and reserves are being replaced.

Derailers. The other aspect of spending the reserves that people find objectionable is that it is risky. However, all strategic choices involve risk and all have potential derailers. It is a matter of discerning which risks seem like the best path for the organization to take, and then being prepared if the assumptions made do not work out. While it is true that "you have to spend money to make money," that rationalization can also lead down a dark path.

In their assumptions, the SDG had identified that they believed that a person with the talent and skill to raise the funds exists and that they could recruit such a person. They also assume that the funding is available. If they are wrong on either of these, the strategy could be derailed.

The assumptions and potential derailers should be taken into consideration by the organization. In making the decision to follow this strategy to spend reserves, the first thing mentioned is that the organization will protect the potential weakness of its cash flow by setting up a line of credit. No other weaknesses or threats are mentioned.

Finally, the organization can protect itself from these potential derailers by setting up a very rigorous set of criteria for hiring the CEO and a set of performance criteria for them to meet once they are hired.

(continued)

If candidates do not meet the criteria, then a search should be extended, rather than hiring the best person in the pool. If performance criteria are not met, then the strategy and/or the hiring decision will need to be revisited.

EXAMPLE: EDUCATIONAL ASSOCIATION

STRATEGY NARRATIVE

We will balance the budget for the first time in 10 years by increasing fees for services and laying off a few of our already limited staff. This will allow us to achieve financial stability, though we will offer services at a bare minimum quality level. It will also allow us funding in the budget to hire a director of development.

The CEO and director of development will work with the board to mobilize volunteers to significantly increase the annual fund and launch an endowment campaign.

As net revenues increase from the annual fund and endowment sources, we will add staffing. We will increase service quality, staffing, staff quality, and staff compensation as net revenues continue to increase. Fees for service will increase regularly according to inflationary pressures. We will continue to increase our impact through our programs over time as funding continues to increase.

KEY ASSUMPTIONS

- Beneficiaries will pay the higher fees even though service quality is lower.
- An effective director of development can be hired.
- The CEO, director of development, board, and volunteers can be effective in raising money.
- Additional potential funding for the organization exists.

COMMENTARY

When I have shared this example with nonprofit executives, most of them think it is a bad strategy. In this case we have to make sure we are not confusing a very bad situation with a bad strategy. This organization is in tough shape. It is, indeed, in crisis. This is why the very first action is to fortify a weakness—the budget deficits—to stabilize the organization. It is, essentially, a "pruning" strategy in which they are cutting back to restabilize and, if they are successful, grow again.

Levers. The main lever here is using the combined new strength of a new director of development, the CEO, the board, and a group of volunteers to raise more money for the annual fund and start an endowment campaign. These may or may not end up being strong levers, but they seem to be the best that the organization has to work with. Poker players know that sometimes you are not dealt a strong hand, and you have to play the hand you are dealt. If the organization hires a strong director of development and the CEO, board, and volunteers are exceptionally motivated due to the crisis they are in, then it makes the lever seem a bit stronger. However, the organization is clearly overreaching by trying to increase the annual fund and trying to launch a capital campaign at the same time. They need to get their operations stabilized and demonstrate positive results in the annual fund. After growing that for a few years and establishing operational credibility, they may be ready for a longer-term endowment campaign.

Integration and Balance. Through years of deficits, program/services beneficiaries have been subsidized heavily by the spending of reserves. Apparently, the board of directors feels that they are finally in crisis and that this has to end. In a move that will be a shock to program/services beneficiaries, fees are increasing and service quality is being lowered. But the budget will be balanced. It would have been much better if less dramatic actions like this had taken place years earlier, before the situation escalated to a crisis.

The strategy is a dramatic effort to get the organization's operations integrated and back in balance among its funding, staffing, and programs/services areas of operation. Once they are back in balance, the strategy explains that the quality of services and staffing will improve, but only as additional funds are available. This should keep the organization in balance and in an integrated positive reinforcing cycle as they are assuring that funding is available before spending it. This is not always done in organizations from all sectors.

Derailers. The strategy assumptions state that the board believes that program/service beneficiaries will continue to pay the increased fees for lower-quality services. If they are wrong, then they need to be ready to backtrack quickly. The rest of their assumptions combine into one final big potential derailer—they believe they can mobilize

(continued)

themselves to raise a lot of money and transform the organization into a quality operation. The potential donors really have to be out there and the CEO, director of development, board, and group of volunteers have to prove to be successful fundraisers. It is certainly possible, but will require talent, skill, and a lot of hard work. Essentially, it is a desperate strategy for a desperate time.

EXAMPLE: HUMAN SERVICES ORGANIZATION

STRATEGY NARRATIVE

We will continue our current staffing level with the good people who work here because they care for the mission, even though we can't pay much and do not have funding to increase compensation.

We will continue our fees for services at their current level, as people cannot afford to pay more. Under these conditions, we will provide as many services and programs as possible so we can make a difference. We will continue to subsidize our fees for services with grants from United Way and government funding. We will attempt to balance the budget in this way.

Our limited staff will continue to do the best they can with an overload of needs until things get better.

KEY ASSUMPTIONS

* Funding from United Way and government sources will continue.
* Staff will continue doing the best they can.

COMMENTARY

The three examples in this section are all hypothetical, but many nonprofit executives with whom I have shared this example claim to have worked for this organization at one time in the past. It is an all-too-familiar story!

Levers. What are this organization's levers? This is a trick question, but the clue can be found in the last four words of the strategy narrative: "until things get better." Hope. The truth is that this organization has no strategy. All it has is hope, and we know that hope is not a strategy. There are no levers except for hope. There is no real vision to which they are aspiring. The strategy narrative is simply an explanation of how the organization is going to continue as long as they can the way they are going—treading water in maintenance mode.

Integration and Balance. This organization has pushed itself to provide more programs/services for beneficiaries, at the service fee level they have set, than it has the capacity to provide. By doing this, their funding and staffing areas are not integrated. Funding is barely covering costs, but without providing proper compensation for the staffing function. They are probably not attracting the quality of staff they would like because of this. They are out of balance and their strategy does not address this. To get itself out of this morass, the organization will need to create an aspirational vision and find some kind of strength or opportunity to leverage—perhaps a new and inspired board member—to move forward.

Derailers. The threat of losing any of the funding this organization has is—given their situation—very real. They are in such a precarious situation that they are one missed grant away from falling into a vicious downward spiral. The threat of losing staff is also real, but one can imagine that when that has happened in the past someone else has come along willing to try the work. Organizations like this are typified by high turnover. This organization has positioned itself for failure.

APPLICATION TO HYPOTHETICAL ORGANIZATIONS

This is the final set of examples for these hypothetical organizations, as this is the final recommendation that the SDG will provide to the board.

The following discussions, as in the other chapters, are representative dialogue. The actual process and conversations for crafting the strategy would, of course, take much longer. Developing a strategy narrative can easily take a half-day or more.

As Jeff completed his discussion of the strategy development process, Bob jumped in quickly with an enthusiastic comment. "Folks, as you know, I chaired the search committee when we hired Tim. We are about to embark on the kind of effort a number of us had in mind when we brought him here; to take this food bank to the next level—and more."

"Bob, not to interrupt," said Stan, one of the newer board members. "I appreciate your enthusiasm. But I have been through these things before, and we are just not structured for this—from a staffing stand-point or volunteer standpoint for that matter."

Bob replied, "We know you have been through these things before— and that's one of the reasons you are here!"

"I know, I know," smiled Stan sheepishly.

"Folks," said Jeff. "I love the enthusiasm as well, and the strategic conversation, but I want to slow us down for just a moment and then we can connect right back to this exact point. Remember, I said that one of the first things we want to do as we write down our strategic actions is to look at our threats and weaknesses to make sure that we don't get derailed before we even leave the station, if you will. As you look at the strategy development map I put up on the wall and you look at the interactions of weaknesses and threats, or any of the threats and weaknesses, do you see anything there that we need to address early on in our strategy?"

"Well," replied Stan, "the first two weaknesses–threats interactions we have listed are what I am talking about. We have this environment that includes the threat of increased competition for contributions, and we have too few development staff and a board that has not had much experience raising money. Tim and Brian are great, but we need more development staff if we are going to begin addressing those wild stretch goals we created. Plus, with everything else on Tim's plate, he does not have much time to devote to fundraising."

"Exactly," said Jeff. "I just wanted us to focus the conversation on our process. So one of the first things you should consider is whether there is something you think you need to do about that early on with your strategy."

"For sure," said Doug, another Executive Committee member. "And when we do that we will not only be addressing the weaknesses and the threat, we will be taking aggressive action to move forward. Tim, how do you feel about the staffing situation given the goals we are embark-ing on?"

"Thanks for asking Doug," said Tim. "And thanks for the kind comments others of you have made about me and about Brian. And you are right, Stan, I don't have enough time right now to devote to fundraising. What I have been thinking of is restructuring the organization. Ralph and I have discussed this possibility and the first thing I would like to do is to appoint him as Chief Operating Officer, which will give me much more time to devote to our campaign. We have a great young woman, Joanna—you all know her—whom we have been grooming, who can be our new VP of Finance. Then I think we need to initially add two more positions—a Director of Development and a Director of Marketing. The marketing position will address the other weakness up there, Jeff, of our marketing program."

"That's excellent, Tim," said Stan. "I think that sounds like it is exactly what we need to do."

"Other reactions?' asked Jeff.

"Tim," asked Al, "based on what you said, may I assume you have figured out that we can afford all of this?"

"Great question, Al," said Tim. "Given last year's surplus of $250,000, we should be able to work these changes into the budget for the coming fiscal year. However, I will point out that—as we stated in the SWOT analysis—there are uncertainties out there with some of our funding. So, the possibility exists that we could have a deficit for a year before new fundraising dollars start to come in."

"That's certainly a risk I am willing to take," said Bob.

"Other thoughts?" asked Jeff.

"Sounds like the right way to go," said Stan. And others agreed.

"All right, then," said Jeff. "You have your first strategic action. What's next?"

"Well," said Stan, "as I said earlier, I have been through this before and we should consider hiring a consultant to do a feasibility study for us on the campaign we want to run. For those of you who are unfamiliar with the process, a consultant would interview potential donors and review other data to give us a forecast of how much they think we can realistically raise. I know how much we *want* to raise, but since this is going to be very public we can't run the risk of falling exceptionally short of our goal—people will think we are failures. We can keep our stretch goal as our 'quiet goal.' And while the feasibility study is going on, we can begin forming a campaign cabinet so we involve more

(continued)

community leaders who can help us raise the kind of money we are talking about."

"I sure am glad we brought you onto the board," said Bob. "Great ideas. But there's more expense again."

"I think we can legitimately call that an investment, Bob," said Doug. "This is one of those situations where we have to spend some money to make some money—even if it means we take a hit for a year or two."

"We certainly don't want to run a deficit," said Tim. "But you all have been good stewards of this organization's finances for years. So we are fortunate to have a cushion if we need it. The other thing a consultant will do is to give us an idea of what kind of budget we will need to run the campaign during the next five years."

"Please mark me down as supportive, yet uncomfortable," said Al. "I do think we need to do what we are talking about—but my conservative bones will never let me feel comfortable about it."

"As always," said Bob, "we appreciate your honesty and your support, Al."

"I'm in," said Andy. "Me too," chimed in others.

"Okay then," said Jeff. "We have our next strategic action. Let's keep going."

By the end of the process, the SDG developed the following strategy narrative to submit as a recommendation to the board of directors.

Strategy Narrative

We will restructure the staff by adding a Chief Operating Officer position and allow our CEO to focus on development. We will also add a Director of Marketing position and Director of Development position to work with the CEO and Vice President of Development to significantly increase funding and the amount of food contributed. We will ideally operate with surplus budgets, while maintaining our commitment to competitive staff compensation. However, we will accept short-term deficits if necessary to spark this movement forward.

We will launch a comprehensive, five-year campaign—targeted for $150 million—for a new building and improved mission impact through significant increases in the annual fund, the initiation of a planned giving program, and a tripling of the amount of food donated. A campaign plan will be developed along with an integrated marketing plan following a feasibility study, and a cabinet of influential volunteer community leaders will be recruited.

As the campaign plan and marketing plan bring in more dollars and contributed food, we will aggressively recruit more volunteers. This growth will continue as we move into the new building and as our capacity continues to expand we will add staffing to support the growth. Our intent is to close the meal gap within five years and to keep it closed in the future.

Key Assumptions

- The community will respond enthusiastically to the overwhelming hunger needs in our area, which we will communicate using our meal gap data.
- We can recruit an influential campaign cabinet.
- Our staff, board, and newly created campaign cabinet can successfully raise $150 million in five years and triple the amount of donated food.

Commentary

While this formal strategy development process just got under way, a number of strategic moves have been made in the past few years to set this organization up for embarking on its new strategy. When Tim was hired, some board members clearly wanted to bring someone in who had the ability to lead a major fund drive. His background as a VP of development and marketing had to be a major attraction to them. And they have added some board members who have been through campaigns before and have clout within the community—a good beginning to the campaign cabinet they want to form.

Levers. Tim has been preparing for this meeting, it seems, for a couple of years. He has his reorganization plan set that will allow him to provide staff leadership to the campaign and give him a solid team to work with, while also making sure that operations are well run as he takes on this new role. They are planning a huge campaign, from an historical perspective, and their success in recruiting the right people on the campaign cabinet will be key. If they get the right people on the cabinet, they seem poised for major accomplishments.

Integration and Balance. At some point in the past, this board decided that they should compensate their staff competitively. This has likely allowed them to recruit and retain very good staff throughout the organization—which will pay special dividends in this restructuring. It

(continued)

will also be helpful in replacing senior staff as they retire. And they have been fiscally responsible. It seems that the organization has been in balance and has had a solid integration of funding, staffing, and programs/services. As they seek to increase their impact, they are being careful to maintain that balance. They will add the staffing they need to begin moving forward and maintain competitive salaries even if it means running short-term deficits. They are prepared to "invest" some of their reserves in maintaining that balance and driving the organization forward.

Derailers. The staff restructuring helps fix a number of weaknesses and helps to block some of the threats of reduced funding. They are aggressively facing these possible derailers. Their biggest derailer could be a public relations problem if they were to announce an unbelievable fundraising campaign goal and then not come even close to it. While they are passionate about closing the meal gap within five years, it is a huge stretch. The feasibility study will give them a realistic pulse on the current fundraising climate and help them temper their public language. Even if they decide on a smaller goal for the immediate campaign, there is nothing stopping them from saying something like "We are embarking on a $75 million campaign as a down payment on the full $150 million we know it will take to fully close the meal gap in our community." The feasibility study will give them some outside perspective on how tenuous their fundraising assumptions might be.

BIG RIVER REGIONAL HOUSING SERVICES

Tom prepared the strategy development map while the group was on a break and gave them a presentation on the strategy development process as they reconvened. "Now this is what you have been waiting for, the time to put all the pieces together and come up with the strategy," he said. "I'll ask you to look at the strategy development map and first pay special attention to the threats and weaknesses, and their interactions with other SWOTs, to see if there are some initial actions that you should take to address those potential concerns."

The group was quiet for a few moments, when Troy said, "I really don't see anything that troubling. It does not seem that any threats are really imminent."

"I would agree that none seem real imminent, but the staff compensation issues really concern me," said Elaine. "Not only might some other organizations come along and steal some of these great folks, we really should be paying them more. I think we need immediate action on that." Heads nodded.

"As far as what we should say our first strategic action is going to be," said Kendra, "I am thinking that the headline of our strategy needs to address what we are going to do about hiring a new CEO."

"That makes sense to me," said Scott. "And with all the talk we have had about raising money, it seems obvious to me that we need someone who has a proven track record of fundraising successes."

"Yes," said Gale, "we need to build a fundraising capacity that will simultaneously fuel more growth and protect us from our threats. It is a double win. But we are going to need more than just a new CEO to make progress on our stretch goals. We are going to need to let them hire a director of development to help out. And, most importantly, we are going to have to go on the record that we are ready to step up as a board and provide leadership to this fundraising activity."

"Tom," asked Kendra, "do you think you can write a couple of sentences up there that capture what we are talking about as our first strategic actions?"

"And while he is doing that," said Elaine, "how do the rest of you feel about the very next thing we say having something to do with staff compensation?"

"I think that's good, and I think we should be aggressive about it over the next five years," said Gale. "We need to send a message that our staff is important and we are going to take care of them."

When Tom finished writing, he asked, "Okay, where is everyone on this? How do you feel about how I captured the first set of actions you want to take and what's next?"

"Is everyone okay with what Tom has written?" asked Kendra. Heads nodded. "What do you think about Elaine's suggestion then?"

"Increasing staff compensation will divert money away from what we could do to acquire more properties," said Don, a board member. "But I guess the point that was made earlier is that we are out of balance in terms of staffing. We have diverted money away from compensation into other activities and maybe we need to get back in balance. I am seeing that it is more fair. I support what Elaine is saying."

"Other thoughts?" asked Tom.

"Well," said Allison, "I can tell you that I have heard some of my superiors in the county government talk about the very thing we mentioned in the SWOT analysis. People in government are starting to retire and our leaders realize that there are a lot of good people out in

(continued)

nonprofits that they could attract. So, I am saying that the threat is real. But I think we should put it in the strategy because it is the right thing to do."

"Any disagreements?" asked Tom. "Okay, we have another strategic action. Do you see any opportunities listed on the strategy development map that you want to seize?"

"I guess we need to add something next about what we will do once this increased funding comes in," said Pat, "like take advantage of any good properties we come across."

"I agree," said Erin, "and we also need to talk about the fact that we're not the only ones out there working on this problem. Let's do something to leverage our good reputation to rally other organizations together to address housing issues more aggressively."

"Good one, Erin," said Kendra. "Let's brainstorm how we might do that."

The SDG continued their discussions and brainstorming for quite a while. After working through a number of drafts, they agreed on the following strategy narrative.

Strategy Narrative

We will hire a new CEO who has a proven track record of fundraising success, as well as a community development background. We will add a director of development position to the staff for the new CEO to hire. The new CEO will have a mandate to develop a comprehensive and successful fundraising program. Aggressive activity will be implemented to increase giving by individual donors, corporations, and foundations. The board is committed to leadership and active participation in these fundraising activities.

We will immediately begin a process of increasing staff compensation and benefits that will continue during the next five years to make it much more competitive. Professional development plans will be created for all employees and succession planning will be implemented.

Additional increased funding will be used to acquire or build new multifamily or senior affordable housing units. We will be opportunistic, about acquiring property that is value priced. Rents and other fees for service will be monitored carefully and increased if market conditions dictate. We will continue producing annual surpluses to build our reserves higher.

*We will initiate a collaborative regional summit on affordable hous-
ing issues among key stakeholders—community development organizations, lenders, government leaders, businesses, and residents. We
will work with collaborators to attract funding to the area to make the
Big River Region a demonstration site for innovative approaches to
solve affordable housing issues. Collectively, these efforts will produce
significantly more affordable, safe, decent, housing for the Big River
Region.*

KEY ASSUMPTIONS

- We can attract a CEO with the type of background we want.
- The CEO and director of development we hire will be successful raising additional funds.

COMMENTARY

This is an example of an organization that was doing just fine prior to
their strategy sessions. In fact, had they not done strategy prior to hiring a new CEO they might have hired someone without fundraising
experience. They might have even elevated the COO to that position.
However, by identifying their huge mission gap, they realized that "doing just fine" was not going to be enough to make a major change in the
mission gap. They needed to try some new, different, more aggressive
ways to bring in funding to more effectively close the mission gap.

Levers. This organization is choosing to make aggressive moves to
leverage the hiring of a CEO with development experience and add a
director of development in the midst of an economic downturn. At the
same time, other organizations are laying off development staff. This
could prove to be an excellent move. The new staff team, along with
board members, could initiate the process of developing relationships
with potential donors and funders—knowing that it may take two to
three years before funds are available to contribute. But when that time
comes and other nonprofits are adding back their development people,
BRRHS will already have relationships with funders and will be in position to access renewed funding sources.

BRRHS is also leveraging its financial reserves as a strength in this
situation. Building up their reserves over time has given them the ability
to take a risk by spending money on their fundraising strategy.

(continued)

The other interesting lever here is their use of the strength of their strong reputation to initiate a summit on affordable housing issues. They realize that the region's housing problems will not be solved by them alone, and they are seeking collaborators.

Integration and Balance. Even though BRRHS has built up reserves over time, they have not used their annual surpluses to make sure that staff compensation remains competitive. They are out of balance in this dimension. Their very specific strategic action to increase compensation and set development plans for the staff will help get them back into balance in this way.

Even as they seek to raise money and increase staff compensation, the organization seeks to continue to build reserves. While opinions vary widely in the nonprofit world on the appropriate level of reserves, their reserve is still relatively low for the size of the organization. The plan to increase the reserves further will keep their funding dimension in balance.

Derailers. BRRHS has responded to its staffing-related weaknesses and threats by planning to hire staff with fundraising experience, increasing compensation, providing development plans, and implementing succession planning. If by "succession planning" they mean that staff will be developed so that they are candidates for some of the senior positions that may be vacated by retirements, then they are on the right track.

Otherwise, their strategy is relatively low risk. They are assuming that they can hire a CEO with the talents they seek, and that they will be successful. Their utilization of the search firm is a helpful hedge against this possible derailer of their strategy. They are counting on their strong reputation in the community to support their fundraising success, which seems reasonable.

By being aggressive with their new fundraising program, they are also protecting themselves from some other possible derailers, such as deeper funding reductions from other sources.

The remaining derailer of interest is the board. Is this the right board to work successfully with the new CEO on fundraising activities? It is unknown from the information presented, but seems unlikely. Otherwise, they would have been active in this way in the past. The new CEO may need to work with the board to bring in some new members who are more oriented toward fundraising.

MERRILL COUNTY LITERACY COUNCIL

Mark set up the strategy development map with all of the flip-chart lists he had been making, and he gave the SDG an overview of the process they were about to go through.

"All right, and now we begin," he said. "As I mentioned, our first task is to deal with potential vulnerabilities and we will first look at that list of interactions of weaknesses–threats. Should anything concern us there that we should address first?"

"I'm very concerned about a number of things," said John, the assistant superintendent of schools, "and they seem to revolve around our finances. I wasn't so excited when Colleen recommended that we not fill the director of programs position that she vacated. But now I really see the wisdom of that. We are in a precarious financial situation, and we already do not pay our staff what they deserve. We need to be financially conservative and we need to bring in some more money."

"You are right on, John," said Donta', "and we need to go on the record that as we bring in some additional revenue that we will begin — and then continue — a process of increasing staff compensation and benefits."

"We have a recommendation that one of your first strategic actions should be conservative budgeting to maintain stability," said Mark. "Does that work for everyone?" Heads nodded. "Are there other threats or weaknesses that we need to address before we look toward the future?"

"Everything else that I see is, like John said, tied to finances, which really is what our future depends on," said Colleen. "I can't think of anything else to stabilize us at this point."

"Neither can I accept asking you and the rest of the staff to please be patient with us until we can bring in some more funding to pay you all more fairly," said John.

"I think the rest of the staff will be and I know I will be patient," said Colleen. "It means a lot to know that you feel it is something to address in the near future."

"Okay, it seems that we have taken actions to stabilize MCLC for moving into the future," said Mark. "Now that we are stable, let's imagine ourselves out there on the map at year five, and we have accomplished all of those strategic stretch goals. What must we have done to make it there? What leverage do you see that we might utilize as you

(*continued*)

look back at the current reality? What do you see on the SWOTs or inter-actions list that we can leverage to move forward?"

"Well," sighed Donta', "I know that this is the hand we have been dealt and I am sorry we don't have any interactions in the strengths–opportunities list to leverage. It looks like we are going to have to play this hand without any aces."

"I see two very good things we have going for us that we can use to begin the move forward," said Ellen. "We have this young, energetic, and talented CEO and we have a great program. Folks, I think it is time that we face the fact that we need more well-connected people from this county on this board. And I think that Colleen has the right stuff to go out and help us recruit them."

"I couldn't agree more, Ellen" said Donta'. "And another thing, we need to be straight up with them when we ask them to join the board that we need them to be strong donors and we need them to work with the rest of us to go out there and raise more money for this important cause. I'll work with you, Colleen."

"Actually folks," said Colleen, "that really excites me. And I look for-ward to working in partnership with you on that."

"And once we get some of those new people in here, we need to learn how to toot our own horn better and how to raise money," exclaimed Ellen.

"Sounds like another strategic action," replied Mark.

The MCLC strategy development group continued their discussion on and on. The result was the following strategy narrative.

STRATEGY NARRATIVE

We will maintain a conservative, balanced budget and not increase expenses until surpluses are available. We will leverage our CEO's tal-ent, along with our program effectiveness, to recruit new board mem-bers who are well connected within the county. We will secure agreements from them to be actively involved in fundraising and build-ing community awareness of literacy issues.

With initial increases in the annual fund, we will make improvements to staff compensation. As the annual fund continues to increase, we will retain a consultant to develop an integrated marketing and fundraising plan. The annual giving plan will be upgraded and fundraising training will be given to staff and board. The marketing plan will raise awareness of literacy issues and help recruit more volunteers, as well as support fundraising initiatives. We will continue to expand the board with well-connected community members who are committed to giving and raising funds. We will seek significant United Way funding increases.

We will phase in these plans to balance increased costs with increased funding. As net revenues from fundraising successes are available they will be divided among staff compensation increases, hiring new staff to manage increased numbers of volunteers, and building reserves. We will closely monitor program quality as we increase program offerings. More and more people in Merrill County will become literate.

As we recruit new board members and annual fund donors, we will seek to identify potential major donors for an endowment campaign for $5 million, which will be launched in five years with a $500,000 lead gift. This will be a springboard to the future, which will continue to increase the literacy rates in Merrill County.

KEY ASSUMPTIONS

- Our CEO can recruit new board members who are well connected within the county.
- We can effectively learn how to raise money.
- We can find a $500,000 lead donor.

COMMENTARY

This organization is in a tough situation, but they definitely have some signs of life with their talented and energetic CEO, their newest board member, Donta', and some committed aspirations.

Levers. As Donta' said, this organization has not been dealt any aces, but they do seem to have a queen of hearts in their new CEO. Utilizing her to go out, with Donta', to recruit new board members is a solid move. She probably has a couple of people who agreed to serve on the SDG in mind already. Some would say that the board should be taking more responsibility to work with Colleen on recruiting new board members. Theoretically, this is correct. However, the reality is that this board needs to change. They need more people like Donta' and most of the other board members, besides him, would not carry the weight necessary in recruitment meetings. Better for her to go alone and/or with Donta'.

Otherwise, the idea of putting together a comprehensive marketing and development plan leverages the strong program they already have.

(continued)

They need to get the word out and, then—yes—they need fundraising training.

The $5 million endowment campaign may be a bit ambitious, but they are taking the healthy disregard for the impossible mind-set seriously. At least they are not starting it immediately and realize that it is something that would come down the line if they are successful identifying significant major donors.

Integration and Balance. This organization is way out of balance when it comes to funding and staffing, particularly compensation for staff. It has been so focused on the programs/services that it has neglected the other two areas—and this is simply not sustainable. Unless they do something different, they will sooner or later lose some grants they have been counting on and begin a downward financial spiral. Or they may lose staff due to the low compensation. The actions they are taking in their strategy may be the best ones they have the capacity for at this point to get back into balance. They have adopted a conservative budget approach and they are sending a message to the staff that they are important. As they are successful with raising additional funds, they are planning on increases in staff compensation while also building up some reserves. They have set out a path that will get them back into balance if they are successful bringing in those additional funds.

They are wise to state that they will need additional staff to manage the increased number of volunteers they intend to recruit. Some organizations will attempt to operate with very little volunteer management by staff and this often results in breakdowns in program quality.

Derailers. This organization is in a precarious situation and there are a number of things that could derail them. These have been identified both in their SWOTs and their assumptions about the strategy. They should take some time to discuss contingency plans if some of their funders do not come through as they have in years past. They may need to cut expenses further in the short term to stay in business until they are successful in attracting new funding.

They are wise to go on the record about increasing staff compensation. They would be even wiser to make some very specific commitments to Colleen for some increases in the near term. She would not be the first good-hearted CEO who took another nonprofit job that paid better "to do the right thing for her family." Right now, she and Donta' are the key to keeping this strategy on the rails.

CHAPTER 8

Strategy Implementation and Management

Now that the organization has prepared its breakthrough strategy, it is time for implementation. This begins by making sure that all aspects of the organization, especially the culture, are aligned with the strategy. The strategic stretch goals are then integrated into the annual planning process, while the strategy guides the development of the action plans. The organization and external environment are continually monitored for changes—and the organization prepares itself to engage those changes. Implementing and managing the strategy requires comprehensive effort from everyone within the organization. Concepts and tools to help support the implementation are provided at the end of this chapter including ideas on Quality Management, the Balanced Scorecard, and Strengths-Based Management.

STRATEGY FIRST

A number of times I have mentioned the work of Dr. Russell Ackoff with respect to Systems Thinking and Idealized Design. When he discusses the importance of doing the thoughtful work necessary to discern the correct direction for an organization, I have heard him say:

The righter we do the wrong thing, the wronger we become.

You can read the same quote in one of his books, but when you hear him say it in person it sounds quite ominous. And when you think about it, it is.

The faster you run in the wrong direction, the further you are from where you need to be. You are worse off. You would have been better off sitting still.

The more money you spend, the more time you spend, the more effort you exert—heading in the wrong direction—the more you just wastes resources.

There exists some wishful thinking among many people that they can take an afternoon with their board and senior staff to set an effective strategic plan for the next five years. They want to be able to jump into the implementation phase as quickly as possible and "get to work!" I respect and appreciate this wish. The work of a nonprofit executive and a board member is never done. Time is at a premium for everyone. And funding is always scarce. So investing both of those resources in this process may be challenging. But the returns on those investments are very significant—and it is in the implementation of the strategy that they are realized.

By taking the time to follow the strategy development process that has been explained in this book, an organization will have:

- Decided upon the mission accomplishment measures that everyone in the organization will understand as the primary performance indicators for the organization. Everyone will understand where the goal line is for their team.

- Articulated a mission gap that they have taken time to really look at, be challenged by, maybe saddened by, but ultimately inspired by to step up and make a difference. It is a gap that they can articulate in a measurable way to those who do not fully understand the extent of the organization's mission challenge.

- An aspirational vision that has been created out of dreams to imagine how much more of a difference they can make if their organization existed in an ideal state—if they could have it any way they wanted. It is a vision that they can share with others and ask for input to make it even more compelling.

- Strategic stretch goals that are the beginning point for taking dreams and bringing them into reality. These goals will direct action and stretch the imagination for ways to pursue the vision that the organization had never thought of before.

- A focused breakthrough strategy that is grounded in the reality of the SWOTs, but guided by the dreams of the vision. It is a strategy designed to guide the organization toward closing the mission gap with new, innovative ideas as effectively as possible during the next three to five years.

Just as importantly, by following the recommended process the organization will have involved and empowered stakeholders who are now prepared to support and participate in the implementation of the strategy. This will include all board and staff, volunteers, beneficiaries of services, donors, funders, and collaborators.

The first seven chapters of the book outlined the process of designing the breakthrough strategy. It is here and now at the stage of implementation, that it is time to reap the benefits of the investment of time the organization has made by putting the breakthrough strategy into action.

First, the senior management of the organization needs to make sure that the organization is properly aligned to implement the new breakthrough strategy. Then annual plans, guided by the strategy, need to be created, implemented, and managed in order to accomplish the strategic stretch goals. The rest of this chapter will provide an overview of these activities. Volumes of books have been written on the implementation and the management aspects of nonprofit organizations, and they are good supplements to this book—which is mostly devoted to the development of strategy. What follows are some general ideas on the implementation process as well as some concepts and tools to further support that process.

ALIGNING THE ORGANIZATION

Once the board of directors approves the recommendations of the strategy development group (SDG), the first implementation task of senior management is to assure that the entire organization is aligned to support its new future. The Venture Philanthropy Partners Capacity Framework, discussed in Chapter 6, is not only an excellent tool for assessment but is also very helpful for achieving alignment.

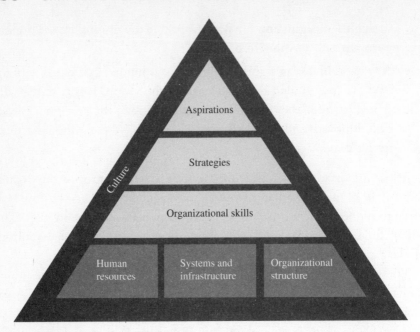

FIGURE 8.1   **VPP Pyramid**

As pictured in the VPP pyramid (Figure 8.1), the top two elements—aspirations and strategy—have now been set during the strategy development process. The task now is to examine the other five elements to assure that the organization's operations in those other areas support the mission, vision, strategic stretch goals, and strategy.

For organizational skills, senior management will want to consider the extent to which it may need to develop its overall capabilities in some particular areas. The example was given earlier in the book about an organization that wanted its board to start making personal solicitations for the fundraising program. Since this was not something they had done before, they would need to develop the skills through training.

The human resources operational area could be impacted as the organization assesses the staff, board, and other volunteer needs. If additional people or different people are needed for key positions, then changes, reorganizations, and the like will have to be made.

Systems and infrastructure almost always need to be updated when a new strategy is put into place. New strategic actions will be taken and new standard operating procedures will need to be developed. The organization will need to make sure that old systems are changed and/or streamlined so that action on the new strategy is supported and not slowed down by antiquated processes.

The new strategy could very well result in a change in organizational structure. As the organization begins to implement the strategy and make plans for acting on the strategic stretch goals, it may see that job descriptions and/or reporting relationships need to change. It may see the need to restructure the board in various ways to support the strategy.

My experience has been that most nonprofit senior managers have a reasonable level of experience looking at issues of organizational skills, human resources, systems and infrastructure, and organizational structure. Culture change and alignment, however, can be more challenging.

VPP defines culture as the connective tissue that binds together the organization, including shared values and practices, behavior norms, and most important, the organization's orientation towards performance. Another shorthand way of thinking about culture is: "This is the way we do things around here."

There are many different perspectives on organization culture and lots of books that senior managers can read to learn more. And there are many consultants who have their own particular way of helping organizations make a culture change. I am going to share an example of one of these approaches that I have used for more than 20 years both as a CEO and a consultant.

A couple of years ago a nonprofit CEO contacted me. His organization had adopted a new strategic plan and vision. He knew he needed to better align the organization to carry out the new plans and he was trying to explain to me some changes he wanted to make. After a while, I said, "It sounds like you want to change the culture." "That's it!" he exclaimed, "but I am not sure how to explain the change."

At this point in the conversation I gave him a brief overview of the "Competing Values" approach to understanding organization culture. It is based on work that Robert Quinn (1988) and others have done on organization effectiveness and culture. Essentially, this model explains that organizations experience a natural tension around two sets of forces. The first tension is between stability and control versus flexibility and discretion. The other tension is between an internal focus versus an external focus. The choices that organizations make on which of these "values" they will most emphasize, determines their particular culture. In this approach to culture, there is not necessarily a right or wrong culture for an organization, but it does have to choose a culture that is the right fit for its purpose, strategy, and environment.

Based on the choices the organization makes on what it values, its culture can be broadly described as one of four general types. Those types are procedural (or hierarchical), cohesion (or clan), innovation (or adhocracy), and achievement (or market). For those interested, this approach to organization culture is thoroughly explained in Cameron and Quinn's book (1999), *Diagnosing and Changing Organizational Culture Based on the Competing Values Framework*. A description of the different cultures follows below. It is important to point out that these are general descriptions and that every organization would have some of the characteristics of all of the other cultural types. But an organization will have a dominant type that characterizes its tendencies.

The Procedural Culture is one in which organizations value an internal focus and stability and control. They are characterized as being very formalized and structured places to work. Procedures and specific processes govern what the people do. They are interested in efficiency, stability, and predictability. Senior managers who perform well in this culture are very good at coordination, organization, and detail. An example of a type of organization for which the Procedural Culture would be a good fit would be a nuclear power plant. As I think about it, I am really happy about the idea of nuclear power plants following a Procedural Culture and all of the rules necessary to allow us to safely use that power.

The Cohesion Culture values an internal focus and flexibility and discretion. It is characterized by high levels of employee participation, having a friendly climate, and putting a strong emphasis on staff development. They have high levels of employee commitment and satisfaction, and they often operate on a consensus decision-making model. Senior managers in this type of culture empower employees, take a mentoring approach to supervision, and are good facilitators. Southwest Airlines is often thought of as an example of this type of culture. Their flight crews have fun and act like family. Off-duty employees regularly help an on-duty crew clean up a plane or hand out peanuts if they happen to be taking a flight.

The Innovation Culture values external focus and flexibility and discretion. Organizations of this culture type emphasize risk taking, being on the cutting edge, and having an entrepreneurial approach to their work. They encourage creativity, flexibility, and adaptability. Successful senior managers in this culture are described as visionary; they support risk taking, and encourage innovation. In Chapter 4, examples of the innovative culture at Google were given, and it is held up as an example of an Innovation Culture. *Fast Company* magazine named it as the most innovative company in the world in 2008.

The Achievement Culture values an external focus and stability and control. This culture type is very results oriented, highly competitive, and driven for success. Goal achievement, productivity, and high performance are very high priorities. Senior managers who thrive in this culture are hard-driving producers who won't accept anything but victory. They stress bottom-line results. General Electric is often held up as a corporate example of this culture. With the exception of using stretch goals as a way to make the company more innovative, failure has not been tolerated at GE. Winning is everything, and they want all their businesses to be leaders in their markets. I was teaching about this one day, and I looked at someone in the class who had just bought a book by the former CEO of GE, Jack Welch. What's the title? *Winning* (2005). And that says it all.

It's often a struggle for leaders to figure out which of these cultures is the best fit, because they all sound good. And that is part of the point. They are all good, and, as mentioned earlier, every organization will have a mix of all of these. What is necessary is to figure out how much emphasis should be placed on each one within an organization so that there is a fit between culture and strategy, purpose, and the organization's environment.

One pitfall for leaders to watch out for, as they discern the type of culture that is the right fit for their organization, is choosing the one that they themselves feel most comfortable with—regardless of the needs of the organization. This problem can be most pronounced during leadership transitions. When a new CEO comes in, for example, it is wise for him or her to take the time to learn the current culture and to see if it is a fit for the organization's strategy, purpose, and environment. If it is a good fit, then the CEO should adapt to it. If a change does need to be made, then it should be based on the needs of the organization.

This Competing Values approach to culture gives some language and different perspectives to culture change. When I gave the explanation to the CEO I mentioned a few paragraphs earlier, he found it very helpful. "That's it," he said, "we need to be more innovative. How do I make that happen?"

We decided that the first step would be to make sure we fully understood the current culture. I directed him to the book I mentioned earlier (Cameron & Quinn, 1999) which includes in it an Organization Culture Assessment Instrument (OCAI). He administered the OCAI to his entire staff and sent me the results. Through a series of questions, the OCAI reports back the extent to which each of the different cultures are exhibited in the organization on a percentage basis. The results of his organization looked like this:

- Procedural: 20.2 percent
- Cohesion: 25.7 percent
- Innovative: 21.1 percent
- Achievement: 32.9 percent

The CEO reviewed the results with the rest of the senior management team and decided that the changes they wanted to see were as follows:

- Procedural: 20.2 percent changed to 20 percent
- Cohesion: 25.7 percent changed to 20 percent
- Innovative: 21.1 percent changed to 35 percent
- Achievement: 32.9 percent changed to 25 percent

The major change the CEO and senior management team wanted to stress with the rest of the staff is that they had to become less insular, more outward thinking, and more creative—more risk taking. They were willing to give up achievement for innovation in order to make a longer term investment in success.

We scheduled a staff retreat, which first involved my explaining the theory behind the different culture types. Then we revealed the results of the survey. Next, the CEO gave a presentation on the rationale for change and he showed them the direction he thought they needed to go to be more successful. He included in his remarks that "Rob has made it clear to me that in making this kind of change it is going to fall onto me to make sure to actually *reward* the first person who tries something very innovative and fails. I promise you I will do that. And we will continue to reward all innovations—the great successes and the ones we wish were successful. This is the only way we can make even more of a difference in the community in the future. We need to find new ways of doing things."

We spent the rest of the time together in small groups brainstorming how to make changes in the organization's operations and systems to encourage innovation. These were then shared in a final large group meeting. The CEO and senior management team then worked at implementing the ideas over the course of the coming months.

The process we put into place for this organization was following the Kotter eight-step model of change mentioned earlier in Chapter 4. This organization had already (1) established a sense of urgency and had a (2) guiding coalition and a new (3) strategy and vision. They needed a new culture to align with the strategy and vision, which this process gave to them. They now had to figure out how to (4) communicate the change—and the culture types gave them some helpful language to do that. The CEO was (5) empowering broad-based action by telling the staff he would reward innovative failure. And we were doing more on that step by generating ideas to change systems to help promote innovation. What was then left was for the senior management team to (6) generate short-term wins and continue to (7) consolidate gains until they had (8) anchored the new culture.

There are many other approaches to aligning culture that can work well for organizations. This is just an example of one approach. The main point is that senior management needs to bring about alignment of all operations with the mission, vision, strategic stretch goals, and strategy. Once this is done then it is ready to implement the strategy on an ongoing basis.

ANNUAL OPERATING PLANS

The intention of this section is to provide recommendations for tailoring annual operating plans for organizations that use the breakthrough strategy approach outlined in this book. Again, many good books on annual planning have been written to augment what is suggested here.

The strategic stretch goals and strategy narrative guide the organization's actions over the entire three- to five-year period covered by the planning process. An annual operating plan for each of those years specifies the goals and actions that will be taken during that one year.

Funders may request a formal annual plan or business plan from an organization according to specific formats. The suggestions here are for plans for internal use, though they may be altered for more formal presentation if necessary.

Reality Check: As discussed in Chapter 5, most people operate according to the traditional analytical goal-setting mind-set. Therefore, if annual plans are being prepared for presentation outside of the organization, then the goals in the plans may need to be lowered to a more analytical level. This is not deception; it is a matter of giving outsiders what they want. If they want a forecast of what the organization thinks it can reasonably accomplish, then that is what should be provided. Along with that forecast, the organization could say something like, "Of course, we are devoting our creative energies to accomplishing even more than what our report is forecasting for you." This gives the outsiders what they need and allows the organization to maintain its integrity.

Strategic Stretch Goals

Achieving the strategic stretch goals becomes the main focus of each year's annual operating plan. This helps ensure the connection between strategy and implementation—a connection that is often lost in organizations.

Once senior management has addressed issues of aligning the organization with the strategy, their next focus should be on the strategic stretch goals. Since, by definition, achieving these goals will require new ideas and processes, a group of people need to be assigned to each of the goals to generate those new ideas. Appointing a task force to each strategic stretch goal is a good method to use. Each task force would be given a "learning goal" assignment of exploring and inventing new alternatives to achieving the goal. The task force should include people who will be responsible for doing the work to achieve the goal, but could include others who will not. The strategy narrative provides a beginning point and guide from which each task force can create its new ideas.

The alternative ideas for achieving each strategic stretch goal would be reviewed by senior management and a decision on which alternative to implement would be made. This then guides action planning for the upcoming time period. Senior management would then make sure to integrate all new ideas and plans within the organization for all the goals.

Setting Annual Stretch Goals and Milestones

Once decisions have been made on the new ideas and processes that will be implemented to achieve the strategic stretch goals, annual milestones for each of the goals should be established. The milestones should be SMART goals that will be achieved at the end of each year for the planning period. The annual milestones for the strategic stretch goals become the annual stretch goals for each year's annual operating plan.

Achieving these annual stretch goals becomes the priority for that year's plan. Certainly, all other operations must continue as well. But the annual stretch goals that are connected to the strategic stretch goals are of paramount importance.

As discussed in the review of the goal-setting research, the organization will be more effective if it sets goals in all of its operational areas. All goals should be SMART, and the organization should harness the power of the almost impossible stretch for these goals according to the guidelines in Chapter 5 (e.g., only for goals on which they are willing to fail).

All goals set within each year should also have milestones attached to them so that progress can be tracked. These could be broken down quarterly, monthly, or even weekly. Essentially, a milestone is the answer to the question, "If we are going to accomplish this goal by the end of year, then where should we be in three months, six months, and so forth?" Milestones provide important feedback. If the results produced during a certain time period do not meet the milestone, then the organization will want to consider changing the plans it has in place to achieve the goal. You won't want to abandon too quickly the set of new ideas you are trying. But if it is clear that the new ideas do not hold the promise once thought, then it is time to make a new plan.

Action Plans

Action plans are designed around each goal that the organization sets. While actions are being planned for each goal, special attention should be given to the strategy narrative to ensure that the themes outlined there are being followed if applicable to the goal. This is especially true for any strategy levers discussed in the strategy narrative that may apply to this goal.

My experience is that there is wide variance among and within organizations on how well people do with creating and implementing action plans. Great strategy can easily fail at this level of implementation. Senior management is wise to provide training and support on basic concepts of action planning including time management and project management. One of my favorite recommendations for people is the book *Deadline Busting* (Ford & Ford, 2005). It is a fast read of 85 tips, with brief explanations, on being a "star performer" in an organization. My favorite is number 55: "If you are going to panic, panic early." But number 50 is a close second: "Develop and use routines and checklists." (I can't believe that some people try to work without checklists. How do they get anything done?)

Budgeting

Budgeting should be done according to the traditional, analytical mind-set. Budgets should be forecasts of results the organization believes can be reasonably produced. This can be difficult in any kind of organization, but I find that nonprofits who want to provide badly needed services to beneficiaries can fall into wishful thinking about revenue as a rationale for adding programs/services. I was trained on this point early in my career by a board treasurer (who went on to become a Fortune 500 CEO). He would say, "Surpluses first, add programs and expenses later." Essentially, we had to prove that we could bring in the additional revenue a year before we were able to spend it.

As stewards of organizations and of an organization's finances, this conservative approach seems reasonable. But it can also have a positive effect on the creativity of the people within the organization. Knowing that the budget is conservative can help create a safe-fail culture, as discussed in Chapter 5. In order to do this, goals with the almost impossible stretch are set—but those targets are not inserted into the budget. Now people know that the organization is not going to go bankrupt if they come up short. This requires focusing attention on the goals, not the budget, and allows people to work with freedom and creativity.

Monitor SWOTs and Assumptions

The SDG identified important strengths, weaknesses, opportunities, and threats for the organization. It also listed its key assumptions when it created the strategy narrative. These SWOTs and assumptions were generated at a particular snapshot in time. Most certainly, changes will occur in the organization and the environment that will affect these issues. Senior management will need to create a method to monitor the SWOTs for changes and the assumptions for accuracy.

When these changes occur, the strategy and/or the implementation of the strategy may need to be altered somewhat. By maintaining a flexible focus on the key themes of the strategy, an organization is usually able to stay true to its essential strategy as it engages the changes.

If there are certain very important SWOTs or assumptions which—if they change or do not occur as assumed—will significantly impact the success of the strategy, then the organization should develop a contingency plan to react to these changes. This does not mean that every possible scenario needs to be discussed and analyzed. But planning for the most important potential derailers of the strategy is time well invested. Preparing contingency plans is a discipline that many avoid ("We'll cross that bridge if the time comes"). It takes additional time and is often dismissed as negative thinking. However, decision making during an urgent situation can be done more thoughtfully and effectively if done ahead of time.

In the event of very significant and unexpected changes in the SWOTs or assumptions, the organization may need to change its strategy. However, this does not mean that it needs to start the entire process over again. The board of directors can either reconvene the SDG or create a new strategy itself. Often, the vision and strategic stretch goals can remain the same and the strategy development process can be reset with a list of new SWOTs. Once those are established, the new strategy narrative can be created.

Changes in the organization and the environment are inevitable. By preparing itself with this expectation, senior management can proactively engage these changes and keep the organization on course with its break-through strategy.

ADDITIONAL MANAGEMENT CONCEPTS AND TOOLS

Numerous management concepts and tools exist that can support the efforts of senior management in implementing and managing strategy. Three of those concepts and tools that hold promise for nonprofit organizations are reviewed briefly here. These concepts and tools are used significantly in the for-profit world, though less so for nonprofits.

Quality Management

The quality management movement spread throughout the United States significantly during the 1980s and into the 1990s. It continues to influence many of the processes and systems within corporations. While initially very popular with manufacturing organizations, quality management spread to service organizations and can be effectively used by nonprofits as well.

There are different applications of quality concepts by various authors and consultants. Two of the most widely cited are Deming's 14 points for management (1982, 1993) and Juran's trilogy (1989) focusing on the inter-relationship among processes of planning, control, and improvement.

One of the consistent themes of quality management approaches is the importance of an organization maintaining a "constancy of purpose." Deming refers to this as the "aim of the system" (1993, p. 51) and says, "there must evolve a sense of agreement upon the aim that extends through the organization" (p. 53). This is consistent with the importance of establishing agreed-upon mission accomplishment measures for non-profits, as discussed in Chapter 3.

Once constancy of purpose is established in an organization, quality management concepts and tools have been developed to support an organization in maintaining consistency of action as it implements its work. Some of these tools (McConnell, 1989) include:

- *The Pareto Principle.* Identifying the 20 percent of causes that produce 80 percent of the effects.

- *Scatter Plots.* Graphs of two data sets that can provide a visual indicator of potential causal relationships.

- *Control Charts.* Plotting the distribution of data as a way to identify variation so that trends can be recognized and actions can be taken on trends rather than on a single variation which may have a special cause.

- *Flow Charts.* Using pictures, symbols, or text coupled with lines and arrows to show direction and map processes.

- *Fishbone, Ishikawa Diagrams.* A cause-and-effect diagram that specifies the main causes of variation, as well as subcauses, and connects them together to demonstrate how they produce an effect.

Some of these tools are more familiar than others to most in the nonprofit world. For example, in fundraising we have said for years that 80 percent of the money will come from 20 percent of the donors. We therefore expend most of our time focused on identifying that 20 percent group of people. And flowcharts are commonly used to map various projects. The other tools may not be so familiar.

Earlier, in Chapter 5, I alluded to our use of some of these tools during my tenure as CEO at LeaderShape, Inc. In the early 1990s we had a strategic intent to dramatically grow the number of sessions of the six-day leadership program we offered. We were also committed to high-quality delivery of each of these sessions. With that in mind, we realized we needed to learn more about quality management concepts. The two tools that we actively applied were control charts and the fishbone diagram.

Our interest in control charts was based on our commitment to assuring quality delivery of the leadership program we had designed. We created metrics that we collected on each session of the program. Once we had collected enough data for the control charts—Deming suggests 25 to 30 incidents (1993, p. 179)—we were able to identify normal variations in the quality of delivery. Once this normal range of variations was established, we set about doing two things: (1) improving the overall average range of quality metric scores through continued training and development, and (2) giving extra attention to situations in which the quality metrics for a session were lower than the normal range we had identified. These are known as situations with "special causes." Deming explains that "efforts must be directed at identification of the special cause that was responsible for the outcome, and at its removal if it could recur" (1993, p. 188).

With respect to special causes, the control chart helped us identify when a fluctuation in our metrics was normal or special. When it was special, we would investigate further to find out what was going on there. Fortunately, we did not have any sessions that fell far outside the normal range and only a few per year that required special cause investigation.

In designing our fishbone, we created a detailed list of 45 variables that we believed interacted to produce a high-quality session of The Leader-Shape Institute. We were then able to apply in practice what we learned by going through this exercise. For example, we were able to create a detailed program management manual that was organized around the variables we had identified in the fishbone. It also gave us information we then used as our outline for training staff and volunteers who had to manage these sessions. Our ability to maintain high quality was supported by the use of these two tools. We increased the number of sessions we conducted from 5 in 1992 to 46 in 2001 with continued high-quality metrics.

Fishbone diagrams can be applied in a variety of ways in the nonprofit world. In Figure 8.2 is an example of a fishbone developed by a team of undergraduates who are a part of the University of Maryland's QUEST Program. QUEST stands for QUality Enhancement Systems & Teams, and it is co-sponsored by the Clark School of Engineering and the Smith School of Business. This team launched a project called Shutters for Scholars, which now helps provide scholarship funding for orphans in the Ukraine through the creation of an innovative web site (www.Shutters4Scholars .com). The first step in launching this project was the delivery of disposable cameras to children in an orphanage who took photographs of themselves and then sent the cameras back to the United States for uploading onto the web site. It was very important for the process to be implemented flawlessly. This example demonstrates why these diagrams are called "fishbones," and it illustrates how the main causes of success can be identified, along with sub-causes. The project was very successful and, yes, they continue to accept donations via the web site.

This is a brief overview of how these concepts and tools can support the implementation of strategy. For more information, a very good booklet is *Three Experts on Quality Management: Philip B. Crosby, W. Edwards Deming, Joseph M. Juran* by J. Gerald Suàrez (available at www.stormingmedia.us).

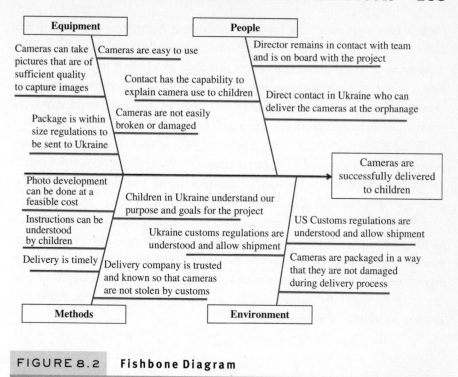

FIGURE 8.2   Fishbone Diagram

If you want even more in-depth information, try *The Deming Management Method* by Mary Walton. In addition, courses in quality management are widely available at various colleges and universities.

The Balanced Scorecard

In 1992, Robert Kaplan and David Norton published their *Harvard Business Review* article "The Balanced Scorecard." Since that time the concept has proliferated in the corporate world and, to some extent, spilled over into the nonprofit world. Numerous articles and books on the Balanced Scorecard have been published during the past 15 years, including a book specifically for government and nonprofits (Niven, 2008).

A number of the motivations behind the creation of the Balanced Scorecard are applicable to nonprofits as well as for profits. First, Kaplan and Norton realized that the financial metrics used by companies were lagging indicators of performance, rather than leading indicators. They wanted some metrics that were drivers of future performance. Next, they appreciated that some of those drivers of future performance would be nonfinancial measures. And finally, they pointed out the importance of monitoring a set of metrics—rather than one or two—in order to appreciate the variety of important activities that go on in an organization. They use the example of all the instrumentation that pilots need to use to effectively fly a plane.

While there is definitely an appeal to provide senior managers of non-profits with a dashboard of metrics that will allow them to monitor their progress, the traditional Balanced Scorecard—as developed for companies—needs to be altered for nonprofits.

Paul Niven, in *Balanced Scorecard for Government and Nonprofit Agencies* (2008), suggests that one important change that needs to be made is a shift in purpose. The original Balanced Scorecard is an input-output model designed to identify the indicators of future financial performance (see Figure 8.3). Niven shifts the intended output to mission, rather than financial output, as indicated in Figure 8.4.

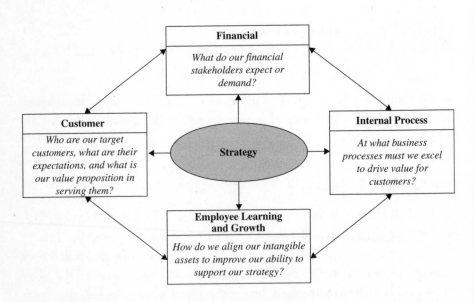

FIGURE 8.3   **The Original Balanced Scorecard**

Source: Paul R. Niven. 2008. *Balanced Scorecard Step-by-Step for Government and Nonprofit Agencies,* 2nd ed. Reprinted with permission of John Wiley & Sons, Inc.

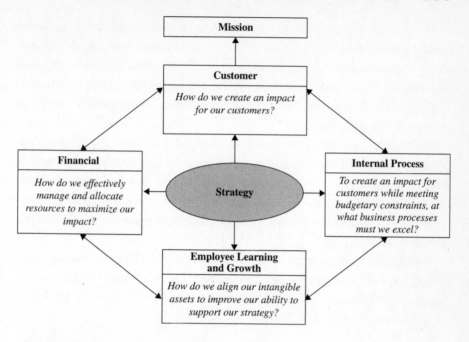

FIGURE 8.4   **Shift to Mission (Rather than Financial Output)**

Source: Paul R. Niven. 2008. *Balanced Scorecard Step-by-Step for Government and Nonprofit Agencies,* 2nd ed. Reprinted with permission of John Wiley & Sons, Inc.

In this way, Niven maintains the main elements of the original Balanced Scorecard: Internal Process, Customer, Financial, Employee Learning, and Growth. But he shifts the design of the layout to demonstrate the higher importance of the customer as the pathway to accomplishing the mission. In both models, strategy is at the core of what generates action.

Kaplan (2002) agrees with the change in primacy from financial output to mission for nonprofits and also suggests that nonprofits need to broaden their definition of *customer,* given their multiple constituencies.

The original logic model of the corporate Balanced Scorecard is that innovations created from improvements in employee learning and growth, along with improvements to internal processes, when combined with improvements to the customer experience, will lead to improvement in various financial metrics, ultimately resulting in enhanced shareholder value.

By making the change in the ultimate output to mission, the logic model for the nonprofit Balanced Scorecard is that innovations created from improvements in employee learning and growth, along with improvements to internal processes, will allow for utilization of finances to most effectively provide an improved customer experience, resulting in mission accomplishment.

Kaplan and Norton (1996a) provide their original logic model as a template and suggest that organizations may want to choose their own models and perspectives they want to measure. With this in mind, organizations can take the general ideas of designing multiple, nonfinancial, leading indicators and design their own arenas of measures to assist them in monitoring their operations.

Kaplan and Norton further extend the use of the Balanced Scorecard to create maps for implementing strategy, which can cascade throughout an organization's divisions—and all the way to the individual level with a Personal Scorecard (Kaplan & Norton, 1996b).

Example: Bethany College

Bethany College in Lindsborg, Kansas, is a small liberal arts school associated with the Lutheran Church (www.Bethanylb.edu). Serving there as president since 2007 is Dr. Ed Leonard. Dr. Leonard earned an MBA and worked in corporate America before later earning his PhD and devoting his career to higher education. Therefore, applying concepts and tools from the for-profit world into the nonprofit world comes naturally to him.

At Bethany, Dr. Leonard has promoted the use of the Balanced Scorecard concept and strategy implementation maps for the college's various operations. In his own words:

> I have been a proponent of Kaplan and Norton's work for over a decade. First as vice president for College Advancement (at Wilmington College of Ohio) and now as president of Bethany College (Kansas), I have utilized the tools of strategy implementation maps and balanced scorecards.
>
> Personally, I have gained great benefit, as a leader, from developing, then using, strategy implementation maps. In the case of the maps, it truly can be said a picture is worth a thousand words. Moreover, I have become persuaded that a well-defined strategy implementation map also serves

the organization as its value chain. That is, the cause-and-effect propositions of value chains can and should be extended to strategy implementation maps—if only at a minimum at the hypothetical level.

Over the last two years at Bethany College, as we developed our vision, strategic directions, and strategic goals, we laid them out on a strategy implementation map (see Figure 8.5). I believe this is a powerful and effective way to share the future with both on-campus as well as off-campus constituents. It also forces us to define our value proposition by also using the strategy implementation map as our value chain. (Heskett, Sasser, and Schlesinger, 2002)

A further benefit gained from the strategy implementation map has been our ability to strategically view the "big picture" and to organize

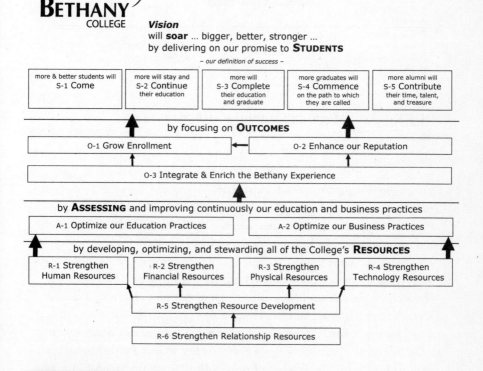

FIGURE 8.5   Strategy Implementation Map

ALIGNING STRUCTURE WITH STRATEGY

Strategic Goals	Board of Director's Committee	College Senior Leadership Team
O-1 Enrollment (recruitment) O-2 Reputation (brand)	Recruitment & Marketing	Dean of Recruitment & Marketing
O-1 Enrollment (retention) O-3 Curriculum O-4 Co-curriculum A-1 Education Practices	Student Experience	Provost / Dean of the College
A-2 Business Practices R-1 Human Resources R-2 Financial Resources	Business & Finance	Vice President for Finance & Operations
R-3 Physical Resources R-4 Technology Resources	Facilities & Technology	
R-5 Resource Development R-6 Relationship Resources	Advancement	Vice President for Advancement

FIGURE 8.6   **Aligning Structure with Strategy**

our college's structure around our strategy. We moved from eight strategic units to four strategic units: student experience, recruitment and marketing, finance and operations, and advancement. Further, we reorganized the committees of the board of directors to align with our strategy, which resulted in the same four as strategic board committees; except we subdivided finance and operations into business and finance and facilities and technology. Because of both reorganizations, we have discovered greater focus on our strategic plans (see Figure 8.6).

As for the Balanced Scorecard, I believe, the balance that is inherent in a well-defined scorecard brings great currency to leading within higher education. That is, the balance of financial and nonfinancial goals, internal and external measures, lagging and leading indicators, hard and soft measures, and, finally, the balance of multiple perspectives (financial, constituent/customer, internal processes, and learning and growth) help the leader to more effectively navigate the institution to its desired future.

However, I have found that the "cascading down" of goals—then the "rolling up"—is the Balanced Scorecard's greatest contribution. Meaning, by delegating leadership, or ownership, of each of the strategic goals shaping the Balanced Scorecard to one of the college's strategic units, the Balanced Scorecard begins to establish accountability (see Figure 8.7). As an example, the value chain concept can be applied directly to the development office. But don't stop there! (Leonard, 2005)

By delegating leadership, or ownership, of each the operational goals shaping the strategic goals to the appropriate operational unit, you are further cementing accountability within the college's culture (see Figure 8.8). But don't stop there!

By finally delegating the strategic and operational goals to the appropriate individual within the operating unit—in other words, that positions performance goals for the ensuing year—you have completely grounded the balanced scorecard and have made strategy everyone's everyday job (see Figure 8.9).

So that at the end of the year, as the individual performances "roll up" to the successful accomplishment of the operational goals, and the operational goals "roll up" to the successful achievement of the strategic goals, you are moving the college strategically to the successful realization of your vision.

Strategy implementation maps and the Balanced Scorecard are, I have found, straightforward to understand and straightforward to develop. I have learned over the last ten years the best overarching strategy with both is, "Ready. Fire. Aim." Which is counterintuitive to higher education, but, then again, so are much of strategy implementation maps and balanced scorecards." (Leonard, 2009)

Another Perspective: The Ethical Scorecard

Author and consultant Doug Smith, whose book *Make Success Measureable* has been mentioned in earlier chapters, takes a different perspective on the Balanced Scorecard. In his book *On Value and Values* (2004), Smith points out that the Balanced Scorecard actually is not balanced. As an input-output linear model that results in financial gain, the Balanced Scorecard uplifts financial returns above everything else. It uses the other elements of

Bethany College
STRATEGIC-LEVEL BALANCED SCORECARD

VISION: Bethany College will soar ... bigger, better, stronger ...

STRATEGIC DIRECTION: by delivering on our promise to STUDENTS — our definition of success —

STRATEGIC GOALS:

		METRICS:	LEAD
S-1 Come	more	TOTAL HEADCOUNT: total headcount enrollment (fall)	Recruitment & Marketing
	better	HS CLASS RANK by Top 25%	Recruitment & Marketing
S-2 Continue		RETENTION RATE: freshmen-to-sophomore retention rate	Student Experience
S-3 Complete		GRADUATION RATE: six-year graduation rate	Student Experience
S-4 Commence		PLACEMENT: rate of acceptance into grad school and rate of job placement within 3 (or 6) months	Student Experience
S-5 Contribute		ALUMNI LOYALTY: % of alumni who contribute	Advancement

STRATEGIC DIRECTION: by focusing on OUTCOMES

STRATEGIC GOALS:

	METRICS:	LEAD
O-1 Grow ENROLLMENT	FTE ENROLLMENT: total full-time equivalent enrollment (fall) @ 12 semester credit hours	Recruitment & Marketing
	NEW STUDENT HEADCOUNT: total headcount of new students (first time first year and transfer)	Recruitment & Marketing
	RETENTION RATE: fall-to-spring retention rate	Student Experience
	RETENTION RATE: spring-to-fall retention rate	Student Experience
O-2 Enhance our REPUTATION	REPUTATION: peer assessment score in *US News & World Report*	Recruitment & Marketing
O-3 Integrate & Enrich the BETHANY EXPERIENCE	ACADEMIC CHALLENGE: NSSE survey score (First Yr / Senior Yr)	Student Experience
	ACTIVE & COLLABORATE LEARNING: NSSE survey score (First Yr / Senior Yr)	Student Experience
	STUDENT-FACULTY INTERACTION: NSSE survey score (First Yr / Senior Yr)	Student Experience
	ENRICHING EDUCATIONAL EXPERIENCES: NSSE survey score (First Yr / Senior Yr)	Student Experience
	SUPPORT CAMPUS ENVIRONMENT: NSSE survey score (First Yr / Senior Yr)	Student Experience

STRATEGIC DIRECTION: by ASSESSING and improving continuously our education and business practices

STRATEGIC GOALS:

	METRICS:	LEAD
A-1 Optimize EDUCATION PRACTICES	OVERALL LEVEL OF IMPLEMENTATION: HLC Assessment of Student Academic Achievement	Student Experience

STRATEGIC DIRECTION: by developing, optimizing & stewarding all of the college's RESOURCES

STRATEGIC GOALS:

	METRICS:	LEAD
R-1 Strengthen HUMAN RESOURCES	RETENTION: % of workforce retention	Finance & Operations
	LENGTH OF SERVICE: average years of employment	Finance & Operations
R-2 Strengthen FINANCIAL RESOURCES	FINANCIAL RATIO: US DoE Financial Responsibility Standards Index	Finance & Operations
R-3 Strengthen PHYSICAL RESOURCES	AGE OF FACILITIES: Accumulated depreciation divided by depreciation expense	Finance & Operations
R-4 Strengthen TECHNOLOGY RESOURCES	IT EXPENDITURES: (including staffing and capital expenditures) as a % of unrestricted expenditures	Finance & Operations
R-5 Strengthen RESOURCE DEVELOPMENT	TOTAL GIVING: total $ of outright and deferred giving	Advancement
	BETHANY FUND: total annual, recurring $ for unrestricted current operations	Advancement
R-6 Strengthen RELATIONSHIP RESOURCES	TOTAL DONORS: # of all donors	Advancement
	BETHANY FUND DONORS: # of donors to the Bethany Fund	Advancement

FIGURE 8.7   Strategic-Level Balanced Scorecard

Office of College Advancement
OPERATIONAL-LEVEL BALANCED SCORECARD

STRATEGIC GOALS:	METRICS:	LEAD
S-5 More alumni will CONTRIBUTE their time, talent & treasure	ALUMNI LOYALTY: % of alumni who contribute	Advancement

STRATEGIC GOALS:	METRICS:	LEAD
R-5 Strengthen RESOURCE DEVELOPMENT	TOTAL GIVING: total $ of outright and deferred giving	Advancement
	BETHANY FUND: total annual, recurring $ for unrestricted current operations	Advancement

OPERATIONAL GOALS:	METRICS:	LEAD
(1) Grow total giving	(a) CURRENT OPERATIONS GIVING: total $ for current operations	Annual Giving
	(b) CAPITAL GIVING: total $ for property, building & equipment	Major Giving
	(c) ENDOWMENT GIVING: total $ for endowment	Major Giving
	(d) DEFERRED GIVING: total $ designated for future support as face value	Planned Giving
(2) Grow the Bethany Fund	(a) BF PERSONAL GIVING: $ contributed through personal solicitation (or unsolicited)	Annual Giving
	(b) BF TELEMARKETING GIVING: $ contributed through telemarketing	Annual Giving
	(c) BF DIRECT MAIL GIVING: $ contributed through direct mail	Annual Giving
	(d) BF INTERNET GIVING: $ contributed through the internet	Annual Giving
	(e) BF PLEDGE FULFILLMENT: % of $ contributed out of $ pledged	Annual Giving
(3) Grow restricted (special) giving	(a) RESTRICTED GIVING: total $ for restricted current operations	Development
	(b) BAA GIVING: $ contributed to the Bethany Athletic Association	Athletic Association
	(c) FOUNDATION GIVING: $ contributed from private foundations	Major Giving
	(i) # of proposals submitted	
	(ii) % of proposals awarded	
	(iii) % of funding secured	

FIGURE 8.8   Operational-Level Balanced Scorecard

STRATEGIC GOALS:	METRICS:	LEAD
R-6 Strengthen RELATIONSHIP RESOURCES	TOTAL DONORS: # of all donors	Advancement
	BETHANY FUND DONORS: # of donors to the Bethany Fund	Advancement
OPERATIONAL GOALS:	METRICS:	LEAD
(1) Get-Keep-Grow donors	(a) DONOR LOYALTY: % who contribute of	Development
	(i) faculty & staff	
	(ii) students	
	(iii) parents	
	(b) BF LEADERSHIP DONORS: # of $1,000+ donors to the Bethany Fund	Annual Giving
	(c) ATHLETIC ASSOCIATION: # of athletic association donors	Athletic Association
(2) Maximize donor reach & outreach	(a) DONOR REACH: # of prospects in the gift pipeline	Advancement Services
	(i) # being actively cultivated or stewarded	
	(ii) # qualified but pending cultivation (inactive)	
	(iii) # to be qualified for capacity & affinity (explore)	
	(b) DONOR OUTREACH: # of face-to-face visits	Development
(3) Expand alumni reach & outreach (someone either been graduated or attended for at least one semester)	(a) ALUMNI REACH: % of alumni reachable by	Alumni Relations
	(i) mail	
	(ii) telephone	
	(iii) email	
	(b) ALUMNI OUTREACH: # of alumni attending all outreach events	Alumni Relations
	(i) # of alumni attending campus outreach events	
	(ii) # of alumni attending regional outreach events	
(4) Engage alumni	(a) LEGACY STUDENTS: % of students who are legacy students	Alumni Relations
	(b) ALUMNI REFERRALS: # of alumni prospective student referrals	Alumni Relations

FIGURE 8.8   Continued

Director of Development
PERFORMANCE-LEVEL BALANCED SCORECARD

PERFORMANCE GOALS	METRICS	TARGET
S-5 More alumni will CONTRIBUTE their time, talent & treasure	ALUMNI LOYALTY: % of alumni who contribute	
R-5 Strengthen RESOURCE DEVELOPMENT	TOTAL GIVING: total $ of outright and deferred giving	
	BETHANY FUND: total annual, recurring $ for unrestricted current operations	
(3) Grow restricted (special) giving	a) RESTRICTED GIVING: total $ for restricted current operations	
R-6 Strengthen RELATIONSHIP RESOURCES	TOTAL DONORS: # of all donors	
	BETHANY FUND DONORS: # of donors to the Bethany Fund	
(1) Get-Keep-Grow donors	(a) DONOR LOYALTY: % who contribute of	
	(i) faculty & staff	
	(ii) students	
	(iii) parents	
(2) Maximize donor reach & outreach	(b) DONOR OUTREACH: # of face-to-face visits	

FIGURE 8.9 Performance-Level Balanced Scorecard

the scorecard as means toward the end of financial return. The parts of the scorecard are not equal or balanced in any way.

In Smith's cycle of sustainable performance, which was discussed in Chapter 1, he points out the importance of the different functional areas of funders/supporters, customers, and employees working together in a relationship of mutual benefit. Each arena of activity both benefits from and contributes to the others. None is more important that the others. Their importance is truly blended because of their cyclical relationship. In *On Value and Values*, he calls this an Ethical Scorecard. It is only sustainable—and therefore ethical—to run an organization in which the importance of all these key arenas of activity are blended together in this way. If one arena of activity is upheld over the other—be it funders/supporters or customers or employees—this will not be sustainable or ethical. So even a Balanced Scorecard that has mission as its ultimate outcome is not balanced unless it blends together the importance of funders and employees, rather than treating them as means to the mission end.

Scoreboard measures can be created for the different arenas of activity that Smith is identifying. In this model, care needs to be taken that the results produced in each arena are blended in a way that they all serve one another.

Strengths-Based Management

Extensive research has been conducted in recent years by The Gallup Organization, which has led to their promotion of new perspectives on the management and development of people. Their research findings and approach are consistent with the positive psychology movement, which encourages people to cultivate what is best within themselves.

What follows is a brief overview of the approach that Gallup advocates in books it has published, including *First, Break All the Rules* (Buckingham & Coffman, 1999), *Now, Discover Your Strengths* (Buckingham & Clifton, 2001), and *StrengthsFinder 2.0* (Rath, 2007). Research demonstrates that their methods lead to higher productivity, fulfillment, and satisfaction for individuals and improved levels of performance for organizations. My personal experience in applying the concepts they recommend has been very beneficial for me and for people I have coached in their approach.

At the outset, I should point out that years ago I partnered with Gallup on some training programs for clients while I worked with the Academy of Leadership at the University of Maryland. However, I am not doing work for them or with them at this time. What I am reporting here is a summary of their books and my observations of the value they provide to individuals and organizations.

In *First Break All the Rules*, Buckingham and Coffman discuss Gallup's research in identifying what strong vibrant workplaces look like and what the world's greatest managers do to find, focus, and keep talented employees. One result of this research is a Gallup instrument called the Q12—a workplace survey which correlates with a vibrant workplace. Responses to the Q12 are a causal link to: productivity, profitability, retention, and customer satisfaction. With the Q12, Gallup can survey companies to discern the level of employee engagement there. More highly engaged employees tend to engage customers effectively, which leads to a variety of positive outcomes for a business.

The Gallup research that created the Q12 survey also reveals what managers need to do to turn their direct reports into engaged employees. First, managers need to understand that many people operate from incorrect assumptions about management. These false assumptions include:

- All behaviors can be learned.
- The "best in role" all get there the same way.
- Weakness fixing leads to success.

These beliefs are pervasive. Think about how many times you have been told, or you told someone else something like: "If you try hard enough, you can do it" or "If you want it badly enough, you can do it" or "If you dream it, you can achieve it." Instead of these incorrect assumptions, Gallup suggests that great managers need to adopt the following assumptions:

- Some behaviors can be learned.
- The "best in role" get the same outcomes using different behaviors.
- Weakness fixing prevents failure, while strength building leads to success. (This does not mean that "weaknesses" can be ignored.)

The Gallup approach advocates the identification and deployment of each individual's natural talents as the way for that person to achieve maximum performance. Instead of obsessing over every weakness that a person may have, we need to provide them with opportunities to grow, develop, and perform in the arenas where they have natural talent.

With this in mind, imagine how things might have turned out for the great golfer Tiger Woods, if someone had obsessed over some of his possible weaknesses. Imagine his junior high school physical education teacher fretting over his grade book and calling young Tiger into his office: "Tiger, I have been looking over your grades on our different activities here in phys ed class. And son, let me tell you, you have that golfing thing down perfectly. However, I am a little concerned about your swimming. You certainly swim well enough not to drown, but I would like to see some improvement there. So, let's take you off the golf course three days per week and give you extra swimming lessons. I am sure that in time you will be as good a swimmer as you are a golfer."

Fictional story? Yes. For all I know, Tiger Woods was and is a fabulous swimmer. But is this not what we do to people in our performance reviews and development plans? Does the Tiger in my example need to learn how to swim better? Maybe—if he wants to. But his golf talent is going to soar if his teacher lets him out on the golf course as much as he wants to go. He can swim well enough not to drown, and these days he can hire a boatload of lifeguards if he ever feels unsafe. He does not need to become as good a swimmer as he is a golfer.

So, while we cannot ignore weaknesses and we need to make sure they do not let us fail—or drown, for example—it is focusing on our natural talents that leads to high performance. And when individuals perform in a superior fashion, so do their organizations.

With this in mind, Gallup says that great managers perform four essential functions to turn their direct reports into engaged, high performers: Select for Talent, Define the Right Outcomes, Focus on Strengths, and Find the Right Fit. Again, all of this is covered in the book *First, Break All the Rules* (Buckingham and Coffman, 1999). Following is a little more detail on each of these functions.

When **Selecting for Talent**, great managers interview candidates while looking for clues such as: yearning—what a person is drawn to; rapid learning, flow—when steps come naturally to someone; almost unconscious glimpses of excellence; and satisfaction in prior roles. I have a friend who, when we were just out of college, told me he thought he would be good at either being a funeral director or a casualty officer—a military officer who visits families to tell them a soldier has died. I thought this a bit unusual at the time, but he was demonstrating a yearning for his talent of empathy. He is now a flight attendant and he loves it. His colleagues give him the angriest passengers. He listens, empathizes, and seemingly absorbs their anger—no more angry passenger after he engages with them. And he derives a great deal of satisfaction from that.

Once in a role, a manager works with a direct report to **Define the Right Outcomes** for the role. Once the outcomes are defined, then the manager lets the direct report use their natural talents to find their own way to the result. Rather than prescribe the "one best way" to carry out a responsibility, the manager gives the person freedom to find their way. Defining outcomes is not as easy for some roles as they are for others. The book has very good ideas for developing outcomes as does Doug Smith's book, *Make Success Measureable* (1999).

The manager allows the direct report to **Focus on Strengths**. Where possible, the direct report is given more responsibilities in arenas where they show natural talent and fewer where they do not. This requires treating people uniquely rather than as machines where every person in the same role has the exact same responsibilities. If a person must perform a duty they are not ideally suited for, then they try to manage around that weakness. As an example, I was serving as an executive coach for a midlevel executive who was trying to deal with a lesser talent—he disliked the small talk at the receptions he was required to attend now and then for members of his association. I asked him if any of his colleagues were great at that and he quickly named three or four. "Great," I said, "the next time you have an event like that to attend, simply ask them if you can stick by their side for the evening. People like that enjoy connecting others—they have a natural talent for it."

The fourth function, **Find the Right Fit**, I think presents some of the greatest challenges to organizations. This is because sometimes a person is in a job that is actually a wonderful fit for them and for their talents—but we want to promote them so we can reward them with better pay. This is the classic "Peter Principle," which suggests that people are promoted to their highest level of incompetence. Rather than doing that, Gallup suggests that organizations reward achievement and consider increasing compensation for people in the role they are already in. Finding the right fit also comes into play when working with them individually on their career development and the organization's succession plans. If we see that a person can use more of their natural talents in other roles in the organization, then we should guide them into those roles. It is good for the organization and the individual.

In two of the other books I mentioned, *Now, Discover Your Strengths* and *StrengthsFinder 2.0,* The Gallup Organization provides the opportunity for individuals to take an assessment which will identify their top talents. This instrument, The Clifton StrengthsFinder™, is named for Dr. Donald O. Clifton, the former Chairman and CEO of Gallup who did pioneering work on the instrument and has been cited as a grandfather of the positive psychology movement. By purchasing either one of these books, a person can go to the Internet with an individualized code provided in the book to take the assessment.

Once the online assessment is completed, a computer-generated report automatically produces a list of the top five natural talents for that individual, in order of their strength. There are a total of 34 talent themes that Gallup has identified that each person has, naturally, to one extent or another. Once a person knows their top talents, they are encouraged to use them more to enhance their performance.

One way that a person can be even more successful in using their top talents is to purposely develop them—to get even better at the things they are already good at. This is what converts a natural talent into a strength. By adding more knowledge and skill to a talent area, and then applying the knowledge and skills in practice, strength is developed.

Notice how this is practically the opposite of how people are typically developed according to the usual performance review and development plan processes. Like the phys ed teacher in the Tiger story, we typically spend time looking for weaknesses and how we can fix people. While glaring weaknesses cannot be ignored, people will be much more successful if they are placed in roles where they can use and develop their natural talents into significant strengths.

As an example, I remember when my top five talents popped up on my computer screen. My first reaction was "This is why I have loved every job I have ever had." I am one of those fortunate people who has had jobs that fit their natural talents very well. Not long after I took the Clifton

StrengthsFinder, I was at an event where I had the opportunity to ask Dr. Clifton to sign my copy of the book *Now, Discover Your Strengths*. He would ask each person in line what their number one talent was and included that in his inscription. For me, he wrote: "Rob, Use your Strategic and soar!" That sums up the Gallup philosophy regarding strengths—use them and you will soar.

Seeing the talent of Strategic as number one on my list has made more sense to me over time. One thing about a top talent is that it is so natural to you that you think other people experience the world in the same way. And when they don't it can be very frustrating. It used to confuse me when others in organizations could not see the obvious strategic direction we should take. Now it makes sense—I just naturally see strategy patterns more clearly than some other people. At the same time, I also have become more aware of my lesser talents—those that I can tell are low on my list. And I am sure that I frustrate others who are high in those talent areas. For example, give me a set of routine detailed tasks and, unless I am remarkably focused, watch me fail. I try to make sure that people I work with understand my lesser talents as well as my top talents.

Given the important role of the senior management team in implementing the breakthrough strategy, there are very helpful lessons to be learned through the research that Gallup has done on strengths-based management and development. The better the senior management team can work together and with followers, the more effectively the organization will bring its vision into reality, close its mission gap, and accomplish its mission.

LEVERAGING YOUR COMMITMENT AND HARD WORK

Creating and implementing breakthrough strategy toward high levels of mission accomplishment is no easy task. But, for those of us committed to making a significant impact for the benefit of others, it is the path to take. This book is intended to provide you with the leverage to take the commitment and hard work you have been giving to your organization and produce a breakthrough in your mission impact.

Best wishes to you and your colleagues as you undertake your organization's strategy development and implementation process. And, most importantly, thank you for your commitment to making a difference for others through the nonprofit organizations you are connected to. Working together, we can make a breakthrough impact in the quality of life for others on our planet. We can create a more just, equitable, and thriving society.

The Seven Deadly Sins of Nonprofit Strategy

Nonprofit organizations frequently fall into different, predictable traps when they go about creating strategy. I have labeled the most common of these as *The Seven Deadly Sins of Nonprofit Strategy*. The strategy development process provided in this book is designed to produce a breakthrough strategy that, if effectively implemented, will make a significant difference in the organization's mission impact. However, if you begin to see yourself or your organization starting to fall into any of these traps, then it may be time to confront those "sins" and get the organization back on the right path—to breakthrough strategy salvation.

1. **"It's Just Sitting on the Shelf."** The rest of the sins are not necessarily in order of severity, but this is clearly number one because it is so pervasive and represents a huge waste of money and time—from staff and volunteers. This sin can be deadly, indeed, when board members realize the hours they have wasted making strategic plans that are never implemented. And for the attorneys on your board, those are billable hours.

2. **Insular Mountaintop Planning.** It can be good for a strategy-planning group to go to the "mountains" to get away from distractions to do work together. But, before you go, gather input regarding the organization's future from stakeholders—and check in with them

when you get back for more input before you publish and laminate the plan (Peter Block calls this error leadership by "lamination").

3. **Overemphasis on Fundraising.** "What?!?" "Impossible!" I can just hear my fundraising colleagues' reaction. Of course, we frequently find new fundraising initiatives as a part of a new strategy. The problem is that as these efforts are highlighted, other important aspects of a strategy are underemphasized—such as program innovation, leadership succession, strategic partnerships, board recruitment, and more.

4. **Too Rushed.** Rather than rushing (e.g., "We are doing our strategic plan at an all-day retreat two weeks from Friday, are you available?"), it is wiser to take the time to thoughtfully design and implement a strategy development process. Of course, it should not take forever, either. Taking the time can lead to inspiring visions, innovative strategies, and empowered stakeholders, which produce higher performance.

5. **Lots of Plans, No Strategy.** Strategic-planning documents can contain volumes of plans, activities, and environmental analysis, but many don't include a real "strategy." A true strategy articulates the dynamic levers which will catapult an organization toward its desired future, as well as how its key operational areas will interact to create a cycle of higher performance.

6. **No Annual Review.** No one can see into the future when developing a strategic plan! So we make certain measured assumptions about the future, including changes in our internal and external environments. An annual review of assumptions and results is important to keep the plan relevant. You may not change your mission or vision, but you may need to change plans and activities.

7. **Not Ambitious Enough.** A strategy and its associated goals and plans should be focused on a vision that is big, bold, and inspiring. Many strategic plans are based simply on an analytical forecast of the way things are currently headed. How dull. It was Goethe who said, "Dream no small dreams for they have no power to move the hearts of men," and Mandela who stated, "Your playing small does not serve the world."

Venture Philanthropy Partners Capacity Assessment Grid

DESCRIPTION

- The McKinsey Capacity Assessment Grid is a tool designed to help nonprofit organizations assess their organizational capacity. The grid should be used in conjunction with the Capacity Framework (discussed in Chapter 6 of this book) which explains the seven elements of organizational capacity and their components. The grid asks the reader to score the organization on each element of organizational capacity, by selecting the text that best describes the organization's current status or performance. The framework and the descriptions in the grid were developed based on our team's collective experience as well as the input of many nonprofit experts and practitioners.

- The grid may be used by nonprofit managers, staff, board members and external capacity builders and funders with the following objectives:

  - To identify those particular areas of capacity that are strongest and those that need improvement

  - To measure changes in an organization's capacity over time

  - To draw out different views within an organization regarding its capacity; different responses to the grid among staff, board members and funders, for example, can be a valuable discussion-starter within an organization

- The grid is not a scientific tool, and should not be used as one. It is very difficult to quantify the dimensions of capacity, and the descriptive text under each score in the grid is not meant to be exact. The scores are meant to provide a general indication—a "temperature" taking, if you will—of an organization's capacity level, in order to identify potential areas for improvement. Furthermore, the results of the exercise should be interpreted in the context of the organizatins stage of development. For example, a score of "2" on organizational processes may be sufficient for a new organization, and this area may not merit immediate attention. In fact, many organizations may never get to level 4 on many elements.

- This tool is meant to be a starting point only. We encourage you to adapt the grid to meet your own organization's capacity assessment needs.

INSTRUCTIONS

Guidelines for Survey Administrators

Decide for which point(s) in time you want to assess the nonprofit's organizational capacity—e.g., today, beginning of last year, three years ago, etc. You may choose to assess the organization at two different points in time, in order to measure changes in capacity.

Select the people whom you want to assess the nonprofit (assessors); these can include nonprofit staff members, board members, or external parties. Ideally, assessors should have a good knowledge of the organization for all points in time chosen for the assessment.

For the human resources section, decide whom you wish to evaluate in the set of rows pertaining to "CEO/ED and/or senior management team." Options include 1) CEO/ED only; 2) CEO/ED and senior management team considered collectively; 3) CEO/ED on the one hand and senior management team on the other; or 4) individuals taken separately. If you choose option 3 or 4, you may need to copy the relevant section for each separate person or group of persons covered by the assessment.

Guidelines for those Filling Out the Survey (Assessors)

For each row, determine the description most suitable for the point in time chosen and write the date (e.g., 6/99) in that box. If you are also conducting the assessment for a second point in time, repeat the procedure with the corresponding date (e.g., 6/01).

Mark the box that is closest to describing the situation at hand; descriptions will rarely be perfect. Interpret the text loosely when necessary and keep in mind that you are trying to score your organization on the continuum of "1" to "4." You may select the limit between two boxes if this seems most accurate.

If a row is not relevant to the organization assessed, designate the row "N/A"; if you simply have no knowledge, mark the row "N/K."

A PDF file of the Capacity Assessment Grid can be obtained on Venture Philanthropy Partners' Web site, www.vppartners.org

Contents

I. Aspirations

- Mission
- Vision—clarity
- Vision—boldness
- Overarching goals

II. Strategy

- Overall strategy
- Goals/performance targets
- Program relevance, and integration
- Program growth and replication
- New program development
- Funding model

III. Organizational skills

- Performance management
  - Performance measurement
  - Performance analysis and program adjustments
- Planning
  - Monitoring of landscape
  - Strategic planning
  - Financial planning/budgeting
  - Operational planning
  - Human resources planning
- Fundraising and revenue generation
  - Fundraising
  - Revenue generation
- External relationship building and management
  - Partnership and alliances development and nurturing
  - Local community presence and involvement

- Other organizational skills
  - Public relations and marketing
  - Influencing of policy-making
  - Management of legal and liability matters
  - Organizational processes use and development

IV. Human resources

- Staffing levels
- Board—composition and commitment
- Board—involvement and support
- CEO/executive director and/or senior management team
  - Passion and vision
  - Impact orientation
  - People and organizational leadership/effectiveness
  - Personal and interpersonal effectiveness
  - Analytical and strategic thinking
  - Financial judgment
  - Experience and standing
- Management team and staff—dependence on CEO/executive director
- Senior management team (if not previously covered)
- Staff
- Volunteers

V. Systems and infrastructure

- Systems
  - Planning systems
  - Decision-making framework
  - Financial operations management
  - Human resources management—management recruiting, development, and retention
  - Human resources management—general staff recruiting, development, and retention

- — Human resources management—incentives
- — Knowledge management
- Infrastructure
  - — Physical infrastructure—buildings and office space
  - — Technological infrastructure—telephone/fax
  - — Technological infrastructure—computers, applications, network, and e-mail
  - — Technological infrastructure—Web site
  - — Technological infrastructure—databases and management reporting systems

VI. Organizational structure

- Board governance
- Organizational design
- Interfunctional coordination
- Individual job design

VII. Culture

- Performance as shared value
- Other shared beliefs and values
- Shared references and practices

McKinsey Capacity Assessment Grid

I. ASPIRATIONS	1 Clear need for increased capacity	2 Basic level of capacity in place	3 Moderate level of capacity in place	4 High level of capacity in place
Mission	No written mission or limited expression of the organization's reason for existence; lacks clarity or specificity; either held by very few in organization or rarely referred to	Some expression of organization's reason for existence that reflects its values and purpose, but may lack clarity; held by only a few; lacks broad agreement or rarely referred to	Clear expression of organization's reason for existence which reflects its values and purpose; held by many within organization and often referred to	Clear expression of organization's reason for existence which describes an enduring reality that reflects its values and purpose; broadly held within organization and frequently referred to
Vision—clarity	Little shared understanding of what organization aspires to become or achieve beyond the stated mission	Somewhat clear or specific under-standing of what organization aspires to become or achieve; lacks specificity or clarity; held by only a few; or "on the wall," but rarely used to direct actions or set priorities	Clear and specific understanding of what organization aspires to become or achieve; held by many within the organization and often used to direct actions and set priorities	Clear, specific, and compelling understanding of what organization aspires to become or achieve; broadly held within organization and consistently used to direct actions and set priorities
Vision—boldness	No clear vision articulated	Vision exists but falls short of reflecting an inspiring view of the future and of being demanding yet achievable	Vision is distinctive along only one of following two attributes: reflects an inspiring view of future; demanding yet achievable	Vision reflects an inspiring view of future and is demanding but achievable

Overarching goals	Vision (if it exists) not explicitly translated into small set of concrete goals, though there may be general (but inconsistent and imprecise) knowledge within organization of overarching goals and what it aims to achieve	Vision translated into a concrete set of goals; goals lack at least two of following four attributes: clarity, boldness, associated metrics, or time frame for measuring attainment; goals known by only a few, or only occasionally used to direct actions or set priorities	Vision translated into small set of concrete goals, but goals lack at most two of following four attributes: clarity, boldness, associated metrics, or time frame for measuring attainment; goals are known by many within organization and often used by them to direct actions and set priorities	Vision translated into clear, bold set of (up to three) goals that organization aims to achieve, specified by concrete to measure success for each criterion, and by well-defined time frames for attaining goals; goals are broadly known within organization and consistently used to direct actions and set priorities

McKinsey Capacity Assessment Grid

II. STRATEGY	1 Clear need for increased capacity	2 Basic level of capacity in place	3 Moderate level of capacity in place	4 High level of capacity in place
Overall strategy	Strategy is either nonexistent, unclear, or incoherent (largely set of scattered initiatives); strategy has no influence over day-to-day behavior	Strategy exists but is either not clearly linked to mission, vision, and overarching goals, or lacks coherence, or is not easily actionable; strategy is not broadly known and has limited influence over day-to-day behavior	Coherent strategy has been developed and is linked to mission and vision but is not fully ready to be acted upon; strategy is mostly known and day-to-day behavior is partly driven by it	Organization has clear, coherent medium- to long-term strategy that is both actionable and linked to overall mission, vision, and overarching goals; strategy is broadly known and consistently helps drive day-to-day behavior at all levels of organization
Goals/performance targets	Targets are nonexistent or few; targets are vague, or confusing, or either too easy or impossible to achieve; not clearly linked to aspirations and strategy, and may change from year to year; targets largely unknown or ignored by staff	Realistic targets exist in some key areas, and are mostly aligned with aspirations and strategy; may lack aggressiveness, or be short-term, lack milestones, or mostly focused on "inputs" (things to do right), or often renegotiated; staff may or may not know and adopt targets	Quantified, aggressive targets in most areas; linked to aspirations and strategy; mainly focused on "outputs/outcomes" (results of doing things right) with some "inputs"; typically multiyear targets, though may lack milestones; targets are known and adopted by most staff who usually use them to broadly guide work	Limited set of quantified, genuinely demanding performance targets in all areas; targets are tightly linked to aspirations and strategy, output/outcome-focused (i.e., results of doing things right, as opposed to inputs, things to do right), have annual milestones, and are long-term nature; staff consistently adopts targets and works diligently achieve them
Program relevance and integration	Core programs and services vaguely defined and lack clear alignment with mission and goals; programs seem scattered and largely unrelated to each other	Most programs and services well defined and can be solidly linked with mission and goals; program offerings may be somewhat scattered and not fully integrated into clear strategy	Core programs and services well defined and aligned with mission and goals; program offerings fit together well as part of clear strategy	All programs and services well defined and fully aligned with mission and goals; program offerings are clearly linked to one another and to overall strategy; synergies across programs are captured

Program growth and replication	No assessment of possibility of scaling up existing programs; limited ability to scale up or replicate existing programs	Limited assessment of possibility of scaling up existing programs and, even when judged appropriate, little or limited action taken; some ability either to scale up or replicate existing programs	Occasional assessment of possibility of scaling up existing programs and when judged appropriate, action occasionally taken; able to scale up or replicate existing programs	Frequent assessment of possibility of scaling up existing programs and when judged appropriate, action always taken; efficiently and effectively able to grow existing programs to meet needs of potential service recipients in local area or other geographies
New program development	No assessment of gaps in ability of current program to meet recipient needs; limited ability to create new programs; new programs created largely in response to funding availability	Limited assessment of gaps in ability of existing program to meet recipient needs, with little or limited action taken; some ability to modify existing programs and create new programs	Occasional assessment of gaps in ability of existing program to meet recipient needs, with some adjustments made; demonstrated ability to modify and fine-tune existing programs and create new programs	Continual assessment of gaps in ability of existing programs to meet recipient needs and adjustment always made; ability and tendency efficiently and effectively to create new, truly innovative programs to the needs of potential service recipients in local area or other geographies; continuous pipeline of new ideas

McKinsey Capacity Assessment Grid

II. STRATEGY	1 Clear need for increased capacity	2 Basic level of capacity in place	3 Moderate level of capacity in place	4 High level of capacity in place
Funding model	Organization highly dependent on a few funders, largely of same type (e.g., government or foundations or private individuals)	Organization has access to multiple types of funding (e.g., government, foundations, corporations, private individuals) with only a few funders in each type, or has many funders within only one or two types of funders	Solid basis of funders in most types of funding source (e.g., government, foundations, corporations, private individuals); some activities to hedge against market instabilities (e.g., building of endowment); organization has developed some sustainable revenue-generating activity	Highly diversified funding across multiple source types; organization insulated from potential market instabilities (e.g., fully developed endowment) and/or has developed sustainable revenue-generating activities; other nonprofits try to imitate organization's fundraising activities and strategies

McKinsey Capacity Assessment Grid	III. ORGANIZATIONAL SKILLS	1 Clear need for increased capacity	2 Basic level of capacity in place	3 Moderate level of capacity in place	4 High level of capacity in place
	Performance management				
	Performance measurement	Very limited measurement and tracking of performance; all or most evaluation based on anecdotal evidence; organization collects some data on program activities and outputs (e.g., number of children served) but has no social impact measurement (measurement of social outcomes, e.g., drop-out rate lowered)	Performance partially measured and progress partially tracked; organization regularly collects solid data on program activities and outputs (e.g., number of children served) but lacks data-driven, externally validated social impact measurement	Performance measured and progress tracked in multiple ways, several times a year, considering social, financial, and organizational impact of program and activities; multiplicity of performance indicators; social impact measured, but control group, longitudinal (i.e., long-term) or third-party nature of evaluation is missing	Well-developed comprehensive, integrated system (e.g., Balanced Scorecard) used for measuring organization's performance and progress on continual basis, including social, financial, and organizational impact of program and activities; small number of clear, measurable, and meaningful key performance indicators; social impact measured based on longitudinal studies with control groups, and performed or supervised by third-party experts
	Performance analysis and program adjustments	Few external performance comparisons made; internal performance data rarely used to improve program and organization	Some efforts made to benchmark activities and outcomes against outside world; internal performance data used occasionally to improve organization	Effective internal and external benchmarking occurs but driven largely by top management and/or confined to selected areas; learnings distributed throughout organization, and often used to make adjustments and improvements	Comprehensive internal and external benchmarking part of the culture and used by staff in target-setting and daily operations; high awareness of how all activities rate against internal and external best-in-class benchmarks; systematic practice of making adjustments and improvements on basis of benchmarking

Planning

	Minimal	Basic	Solid	Extensive
Monitoring of landscape	Minimal knowledge and understanding of other players and alternative models in program area	Basic knowledge of players and alternative models in program area but limited ability to adapt behavior based on acquired understanding	Solid knowledge of players and alternative models in program area; good ability to adapt behavior based on acquired understanding, but only occasionally carried out	Extensive knowledge of players and alternative models in program area; refined ability and systematic tendency to adapt behavior based on understanding
Strategic planning	Limited ability and tendency to develop strategic plan, either internally or via external assistance; if strategic plan exists, it is not used	Some ability and tendency to develop high-level strategic plan either internally or via external assistance; strategic plan roughly directs management decisions	Ability and tendency to develop and refine concrete, realistic strategic plan; some internal expertise in strategic planning or access to relevant external assistance; strategic planning carried out on a near-regular basis; strategic plan used to guide management decisions	Ability to develop and refine concrete, realistic and detailed strategic plan; critical mass of internal expertise in strategic planning, or efficient use of external, sustainable, highly qualified resources; strategic planning exercise carried out regularly; strategic plan used extensively to guide management decisions
Financial planning/budgeting	No or very limited financial planning; general budget developed; only one budget for entire central organization; performance against budget loosely or not monitored	Limited financial plans, ad hoc update; budget utilized as operational tool; used to guide/assess financial activities; some attempt to isolate divisional (program or geographical) budgets within central budget; performance-to-budget monitored periodically	Solid financial plans, regularly updated; budget integrated into operations; reflects organizational needs; solid efforts made to isolate divisional (program or geographical) budgets within central budget; performance-to-budget monitored regularly	Very solid financial plans, continuously updated; budget integrated into full operations; as strategic tool, it develops from process that incorporates and reflects organizational needs and objectives; well-understood divisional (program or geographical) budgets within overall central budget; performance-to-budget closely and regularly monitored

McKinsey Capacity Assessment Grid	III. ORGANIZATIONAL SKILLS	1 Clear need for increased capacity	2 Basic level of capacity in place	3 Moderate level of capacity in place	4 High level of capacity in place
	Planning				
	Operational planning	Organization runs operations purely on day-to-day basis with no short- or longer-term planning activities; no experience in operational planning	Some ability and tendency to develop high-level operational plan either internally or via external assistance; operational plan loosely or not linked to strategic planning activities and used roughly to guide operations	Ability and tendency to develop and refine concrete, realistic operational plan; some internal expertise in operational planning or access to relevant external assistance; operational planning carried out on a near-regular basis: operational plan linked to strategic planning activities and used to guide operations	Organization develops and refines concrete, realistic, and detailed operational plan; has critical mass of internal expertise in operational planning, or efficiently uses external, sustainable, highly qualified resources; operational planning exercise carried out regularly; operational plan tightly linked to strategic planning activities and systematically used to direct operations
	Human resources planning	Organization uncovers and/ or addresses HR needs only when too large to ignore; lack of HR planning activities and expertise (either internal or accessible external); no experience in HR planning	Some ability and tendency to develop high-level HR plan either internally or via external assistance; HR plan loosely or not linked to strategic planning activities and roughly guides HR activities	Ability and tendency to develop and refine concrete, realistic HR plan; some internal expertise in HR planning or access to relevant external assistance; HR planning carried out on near-regular basis; HR plan linked to strategic planning activities and used to guide HR activities	Organization is able to develop and refine concrete, realistic, and detailed HR plan; has critical mass of internal expertise in HR planning (via trained, dedicated HR manager), or efficiently uses external, sustainable, highly qualified resources; HR planning exercise carried out regularly; HR plan tightly linked to strategic planning activities and systematically used to direct HR activities

Fundraising and revenue generation

Fundraising	Generally weak fundraising skills and lack of expertise (either internal or access to external expertise)	Main fund-raising needs covered by some combination of internal skills and expertise, and access to some external fundraising expertise	Regular fund-raising needs adequately covered by well developed internal fundraising skills, occasional access to some external fund-raising expertise	Highly developed internal fund-raising skills and expertise in all funding source types to cover all regular needs; access to external expertise for additional extraordinary needs
Revenue generation	No internal revenue-generation activities; concepts such as cause-related marketing, fee-for-services and retailing are neither explored nor pursued	Some internal revenue-generation activities, however financial net contribution is marginal; revenue-generation activities distract from programmatic work and often tie up senior management team	Some proven internal revenue-generation activities and skills; these activities provide substantial additional funds for program delivery, but partially distract from programmatic work and require significant senior management attention	Significant internal revenue-generation; experienced and skilled in areas such as cause-related marketing, fee-for-services and retailing; revenue-generating activities support, but don't distract from focus on creating social impact

External relationship building and management

Partnerships and alliances development and nurturing	Limited use of partnerships and alliances with public sector, nonprofit, or for-profit entities	Early stages of building relationships and collaborating with other for-profit, nonprofit, or public sector entities	Effectively built and leveraged some key relationships with few types of relevant parties (for-profit, public, and nonprofit sector entities); some relations may be precarious or not fully "win-win"	Built, leveraged, and maintained strong, high-impact, relationships with variety of relevant parties (local, state, and federal government entities as well as for-profit, other nonprofit, and community agencies); relationships deeply anchored in stable, long-term, mutually beneficial collaboration

McKinsey Capacity Assessment Grid	III. ORGANIZATIONAL SKILLS	1 Clear need for increased capacity	2 Basic level of capacity in place	3 Moderate level of capacity in place	4 High level of capacity in place
	Local community presence and involvement	Organization's presence either not recognized or generally not regarded as positive; few members of local community (e.g., academics, other nonprofit leaders) constructively involved in the organization	Organization's presence somewhat recognized, and generally regarded as positive within the community; some members of larger community constructively engaged with organization	Organization reasonably well-known within community, and perceived as open and responsive to community needs; members of larger community (including a few prominent ones) constructively involved in organization	Organization widely known within larger community, and perceived as actively engaged with and extremely responsive to it; many members of the larger community (including many prominent members) actively and constructively involved in organization (e.g., board, fundraising)
Other organizational skills					
	Public relations and marketing	Organization makes no or limited use of PR/marketing; general lack of PR/marketing skills and expertise (either internal or accessible external or expertise	Organization takes oppor-tunities to engage in PR/marketing as they arise; some PR/ marketing skills and experience within staff or via external assistance	Organization considers PR/ marketing to be useful, and actively seeks opportunities to engage in these activities; critical mass of internal expertise and experience in PR/marketing or access to relevant external assistance	Organization fully aware of power of PR/marketing activities, and continually and actively engages in them; broad pool of nonprofit PR/marketing expertise and experience within organization or efficient use made of external, sustainable, highly qualified resources
	Influencing of policy-making	Organization does not have ability or is unaware of possibilities for influencing policy-making; never called in on substantive policy-discussions	Organization is aware of its possibilities in influencing policy-making; some readiness and skill to participate in policy-discussion, but rarely invited to substantive policy discussions	Organization is fully aware of its possibilities in influencing policy-making and is one of several organizations active in policy-discussions on state or national level	Organization pro-actively and reactively influences policy-making, in a highly effective manner, on state and national levels; always ready for and often called on to participate in substantive policy discussion and at times initiates discussions

Management of legal and liability matters	Organization does not anticipate legal issues, but finds help and addresses issues individually when they arise; property insurance includes liability component	Legal support resources identified, readily available, and employed on "as needed" basis; major liability exposures managed and insured (including property liability and workers compensation)	Legal support regularly available and consulted in planning; routine legal risk management and occasional review of insurance	Well-developed, effective, and efficient internal legal infrastructure for day-to-day legal work; additional access to general and specialized external expertise to cover peaks and extraordinary cases; continuous legal risk management and regular adjustment of insurance
Organizational processes use and development	Limited set of processes (e.g., decision making, planning, reviews) for ensuring effective functioning of the organization; use of processes is variable, or processes are seen as ad hoc requirements ("paperwork exercises"); no monitoring or assessment of processes	Basic set of processes in core areas for ensuring efficient functioning of organization; processes known, used, and truly accepted by only portion of staff; limited monitoring and assessment of processes, with few improvements made in consequence	Solid, well-designed set of processes in place in core areas to ensure smooth, effective functioning of organization; processes known and accepted by many, often used and contribute to increased impact; occasional monitoring and assessment of processes, with some improvements made	Robust, lean, and well-designed set of processes (e.g., decision making, planning, reviews) in place in all areas to ensure effective and efficient functioning of organization; processes are widely known, used and accepted, and are key to ensuring full impact of organization; continual monitoring and assessment of processes, and systematic improvement made

McKinsey Capacity Assessment Grid	IV. HUMAN RESOURCES	1 Clear need for increased capacity	2 Basic level of capacity in place	3 Moderate level of capacity in place	4 High level of capacity in place
	Staffing levels	Many positions within and peripheral to organization (e.g., staff, volunteers, board, senior management) are unfilled, inadequately filled, or experience high turnover and/or poor attendance	Most critical positions within and peripheral to organization (e.g., staff, volunteers, board, senior management) are staffed (no vacancies), and/or experience limited turnover or attendance problems	Positions within and peripheral to organization (e.g., staff, volunteers, board, senior management) are almost all staffed (no vacancies); few turnover or attendance problems	Positions within and peripheral to organization (e.g., staff, volunteers, board, senior management) are all fully staffed (no vacancies); no turnover or attendance problems
	Board—composition and commitment	Membership with limited diversity of fields of practice and expertise; drawn from a narrow spectrum of constituencies (from among nonprofit, academia, corporate, government, etc.); little or no relevant experience; low commitment to organization's success, vision and mission; meetings infrequent and/or poor attendance	Some diversity in fields of practice; membership represents a few different constituencies (from among nonprofit, academia, corporate, government, etc.); moderate commitment to organization's success, vision and mission; regular, purposeful meetings are well-planned and attendance is good overall	Good diversity in fields of practice and expertise; membership represents most constituencies (nonprofit, academia, corporate, government, etc.); good commitment to organization's success, vision and mission, and behavior to suit; regular, purposeful meetings are well-planned and attendance is consistently good, occasional subcommittee meetings	Membership with broad variety of fields of practice and expertise, and drawn from the full spectrum of constituencies (nonprofit, academia, corporate, government, etc.); includes functional and program content-related expertise, as well as high-profile names; high willingness and proven track record of investing in learning about the organization and addressing its issues; outstanding commitment to the organization's success, mission and vision; meet in person regularly, good attendance, frequent meetings of focused subcommittees

Board—involvement and support	Provide little direction, support, and accountability to leadership; board not fully informed about 'material' and other major organizational matters; largely "feel-good" support	Provide occasional direction, support and accountability to leadership; informed about all 'material' matters in a timely manner and responses/decisions actively solicited	Provide direction, support and accountability to programmatic leadership; fully informed of all major matters, input and responses actively sought and valued; full participant in major decisions	Provide strong direction, support, and accountability to programmatic leadership and engaged as a strategic resource; communication between board and leadership reflects mutual respect, appreciation for roles and responsibilities, shared commitment and valuing of collective wisdom
CEO/executive director and/ or senior management team				
Passion and vision	Low energy level and commitment; little continued attention to organizational vision	Good energy level; visible commitment to organization and its vision	Inspiringly energetic; shows constant, visible commitment to organization and its vision; excites others around vision	Contagiously energetic and highly committed; lives the organization's vision; compellingly articulates path to achieving vision that enables others to see where they are going

McKinsey Capacity Assessment Grid

IV. HUMAN RESOURCES	1 Clear need for increased capacity	2 Basic level of capacity in place	3 Moderate level of capacity in place	4 High level of capacity in place
CEO/executive director and/ or senior management team				
Impact orientation	Focused purely on social impact; financials viewed as an unfortunate constraint; fails to deliver impact consistently; delays decision making; reluctant to change status quo; mandates rather than leads change	Focused on social impact with some appreciation for cost-effectiveness when possible; constantly delivers satisfactory impact given resources; promptly addresses issues; understands implications and impact of change on people	Sees financial soundness as essential part of organizational impact, together with social impact; focuses on ways to better use existing resources to deliver highest impact possible; has a sense of urgency in addressing issues and rapidly moves from decision to action; develops and implements actions to overcome resistance to change	Guides organization to succeed simultaneously in dual mission of social impact and optimal financial efficiency; constantly seeks and finds new opportunities to improve impact; anticipates possible problems; has sense of urgency about upcoming challenges; communicates compelling need for change that creates drive; aligns entire organization to support change effort
People and organizational leadership/ effectiveness	Has difficulty building trust and rapport with others; micromanages projects; shares little of own experiences as developmental/coaching tool	Is responsive to opportunities from others to work together; expresses confidence in others' ability to be successful; shares own experience and expertise	Actively and easily builds rapport and trust with others; effectively encourages others to succeed; gives others freedom to work their own way; gives people freedom to try out ideas and grow	Constantly establishing successful, win-win relationships with others, both within and outside the organization; delivers consistent, positive and reinforcing messages to motivate people; able to let others make decisions and take charge; finds or creates special opportunities to promote people's development

Personal and interpersonal effectiveness	Fails to show respect for others consistently, may be openly judgmental or critical; has difficulty influencing without using power, limited charisma or influence; limited curiosity about new ideas and experiences	Earns respect of others, takes time to build relationships; has presence, is able to influence and build support using limited communication style; accepts learning and personal development opportunities that arise	Is respected and sought out by others for advice and counsel; has strong presence and charisma; uses multiple approaches to get buy-in, appreciates the impact of his/her words or actions; seeks new learning and personal development opportunities	Is viewed as outstanding "people person"; uses diversity of communication styles, including exceptional charisma, to inspire others and achieve impact; continually self-aware, actively works to better oneself; outstanding track record of learning and personal development
Analytical and strategic thinking	Is uncomfortable with complexity and ambiguity and does whatever possible to reduce or avoid it; relies mainly on intuition rather than strategic analysis	Is able to cope with some complexity and ambiguity; able to analyze strategies but does not yet generate strategies	Quickly assimilates complex information and is able to distill it to core issues; welcomes ambiguity and is comfortable dealing with the unknown; develops robust strategies	Has keen and exceptional ability to synthesize complexity; makes informed decisions in ambiguous, uncertain situations; develops strategic alternatives and identifies associated rewards, risks, and actions to lower risks
Financial judgment	Has difficulty considering financial implications of decisions	Draws appropriate conclusions after studying all the facts; understands basic financial concepts and drives for financial impact of major decisions	Has sound financial judgment; consistently considers financial implications of decisions	Has exceptional financial judgment; has keen, almost intuitive sense for financial implications of decisions

McKinsey Capacity Assessment Grid	IV. HUMAN RESOURCES	1 Clear need for increased capacity	2 Basic level of capacity in place	3 Moderate level of capacity in place	4 High level of capacity in place
	CEO/executive director and/ or senior management team				
	Experience and standing	Limited experience in nonprofit management and few relevant capabilities from other field(s); little evidence of social entrepreneur-like qualities; limited recognition in the nonprofit community	Some relevant experience in nonprofit management; some relevant capabilities from other field(s); emerging social entrepreneur-like qualities; some local recognition in the nonprofit community	Significant experience in nonprofit management; many relevant capabilities from other field(s); significant evidence of social entrepreneur-like qualities; some national recognition as a leader/shaper in particular sector	Highly experienced in nonprofit management; many distinctive capabilities from other field(s) (e.g., for-profit, academia); exceptional evidence of social entrepreneur-like qualities; possesses a comprehensive and deep understanding of the sector; recognized nationally as a leader/shaper in particular sector
	Management team and staff— dependence on CEO/executive director	Very strong dependence on CEO/executive director; organization would cease to exist without his/her presence	High dependence on CEO/ executive director; organization would continue to exist without his/her presence, but likely in a very different form	Limited dependence on CEO/executive director; organization would continue in similar way without his/her presence but areas such as fundraising or operations would likely suffer significantly during transition period; no member of management team could potentially take on CEO/ED role	Reliance but not dependence on CEO/ executive director; smooth transition to new leader could be expected; fundraising and operations likely to continue without major problems; senior management team can fill in during transition time; several members of management team could potentially take on CEO/ED role

244

Senior management team	Team has no or very limited experience in nonprofit or for-profit management; team represents few constituencies (nonprofit, academia, corporate, government, etc.) and has no or very limited capabilities and track record from other fields; limited track record of learning and personal development; mostly energetic and committed	Team has some experience in nonprofit or for-profit management; team represents some constituencies (nonprofit, academia, corporate, government, etc.); some relevant capabilities and track record from other fields; good track record of learning and personal development; energetic and committed	Team has significant experience in nonprofit or for-profit management; team represents most constituencies (nonprofit, academia, corporate, government, etc.); significant relevant capabilities and track record from other fields; good track record of learning and personal development; highly energetic and committed	Team highly experienced in nonprofit or for-profit management; drawn from full spectrum of constituencies (nonprofit, academia, corporate, government, etc.); outstanding capabilities and track record from other fields; outstanding track record of learning and personal development; contagiously energetic and committed
Staff	Staff drawn from a narrow range of backgrounds and experiences; interest and abilities limited to present job; little ability to solve problems as they arise	Some variety of staff backgrounds and experiences; good capabilities, including some ability to solve problems as they arise; many interested in work beyond their current jobs and in the success of the organization's mission	Staff drawn from diverse backgrounds and experiences, and bring a broad range of skills; most are highly capable and committed to mission and strategy; eager to learn and develop, and assume increased responsibility	Staff drawn from extraordinarily diverse backgrounds and experiences, and bring broad range of skills; most staff are highly capable in multiple roles, committed both to mission/strategy and continuous learning; most are eager and able to take on special projects and collaborate across divisional lines; staff are frequent source of ideas and momentum for improvement and innovation

McKinsey Capacity Assessment Grid

IV. HUMAN RESOURCES	1 Clear need for increased capacity	2 Basic level of capacity in place	3 Moderate level of capacity in place	4 High level of capacity in place
Volunteers	Limited abilities; may be unreliable or have low commitment; volunteers are poorly managed	Good abilities; mostly reliable, loyal, and committed to organization's success; volunteers managed but without standards and little accountability	Very capable set of individuals, bring required skills to organization; reliable, loyal and highly committed to organization's success and to "making things happen"; work easily with most staff, but do not generally play core roles without substantial staff supervision; volunteers are managed and contribute to the overall success of the organization	Extremely capable set of individuals, bring complementary skills to organization; reliable, loyal, highly committed to organization's success and to "making things happen"; often go beyond call of duty; able to work in a way that serves organization well, including ability to work easily with wide range of staff and play core roles without special supervision; volunteers managed very well and significantly contribute to overall success of organization

McKinsey Capacity Assessment Grid

V. SYSTEMS AND INFRA-STRUCTURE	1 Clear need for increased capacity	2 Basic level of capacity in place	3 Moderate level of capacity in place	4 High level of capacity in place
Systems				
Planning systems	Planning happens on an ad hoc bases only and is not supported by systematically collected data	Planning done regularly and uses some systematically collected data	Regular planning complemented by ad hoc planning when needed; some data collected and used systematically to support planning effort and improve it	Regular planning complemented by ad hoc planning when needed; clear, formal systems for data collection in all relevant areas; data used systematically to support planning effort and improve it
Decision making framework	Decisions made largely on an ad hoc basis by one person and/or whomever is accessible; highly informal	Appropriate decision makers known; decision making process fairly well established and process is generally followed, but often breaks down and becomes informal	Clear, largely formal lines/ systems for decision making but decisions are not always appropriately implemented or followed; dissemination of decisions generally good but could be improved	Clear, formal lines/ systems for decision making that involve as broad participation as practical and appropriate along with dissemination/ interpretation of decision
Financial operations management	Gifts and grants deposited and acknowledged, bills paid, supporting documentation collected/retained	Financial activities transparent, clearly and consistently recorded and documented, include appropriate checks and balances, and tracked to approve budget	Formal internal controls governing all financial operations; fully tracked, supported and reported, annually audited fund flows well managed; attention is paid to cash flow management	Robust systems and controls in place governing all financial operations and their integration with budgeting, decision making, and organizational objectives/strategic goals; cash flow actively managed

247

Human resources management—management recruiting, development, and retention	Standard career paths in place without considering managerial development; no or very limited training, coaching, and feedback; no regular performance appraisals; no systems/processes to identify new managerial talent	Some tailoring of development plans for brightest stars; personal annual reviews incorporate development plan for each manager; limited willingness to ensure high-quality job occupancy; some formal recruiting networks are in place	Recruitment, development, and retention of key managers is priority and high on CEO/executive director's agenda; some tailoring in development plans for brightest stars; relevant training, job rotation, coaching/feedback, and consistent performance appraisal are institutionalized; genuine concern for high-quality job occupancy; well connected to potential sources of new talent	Well-planned process to recruit, develop, and retain key managers; CEO/executive director takes active interest in managerial development; individually tailored development plans for brightest stars; relevant and regular internal and external training, job rotation, coaching/feedback, and consistent performance appraisal are institutionalized; proven willingness to ensure high-quality job occupancy; well-connected to potential sources of new talent
Human resources management—general staff recruiting, development, and retention	Standard career paths in place without considering staff development; limited training, coaching and feedback; no regular performance appraisals; no systems/processes to identify new talent	No active development tools/programs; feedback and coaching occur sporadically; performance evaluated occasionally; limited willingness to ensure high-quality job occupancy; sporadic initiatives to identify new talent	Limited use of active development tools/programs; frequent formal and informal coaching and feedback; performance regularly evaluated and discussed; genuine concern for high-quality job occupancy; regular concerted initiatives to identify new talent	Management actively interested in general staff development; well-thought-out and targeted development plans for key employees/positions; frequent, relevant training, job rotation, coaching/feedback, and consistent performance appraisal institutionalized; proven willingness to ensure high-quality job occupancy; continuous, proactive initiatives to identify new talent

V. SYSTEMS AND INFRA-STRUCTURE	1 Clear need for increased capacity	2 Basic level of capacity in place	3 Moderate level of capacity in place	4 High level of capacity in place
Systems				
Human resources management—incentives	No incentive system to speak of; or incentive system that is ineffective and/or generates bad will	Some basic elements of incentive system in place; may include one of following: competitive salary (possibly partly performance-based), attractive career development options, or opportunities for leadership and entrepreneurship; some evidence of motivational effect on staff performance	Many elements of incentive system in place; includes a few of following: competitive salary (partly performance-based), attractive career development options, opportunities for leadership and entrepreneurship; obvious effect in motivating staff to overdeliver	Well-designed, clear, and well-accepted incentive system; includes competitive salary (partly performance-based), attractive career development options, opportunities for leadership and entrepreneurship; system effective in motivating staff to overdeliver in their job
Knowledge management	No formal systems to capture and document internal knowledge	Systems exist in a few areas but either not user-friendly or not comprehensive enough to have an impact; systems known by only a few people, or only occasionally used	Well-designed, user-friendly systems in some areas; not fully comprehensive; systems are known by many people within the organization and often used	Well-designed, user-friendly, comprehensive systems to capture, document, and disseminate knowledge internally in all relevant areas; all staff is aware of systems, knowledgeable in their use, and make frequent use of them

Infrastructure

Physical infrastructure— buildings and office space	Inadequate physical infrastructure, resulting in loss of effectiveness and efficiency (e.g., unfavorable locations for clients and employees, insufficient workspace for individuals, no space for teamwork)	Physical infrastructure can be made to work well enough to suit organization's most important and immediate needs; a number of improvements could greatly help increase effectiveness and efficiency (e.g., no good office space for teamwork, no possibility of holding confidential discussions, employees share desks)	Fully adequate physical infrastructure for the current needs of the organization; infrastructure does not impede effectiveness and efficiency (e.g., favorable locations for clients and employees, sufficient individual and team office space, possibility for confidential discussions)	Physical infrastructure well-tailored to organization's current and anticipated future needs; well-designed and thought out to enhance organization's efficiency and effectiveness (e.g., especially favorable locations for clients and employees, plentiful team office space encourages teamwork, layout increases critical interactions among staff)
Technological infrastructure— telephone/fax	Status, lack of sophistication, or limited number of telephone and fax facilities are an impediment to day-to-day effectiveness and efficiency	Adequate basic telephone and fax facilities accessible to most staff; may be moderately reliable or user-friendly, or may lack certain features that would increase effectiveness and efficiency (e.g., individual voice-mail), or may not be easily accessible to some staff (e.g. front-line deliverers)	Solid basic telephone and fax facilities accessible to entire staff (in office and at front line); cater to day-to-day communication needs with essentially no problems; includes additional features contributing to increased effectiveness and efficiency (e.g., individual, remotely accessible voice-mail)	Sophisticated and reliable telephone and fax facilities accessible by all staff (in office and at frontline); includes around-the-clock, individual voice mail; supplemented by additional facilities (e.g., pagers, cell phones) for selected staff; effective and essential in increasing staff effectiveness and efficiency

McKinsey Capacity Assessment Grid	V. SYSTEMS AND INFRA-STRUCTURE	1 Clear need for increased capacity	2 Basic level of capacity in place	3 Moderate level of capacity in place	4 High level of capacity in place
	Infrastructure				
	Technological infrastructure— computers, applications, network, and e-mail	Limited/no use of computers or other technology in day-to-day activity; and/or little or no usage by staff of existing IT infrastructure	Well-equipped at central level; incomplete/limited infrastructure at locations aside from central offices; equipment sharing may be common; satisfactory use of IT infrastructure by staff	Solid hardware and software infrastructure accessible by central and local staff; no or limited sharing of equipment is necessary; limited accessibility for frontline program deliverers; high usage level of IT infrastructure by staff; contributes to increased efficiency	State-of-the-art, fully networked computing hardware with comprehensive range of up-to-date software applications; all staff has individual computer access and e-mail; accessible by frontline program deliverers as well as entire staff; used regularly by staff; effective and essential in increasing staff efficiency
	Technological infrastructure—Web site	Organization has no individual Web site	Basic Web site containing general information, but little information on current developments; site maintenance is a burden and performed only occasionally	Comprehensive Web site containing basic information on organization as well as up-to-date latest developments; most information is organization-specific; easy to maintain and regularly maintained	Sophisticated, comprehensive and interactive Web site, regularly maintained and kept up to date on latest area and organization developments; praised for its user-friendliness and depth of information; includes links to related organizations and useful resources on topic addressed by organization

Technological infrastructure— databases and management reporting systems	No systems for tracking clients, staff volunteers, program outcomes and financial information	Electronic data-bases and management reporting systems exist only in few areas; systems perform only basic features, are awkward to use or are used only occasionally by staff	Electronic data-base and management reporting systems exist in most areas for tracking clients, staff, volunteers, program outcomes and financial information; commonly used and help increase information sharing and efficiency	Sophisticated, comprehensive electronic database and management reporting systems exist for tracking clients, staff, volunteers, program outcomes and financial information; widely used and essential in increasing information sharing and efficiency

VI. ORGANIZATIONAL STRUCTURE	1 Clear need for increased capacity	2 Basic level of capacity in place	3 Moderate level of capacity in place	4 High level of capacity in place
Board governance	Board does not scrutinize budgets or audits, does not set performance targets and hold CEO/ED accountable or does not operate according to formal procedures; executive, treasury, and board functions unclear	Roles of legal board, advisory board and management are clear; board functions according to by-laws, reviews budgets, and occasionally sets organizational direction and targets, but does not regularly review CEO/ED performance, monitor potential conflicts of interest, scrutinize auditors, or review IRS and state filings	Roles of legal board, advisory board, and managers are clear and function well; board reviews budgets, audits, IRS and state filings; size of board set for maximum effectiveness with rigorous nomination process; board co-defines performance targets and actively encourages CEO/ED to meet targets; annual review of CEO's performance, but board not prepared to hire or fire CEO	Legal board, advisory board and managers work well together from clear roles; board fully understands and fulfills fiduciary duties; size of board set for maximum effectiveness with rigorous nomination process; board actively defines performance targets and holds CEO/ED fully accountable; board empowered and prepared to hire or fire CEO/ED if necessary; board periodically evaluated
Organizational design	Organizational entities (e.g., headquarters, regional and local offices) are not "designed," and roles, responsibilities of entities are neither formalized nor clear; absence of organization chart	Some organizational entities are clearly defined, others are not; most roles and responsibilities of organizational entities are formalized but may not reflect organizational realities; organization chart is incomplete and may be outdated	Organizational entities are clearly defined; all roles and responsibilities of organizational entities are formalized but do not necessarily reflect organizational realities; organization chart is complete but may be outdated	Roles and responsibilities of all organizational entities (e.g., headquarters, regional and local entities) are formalized, clear and complement each other; organization chart is complete and reflects current reality

Interfunctional coordination	Different programs and organizational units function in silos; little or dysfunctional coordination between them	Interactions between different programs and organizational units are generally good, though coordination issues do exist; some pooling of resources	All programs and units function together effectively with sharing of information and resources; few coordination issues	Constant and seamless integration between different programs and organizational units with few coordination issues; relationships are dictated by organizational needs (rather than hierarchy or politics)
Individual job design	Lack of positions created to address a number of key roles (e.g. CFO, HR, learning and measurement); unclear roles and responsibilities with many overlaps; job descriptions do not exist	Positions exist for most key roles, with a few still missing; most key positions are well-defined and have job descriptions; some unclear accountabilities or overlap in roles and responsibilities; job descriptions tend to be static	All key roles have associated positions; most individuals have well-defined roles with clear activities and reporting relationships and minimal overlaps; job descriptions are continuously being redefined to allow for organizational development and individuals' growth within their jobs	All roles have associated dedicated positions; all individuals have clearly defined core roles which must be achieved and an area of discretion where they can show initiative and try to make a difference; core roles are defined in terms of end-products and services rather than activities; individuals have the ability to define their own activities and are empowered to continuously reexamine their jobs

McKinsey Capacity Assessment Grid

VII. CULTURE	1 Clear need for increased capacity	2 Basic level of capacity in place	3 Moderate level of capacity in place	4 High level of capacity in place
Performance as shared value	Employees are hired, rewarded and promoted for executing a set of tasks/duties or for no clear reason, rather than for their impact; decisions are mostly made on "gut feeling"	Performance contribution is occasionally used and may be one of many criteria for hiring, rewarding and promoting employees; performance data is used to make decisions	Employee contribution to social, financial and organizational impact is typically considered as a preeminent criterion in making hiring, rewards and promotion decisions; important decisions about the organization are embedded in comprehensive performance thinking	All employees are systematically hired, rewarded and promoted for their collective contribution to social, financial and organizational impact; day-to-day processes and decision making are embedded in comprehensive performance thinking; performance is constantly referred to
Other shared beliefs and values	No common set of basic beliefs and values exists within the organization	Common set of basic beliefs exists in some groups within the organization, but is not shared broadly; values may be only partially aligned with organizational purpose or only rarely harnessed to produce impact	Common set of basic beliefs held by many people within the organization; helps provide members a sense of identity; beliefs are aligned with organizational purpose and occasionally harnessed to produce impact	Common set of basic beliefs and values (e.g., social, religious) exists and is widely shared within the organization; provides members sense of identity and clear direction for behavior; beliefs embodied by leader but nevertheless timeless and stable across leadership changes; beliefs clearly support overall purpose of the organization and are consistently harnessed to produce impact

Shared references and practices	No major common set of practices and references exists within the organization (such as traditions, rituals, unwritten rules, stories, heroes or role models, symbols, language, dress)	Common set of references and practices exists in some groups within the organization, but are not shared broadly; may be only partially aligned with organizational purpose or only rarely harnessed to produce impact	Common set of references and practices exists, and are adopted by many people within the organization; references and practices are aligned with organizational purpose and occasionally harnessed to drive towards impact	Common set of references and practices exist within the organization, which may include: traditions, rituals, unwritten rules, stories, heroes or role models, symbols, language, dress; are truly shared and adopted by all members of the organization; actively designed and used to clearly support overall purpose of the organization and to drive performance

Summary of Hypothetical Organization Strategy Development Outcomes

LARGE CITY METRO FOOD BANK

Location: LCMFB is located in a metropolitan area of more than one million residents. It has a main administration office, which is co-located with its food distribution center. The population of the area is 47 percent White, 29 percent African-American, 18 percent Hispanic, and 6 percent other. Median family income is $47,391.

Staff: The total staff includes 47 people. The senior staff consists of a Chief Executive Officer and three Vice Presidents: Development, Finance, Human Resources. The CEO is 55 years of age and is starting his third year in that position. He came to LCMFB from a similar organization in another city where he had served as the Vice President of Marketing and Development. The VPs of Finance and Human Resources are in their 60s, while the VP of Development is in his 40s. Beyond the senior staff, other program director positions exist. By board policy, staff compensation and benefits are at the 80th percentile for the U.S. nonprofit sector. Volunteers are used extensively.

Board: The board of directors has 18 people, mostly professionals: three attorneys, two CPAs, two MDs, a clergy-person, a university professor, and nine senior business executives. Board members serve a maximum of three 3-year terms. There is an executive committee made up of five board members. The executive committee meets monthly, and the board meets every two months.

Programs/Services: LCMFB collects food from a wide variety of sources and then distributes it to community partners, including food pantries, soup kitchens, shelters, after-school programs, and senior housing sites.

Funding: $55 million annual budget, with a $250,000 net surplus for the most recent fiscal year. Revenue is 80 percent in contributed food, 10 percent from contributions and grants, 10 percent other. The organization has $8 million in net assets.

Mission

To obtain and distribute food through a network of providers.

Revised Mission for Improved Aim and Impact

To feed those who suffer from hunger in the Large City Metro Area by obtaining food and distributing it through a network of providers including food pantries, soup kitchens, shelters, after-school programs, and senior housing sites.

Mission Accomplishment Measures

The number of meals reaching people living in poverty in the Large City Metro area compared to (divided by) the number of meals they need.

Mission Gap

- *Current condition:* Forty million emergency meals are needed by people in the Large City Metro Area annually, and 13 million meals are reaching them.
- *Ideal condition:* Everyone in the Large City Metro area has access to emergency food when they need it.
- *Mission gap:* 27 million meals per year

Vision

- A headquarters for LCMFB that would include five times the square footage of our current building with food storage space, our own pantry, a training room, a full kitchen, quality technology and office furnishings. And it would be "green."
- Triple the number of volunteers we have now
- A staff of 70 who are paid competitively and receive professional development opportunities
- A board of directors who are extremely well connected within the community and have access to considerable funding
- An annual fund of $30 million
- Triple the number of delivery trucks we now have.
- A comprehensive marketing program
- An extensive planned giving program
- Triple the number of food donations per year.
- Community and nonprofit leaders think of us as the exemplary nonprofit in the region.
- A new division of SNAP (Supplemental Nutrition Assistance Program; formerly food stamps) counselors

Strategic Stretch Goals

- Raise $22 million for a new building and move in by June 30, 2013.
- In addition to the building fund, raise $128 million in gifts from individuals, corporations, foundations, and in qualified planned gifts by June 30, 2015 (cumulatively).
- Triple the amount of food donated annually by June 30, 2015.
- Triple the number of volunteers utilized annually by June 30, 2015.
- Close our community meal gap by June 30, 2015.

SWOTS

Strengths

- New, high-profile board members
- Quality and dedicated staff

- Financial reserves
- Competitive staff compensation
- Enthusiastic and committed volunteers

Weaknesses

- Senior staff nearing traditional retirement age
- Too few development staff
- Facilities not large enough to meet needs
- No real marketing program
- Board has not been active in personal fundraising solicitation.

Opportunities

- Surveys show high interest among public in mission.
- Retired volunteers are planned giving prospects.
- Retirees in community are living longer, healthier, and are interested in volunteer activity.
- Foundations exist that support building campaigns.
- The Large City Metro Community Foundation has established basic human needs as a funding priority.

Threats

- Competition for donations is increasing.
- Corporations are cutting back on charitable contributions.
- Rumored corporate mergers may reduce funding.
- Foundation giving is decreasing due to lower endowment income.
- Once economy recovers, interest in hunger issues may ease.

SWOT Interactions

Weaknesses and Threats

- Too few development staff, and Competition for donations is increasing.
- Board has not been active in personal fundraising solicitation, and Competition for donations is increasing.

- No real marketing program, and Once economy recovers, interest in hunger issues may ease.

Strengths and Threats

- Financial reserves, and Competition for donations is increasing
- Financial reserves, and Corporations are cutting back on charitable contributions
- Financial reserves, and Rumored corporate mergers may reduce funding
- Financial reserves, and Foundation giving is decreasing due to lower endowment income

Weaknesses and Opportunities

- Too few development staff, and Retired volunteers are planned giving prospects
- No real marketing program, and Surveys show high interest among public in mission
- Too few development staff, and Foundations exist that support building campaigns
- Board has not been active in personal fundraising solicitation, and Surveys show high interest among public in mission

Strengths and Weaknesses

- Competitive staff compensation, and Senior staff nearing traditional retirement age
- New, high-profile board members, and Board has not been active in personal fundraising solicitation
- Quality and dedicated staff, and Senior staff nearing traditional retirement age

Opportunities and Threats

- Surveys show high interest among public in mission, and Once economy recovers, interest in hunger issues may ease.

- Retired volunteers are planned giving prospects, and Competition for donations is increasing.

- The Large City Metro Community Foundation has established basic human needs as a funding priority, and Foundation giving is decreasing due to lower endowment income.

Strengths and Opportunities

- None

Strategy Narrative

We will restructure the staff by adding a Chief Operating Officer position and allow our CEO to focus on development. We will also add a Director of Marketing position and Director of Development position to work with the CEO and Vice President of Development to significantly increase funding and the amount of food contributed. We will ideally operate with surplus budgets, while maintaining our commitment to competitive staff compensation. However, we will accept short-term deficits if necessary to spark this movement forward.

We will launch a comprehensive, five-year campaign—targeted for $150 million—for a new building and improved mission impact through significant increases in the annual fund, the initiation of a planned giving program, and a tripling of the amount of food donated. A campaign plan will be developed along with an integrated marketing plan following a feasibility study, and a cabinet of influential volunteer community leaders will be recruited.

As the campaign plan and marketing plan bring in more dollars and contributed food, we will aggressively recruit more volunteers. This growth will continue as we move into the new building and as our capacity continues to expand we will add staffing to support the growth. Our intent is to close the meal gap within five years and to keep it closed in the future.

Key Strategy Assumptions

- The community will respond enthusiastically to the overwhelming hunger needs in our area which we will communicate using our meal gap data.

- We can recruit an influential campaign cabinet.

- Our staff, board, and newly created campaign cabinet can successfully raise $150 million in five years and triple the amount of donated food.

BIG RIVER REGIONAL HOUSING SERVICES

Location: BRRHS serves a five-county region that is mostly rural. It has its main administrative offices in the largest city in the area, with satellite offices in two of the other counties. The region includes 500,000 residents and the population is 80 percent White, 9 percent African-American, 7 percent Hispanic, and 4 percent other. Median family income is $41,940.

Staff: The total staff includes 38 people. This currently includes an interim CEO, Pat, who was brought in to serve temporarily until a new permanent CEO is hired. The most recent CEO, Jeff, accepted a position on the domestic policy team of the Obama White House. There is a Chief Operating Officer, a Director of Finance, a Director of Operations, and a number of other program directors and line staff. The COO and Director of Operations are both in their early 60s, and the Director of Finance is in her 50s. Compensation and benefits are generally at the 40th percentile for the U.S. nonprofit sector, although the former CEO was paid at the 65th percentile level. Volunteers are used sporadically for programs.

Board: The board of directors has seven people, including a bank vice president, two residents of the organization's housing units, an attorney, a retired county government worker, a social worker, and a realtor. Board members serve three year terms with no limits.

Programs/Services: Develop and construct affordable housing units which are then either sold or managed by the organization. Currently 360 units, mostly multifamily, are managed and three to four units per year are built and sold. They also conduct other neighborhood revitalization programs.

Funding: $6 million annual budget, which includes 15 percent in government funding and most of the rest from fees for service. The most recent fiscal year ended with a $93,000 surplus. The organization has $1.2 million in net assets.

Mission

To enhance the quality of life of our communities by providing housing services.

Revised Mission for Improved Aim and Impact

To ensure that all citizens within the Big River Region (currently defined as Franklin, Yates, Thompson, Mercer, and Allegheny Counties) have access to safe, affordable, and decent housing.

Mission Accomplishment Measures

Percentage of households within the Big River Region (currently defined as Franklin, Yates, Thompson, Mercer, and Allegheny Counties) which meet the standards we set for affordability, quality, and safety using the Success Measures® surveys.

Mission Gap

- *Current condition:* 80,000 of 250,000 households have housing that is not safe, decent, and affordable.
- *Ideal condition:* All households in our region have housing that is safe, decent, and affordable.
- *Mission gap:* 80,000 households

Vision

- A new main administration building that is four times the square footage of the current facility with up to date technology and furnishings. Two new satellite offices are established in other counties. New and current satellite offices also have up to date technology and furnishings. All facilities are "green."
- Two hundred staff who are paid competitively within the nonprofit and government environments and who each have professional development plans that the organization supports
- A board of directors of 25 people who are well connected within the region, and an executive committee of seven. All board members are active donors, organization promoters, and annual fund solicitors.

- An annual fund of $5 million
- Corporate and foundation funding of $7 million per year
- Collaborations
- Government funding of $4 million per year
- Residents feel proud to be living in our facilities and have a good quality of life.
- We are widely recognized for making a significant impact on the quality of life in the region, including the economic vitality of counties we serve.
- Reserves of $10 million (quasi-endowment)

Strategic Stretch Goals

- Increase annual fund donations from individuals to $150,000 per year by June 30, 2015.
- Increase corporate, foundation, and government grants to $500,000 per year by June 30, 2015.
- Increase reserves by $200,000 by June 30, 2015.
- Acquire or build 1,000 multifamily or senior affordable housing units by June 30, 2015.
- Demonstrate at least a 5 percent improvement (compared to baseline) on all indicators tracked for our region's Success Measures by June 30, 2015.

SWOTs

Strengths

- Financial reserves
- Strong reputation in community
- Quality, hardworking staff
- Engaged residents who care about properties
- Dedicated board

Weaknesses

- Board does not have fundraising experience.
- Staff does not have fundraising experience.
- Compensation packages for staff are very low.
- Office facilities need repair, and technology needs upgrading.
- Senior managers are nearing traditional retirement age.

Opportunities

- The national market for CEOs includes people who have fundraising and community development experience.
- Property values are lower; good time to purchase land or buildings.
- Many individuals within our area are potential donors but have never been asked.
- Potential new board members exist who would be committed to our mission.
- Many companies and foundations have never been asked to contribute.

Threats

- Recent bank mergers may threaten contributions.
- Government or other nonprofits could hire away staff with better compensation.
- State budget crisis could lower grants for years.
- Economic slowdown could cause residents to lose jobs; move or fall behind on payments.
- Economic slowdown will further increase need for safe, decent, affordable housing.

SWOT Interactions

Weaknesses Threats

- Compensation packages for staff are very low, and Government or other nonprofits could hire away staff with better compensation.

- Board does not have fundraising experience, and Recent bank mergers may threaten contributions
- Staff does not have fundraising experience, and Recent bank mergers may threaten contributions.

Strengths and Threats

- Financial reserves, and Recent bank mergers may threaten contributions.
- Financial reserves, and State budget crisis could lower grants for years

Weaknesses and Opportunities

- Staff does not have fundraising experience, and The national market for CEOs includes people who have fundraising and community development experience.

Strengths and Weaknesses

- Financial reserves, and Compensation packages for staff are very low.

Opportunities and Threats

- Many individuals within our area are potential donors; have never been asked, and Recent bank mergers may threaten contributions.
- Many individuals within our area are potential donors; have never been asked, and State budget crisis could lower grants for years.
- Many companies and foundations have never been asked to contribute, and Recent bank mergers may threaten contributions.
- Many companies and foundations have never been asked to contribute, and State budget crisis could lower grants for years.

Strengths and Opportunities

- Strong reputation in community, and Many individuals within our area are potential donors; have never been asked
- Strong reputation in community, and Potential new board members exist who would be committed to our mission

- Strong reputation in community, and Many companies and foundations have never been asked to contribute
- Financial reserves and Property values are lower; good time to purchase land or houses

Strategy Narrative

We will hire a new CEO who has a proven track record of fundraising success, as well as a community development background. We will add a Director of Development position to the staff for the new CEO to hire. The new CEO will have a mandate to develop a comprehensive and successful fundraising program. Aggressive activity will be implemented to increase giving by individual donors, corporations, and foundations. The board is committed to leadership and active participation in these fundraising activities.

We will immediately begin a process of increasing staff compensation and benefits that will continue during the next five years to make it much more competitive. Professional development plans will be created for all employees and succession planning will be implemented.

Additional increased funding will be used to acquire or build new multi-family or senior affordable housing units. We will be opportunistic, about acquiring property that is value priced. Rents and other fees for service will be monitored carefully and increased if market conditions dictate. We will continue producing annual surpluses to build our reserves higher.

We will initiate a collaborative regional summit on affordable housing issues among key stakeholders—community development organizations, lenders, government leaders, businesses, and residents. We will work with collaborators to attract funding to the area to make the Big River Region a demonstration site for innovative approaches to solve affordable housing issues. Collectively, these efforts will produce significantly more affordable, safe, decent, housing for the Big River Region.

Key Strategy Assumptions

- We can attract a CEO with the type of background we want.
- The CEO and director of development we hire will be successful raising additional funds.

MERRILL COUNTY LITERACY COUNCIL

Location: MCLC is located in a county of 125,000 residents. It has a main administration office in the largest city in the county. The population is 68 percent White, 18 percent African-American, 9 percent Hispanic, and 5 percent other. Median family income is $52,628.

Staff: The total staff consists of five people—a CEO, a now vacant Director of Programs position, a part-time Director of Finance, and three program staff. The CEO is 33 years old. When the previous CEO moved out of state during the past year, she was promoted from her post as director of programs. Compensation and benefits for staff are at the 30th percentile for the U.S. nonprofit sector. Volunteers are used extensively as teachers, child care providers, and tutors.

Board: The board of directors currently has five members, but could have as many as eleven. Members include the founding chair of the organization, who is a retired elementary school principal, a clergyperson, an assistant superintendent of one of the county school districts, an attorney, and one of the organization's volunteer tutors who is a homemaker.

Programs/Services: Classes for adults in reading and mathematics literacy, as well as tutoring for adults in the classes. Child care services are also provided for adults who need to bring children to classes.

Funding: $195,000 annual budget and the most recent year ended with a $3,000 deficit. Funding includes 10 percent from individual contributions, and the rest in grants from United Way, local corporations, school districts, and various government entities. The organization has $40,000 in net assets.

Mission

To provide literacy educational services to citizens in Merrill County.

Revised Mission for Improved Aim and Impact

The mission of Merrill County Literacy Council is to assure that all adults age 16 or older in Merrill County are literate.

Mission Accomplishment Measures

The percentage of adults in Merrill County, age sixteen and older, who are literate as measured by the NAAL survey.

Mission Gap

- *Current condition:* Twenty percent of 100,000 adults age sixteen and older in Merrill County are not literate at NAAL Level 3.
- *Ideal condition:* All adults age 16 and older are literate at NAAL Level 3 or higher.
- *Mission gap:* 20,000 adults, age 16 and older

Vision

- Twenty-four total full-time staff (five times current size)—all highly qualified and fully engaged; adding more middle managers, counselors, volunteer managers, child care managers
- Total compensation for all staff is competitive with similar jobs in government and education, including benefits (insurance, retirement, etc.).
- Every employee has a professional development plan that is supported by the organization.
- Fully engaged board with strong community connections
- Five hundred certified literacy teaching and tutoring volunteers (25 times the current number)
- $3 million per year in reliable unrestricted grants
- Five times our current office space with mid-quality furniture and up-to-date equipment and technology for all staff
- Free access to as many quality classrooms as needed at any time
- Free transportation for all volunteers and students to classrooms
- Endowment of $15 million
- Two hundred child care volunteers (30 times current number)

Strategic Stretch Goals

- Unrestricted grants from all sources will increase by 300 percent to $2 million by June 30, 2015.

- The number of certified literacy teaching volunteers will increase by 500+ percent to 100 by June 30, 2015.

- Financial reserves will be increased by $400,000 by June 30, 2015.

- An endowment fundraising campaign for $5 million will be initiated and a lead gift of $500,000 will be pledged by June 30, 2015.

- The literacy rate in Merrill County, as reported by county officials, will be 85 percent by June 30, 2015.

SWOTs

Strengths

- Talented and energetic CEO
- Educational program is very effective—nationally recognized.
- Dedicated and effective volunteer teachers
- Solid, hardworking staff
- Board that cares

Weaknesses

- Limited financial reserves
- Compensation (pay and benefits) for staff is too low.
- Not enough board members have strong community connections.
- Outdated office equipment creates inefficiencies.
- Understaffed—paid staff and volunteers

Opportunities

- Our mission is consistent with new United Way priorities.
- Chamber of Commerce has identified workforce preparation as an important issue for the future.

- Possibility of creating stronger partnerships with schools, churches, service clubs
- Students from local colleges and universities have not been tapped as volunteer resources.
- We are addressing a serious problem with an effective solution (program), yet the seriousness of the ripples of the problem is not well understood. Once people understand, they respond.

Threats

- Increased immigration will increase illiteracy rates.
- Downturn in regional economy could hurt funding.
- General decreases in funding sources as competition for donations increases
- Performance of county schools has been on the decline.
- Government or other nonprofits could "poach" our CEO or other staff with better compensation.

SWOT Interactions

Weaknesses and Threats

- Limited financial reserves, and Potential downturn in regional economy could hurt funding
- Limited financial reserves, and General decreases in funding sources as competition for donations increases
- Compensation (pay and benefits) for staff is too low, and Government or other nonprofits could "poach" our CEO or other staff with better compensation.

Strengths and Threats

- Talented and energetic CEO, and Government or other nonprofits could "poach" our CEO or other staff with better compensation
- Solid, hardworking staff, and Government or other nonprofits could "poach" our CEO or other staff with better compensation

Weaknesses and Opportunities

- Limited financial reserves, and Our mission is consistent with new United Way priorities
- Understaffed—paid staff and volunteers, and Possibility of creating stronger partnerships with schools, churches, service clubs
- Understaffed—paid staff and volunteers, and Students from local colleges and universities have not been tapped as volunteer resources

Strengths and Weaknesses

- Talented and energetic CEO, and Compensation (pay and benefits) for staff is too low
- Solid, hardworking staff, and Compensation (pay and benefits) for staff is too low

Opportunities and Threats

- Our mission is consistent with new United Way priorities, and Potential downturn in regional economy could hurt funding.
- Our mission is consistent with new United Way priorities, and General decreases in funding sources as competition for donations increases

Strengths and Opportunities

- None

Strategy Narrative

We will maintain a conservative, balanced budget and not increase expenses until surpluses are available. We will leverage our CEO's talent, along with our program effectiveness, to recruit new board members who are well-connected within the county. We will secure agreements from them to be actively involved in fundraising and building community awareness of literacy issues.

With initial increases in the annual fund, we will make improvements to staff compensation. As the annual fund continues to increase, we will retain a consultant to develop an integrated marketing and fundraising plan. The annual giving plan will be upgraded and fundraising training will be given to staff and board. The marketing plan will raise awareness of literacy issues and help recruit more volunteers, as well as support fundraising initiatives. We will continue to expand the board with well-connected community members who are committed to giving and raising funds. We will seek significant United Way funding increases.

We will phase in these plans to balance increased costs with increased funding. As net revenues from fundraising successes are available they will be divided among staff compensation increases, hiring new staff to manage increased numbers of volunteers, and building reserves. We will closely monitor program quality as we increase program offerings. More and more people in Merrill County will become literate.

As we recruit new board members and annual fund donors, we will seek to identify potential major donors for an endowment campaign for $5 million, which will be launched in five years with a $500,000 lead gift. This will be a springboard to the future which will continue to increase the literacy rates in Merrill County.

Key Strategy Assumptions

- Our CEO can recruit new board members who are well connected within the county.
- We can effectively learn how to raise money.
- We can find a $500,000 lead donor.

References

Ackoff, R. 1999. *Re-creating the corporation*. New York: Oxford University Press.

Ackoff, R., J. Magidson, & H. Addison. 2006. *Idealized design*. Upper Saddle River, NJ: Wharton School Publishing.

Allison, M., & J. Kay. 2005. *Strategic planning for nonprofit organizations*. Hoboken, NJ: John Wiley & Sons.

Backman, E., A. Grossman, & V. Rangan. 2000. Introduction. *Nonprofit and Voluntary Sector Quarterly* 29(1): 2–8.

Barry, B. 1986. *Strategic planning workbook*. St. Paul, MN: Amherst H. Wilder Foundation.

Block, P. 2000. *Flawless consulting*. San Francisco: Jossey-Bass.

Bradach, J., Tierney, T., & Stone, N. 2008. Delivering on the promise of nonprofits. *Harvard Business Review* 86(12): 88–97.

Bryson, J. 2004. *Strategic planning for public and nonprofit organizations*, 3rd ed. San Francisco: Jossey-Bass.

Buckingham, M., & D. Clifton. 2001. *Now discover your strengths*. New York: Free Press.

Buckingham, M., & C. Coffman, C. 1999. *First, break all the rules*. New York: Simon & Schuster.

Business Roundtable. 2005. Principles of corporate governance. A. White Paper by Business Roundtable, November.

Burns, J. M. 1978. *Leadership*. New York: Harper & Row.

Cameron, K. S., & R. E. Quinn. 1999. *Diagnosing and changing organizational culture based on the competing values framework*. Reading, MA: Addison-Wesley.

Carver, J. 1990. *Boards that make a difference*. San Francisco: Jossey-Bass.

Chait, R., W. Ryan, & B. Taylor. 2005. *Governance as leadership*. Hoboken, NJ: John Wiley & Sons.

Collins, J. 2001. *Good to great*. New York: HarperCollins.

Collis, D. J., & M. G. Rukstad. 2008. Can you say what your strategy is? *Harvard Business Review*, April 2008, pp. 82–90.

Covey, S. 1994. *First things first*. New York: Simon & Schuster.

Deming, W. E. 1982. *Out of the crisis*. Cambridge: Massachusetts Institute of Technology, Center for Advanced Engineering Study.

Deming, W. E. 1993. *The new economics*. Cambridge: Massachusetts Institute of Technology, Center for Advanced Engineering Study.

Drucker, P. 1974. *Management*. New York: Harper & Row.

Drucker, P. 1993. *The five most important questions*. San Francisco: Jossey-Bass.

Drucker, P. 1999. *The Drucker Foundation self-assessment tool*. San Francisco: Jossey-Bass.

Etzioni, E. 1964. *Modern organizations*. Englewood Cliffs, NJ: Prentice Hall.

Forbes, D. 1998. Measuring the unmeasurable: Empirical studies of nonprofit organization effectiveness from1977 to 1997. *Nonprofit and Voluntary Sector Quarterly* 27(2): 183–202.

Ford, J., & L. Ford. 1990. *Designing organizations for growth*. Unpublished working paper. Columbus: Ohio State University.

Ford, J. & L. Ford. 2005. *Deadline busting*. New York: iUniverse.

Ford, J., R. Sheehan, & L. Ford. 1994. *Mission accomplishment: An added dimension to public sector organization effectiveness*. Paper presented at Academy of Management Annual Conference, Dallas, TX.

Friedman, M. 1970. The social responsibility of the corporation is to increase its profits. *New York Times Magazine*, September 13.

Google Press Center. 2009. Larry Page's University of Michigan Commencement Address. May 2.

Hackman, J. R. 2002. *Leading teams*. Boston: Harvard Business Publishing.

Hambrick, D., & J. Fredrickson. 2005. Are you sure you have a strategy? *Academy of Management Executive* 19(4): 51–62.

Hamel, G., & C. K. Prahalad. 1989. Strategic intent. *Harvard Business Review* 67(3): 63–76.

Hamel, G., & C. K. Prahalad. 1993. Strategy as stretch and leverage. *Harvard Business Review* 71(2): 75–84.

Hamel, G., & C. K. Prahalad. 1994. *Competing for the future*. Boston, MA: Harvard Business School Press.

Herman, R., & D. Renz. 1997. Multiple constituencies and the social construction of nonprofit organization effectiveness. *Nonprofit and Voluntary Sector Quarterly* 26(2): 185–206.

Herman, R., & D. Renz. 1998. Nonprofit organizational effectiveness: Contrasts between especially effective and less effective organizations. *Nonprofit Management & Leadership* 9(1): 23–38.

Herman, R., & D. Renz. 1999. Theses on nonprofit organizational effectiveness. *Nonprofit and Voluntary Sector Quarterly* 28(2): 107–126.

Herman, R., & D. Renz. 2004. Doing things right: Effectiveness in local nonprofit organizations, a panel study. *Public Administration Review* 64(6): 694–704.

Herman, R., & D. Renz. 2008. Advancing nonprofit organizational effectiveness research and theory. *Nonprofit Management & Leadership* 18(4): 399–415.

Heskett, J., W. Sasser, & L. Schlesinger. 2002. *The value profit chain: Treat employees like customers and customers like employees.* New York: Free Press.

Hyatt, J. 1994. GE chairman's annual letter notes strides by "stretch" of the imagination. *Wall Street Journal, March* 8, p. 1.

Jacques, M. 1999. Transformation and redesign at the White House Communications Agency. *Quarterly Management Review (American Society for Quality)* 6(3): 8–23.

Juran, J. M. 1989. *Juran on leadership for quality.* New York: Free Press.

Kaplan, R. 2002. *The Balanced Scorecard and nonprofit organizations. Balanced Scorecard Report,* Harvard Business School Publishing, November-December.

Kaplan, R., & D. Norton. 1992. The Balanced Scorecard. *Harvard Business Review,* January-February, pp. 71-79.

Kaplan, R., & D. Norton. 1996a. *The Balanced Scorecard.* Boston: Harvard Business School Press.

Kaplan, R., & D. Norton. 1996b. Using the Balanced Scorecard as a strategic management system. *Harvard Business Review,* January-February, pp. 75-85.

Kearns, K. 1992. From comparative advantage to damage control: Clarifying strategic issues using SWOT analysis. *Nonprofit Management & Leadership* 3(1): 3–22.

Kearns, K. 2000. *Private sector strategies for social sector success.* San Francisco: Jossey-Bass.

Kearns, K., & G. Scarpino. 1996. Strategic planning research knowledge and gaps. *Nonprofit Management & Leadership* 6(4): 429–439.

Kerr, S., & S. Landauer. 2004. Using stretch goals to promote organizational effectiveness and personal growth: General Electric and Goldman Sachs. *Academy of Management Executive* 18(4): 134–138.

Kotter, J. 1995. Leading change: Why transformation efforts fail. *Harvard Business Review.* March-April pp. 59-67.

Kotter, J. 1996. *Leading change.* Cambridge, MA: Harvard Business School Press.

Kotter, J. 1998. Winning at Change *Leader to Leader* 10 (Fall): 27–33.

Kouzes, J., & B. Posner. 2009. To lead, create a shared vision. *Harvard Business Review,* January 2009, pp. 20–21.

Leonard, E. F., III. 2005. The advancement value chain: An exploratory model. *International Journal of Educational Advancement* (5)2: 142–161.

Leonard, E. F., III. 2009. Reflections on Bethany and the Balanced Scorecard. Email. June 24, 2009.

Light, P. 2002. *Pathways to nonprofit excellence.* Washington, DC: The Brookings Institution.

Locke, E., & G. Latham. 1990. *A theory of goal setting and task performance.* Englewood Cliffs, NJ: Prentice Hall.

Locke, E., & G. Latham. 2006. New directions in goal setting theory. *Current Directions in Psychological Science* 15(5): 265–268.

March, J., & H. Simon. 1958. *Organizations.* New York: John Wiley & Sons.

McConnell, J. 1989. *The seven tools of TQC.* Dee Why, Australia: The Delaware Group.

Mintzberg, H. 1994. The fall and rise of strategic planning. *Harvard Business Review* 72(1): 107–114.

Moore, M. 2000. Managing for value: Organizational strategy in for-profit, nonprofit, and governmental organizations. *Nonprofit and Voluntary Sector Quarterly* 29(1): 183–204.

Niven, P. 2008. *Balanced Scorecard for government and nonprofit agencies*, 2nd ed. Hoboken, NJ: John Wiley & Sons.

Nutt, P., & R. Backoff. 1992. *Strategic management of public and third sector organizations*. San Francisco: Jossey-Bass.

O'Connell, B. 1985. *The board member's book*. New York: Foundation Center.

Peters, T. 2001. Tom Peters's true confessions. *Fast Company* 53, November.

Phills, J. 2005. *Integrating mission and strategy for nonprofit organizations*. New York: Oxford University Press.

Porter, M. 1980. *Competitive strategy*. New York: Free Press.

Porter, M. 1996. What is strategy? *Harvard Business Review* 74(6): 61–78.

Prahalad, C.K., & G. Hamel. 1990. The core competence of the corporation. *Harvard Business Review* 68(3): 79–91.

Price, J. 1968. *Organization effectiveness: An inventory of propositions*. Homewood, IL: Irwin.

Quinn, R. 1988. *Beyond rational management*. San Francisco: Jossey-Bass.

Rath, T. 2007. *StrengthsFinder 2.0*. New York: Gallup Press.

Rossi, P. H., & H. E. Freeman. 1985. *Evaluation*. Thousand Oaks, CA: Sage.

Salter, C. 2008. Google. *Fast Company*, March pp. 74–91.

Sawhill, J., & D. Williamson. 2001a. Measuring what matters in nonprofits. *McKinsey Quarterly* 2: 98–107.

Sawhill, J., & D. Williamson. 2001b. Mission impossible? Measuring success in nonprofit organizations. *Nonprofit Management & Leadership* 11(3): 371–387.

Seijits, G., & G. Latham. 2005. Learning versus performance goals: When should each be used? *Academy of Management Executive* (19)1: 124–131.

Senge, P. 1990. *The fifth discipline*. New York: Doubleday/Currency.

Sheehan, R. 1994. *Mission accomplishment as philanthropic organization effectiveness*. Unpublished dissertation.

Sheehan, R. 1996. Mission accomplishment as philanthropic organization effectiveness: Key findings from the excellence in philanthropy project. *Nonprofit and Voluntary Sector Quarterly* 25(1): 110–123.

Sheehan, R. 1999. Achieving growth and high quality by strategic intent. *Nonprofit Management & Leadership* 9(4): 413–428.

Sheehan, R. 2005. *What is nonprofit strategy?* Paper presented at the annual meeting of the Association of Research on Nonprofit Organizations & Voluntary Action, Washington, DC.

Sheehan, R. 2009. *Mission gap: The missing driver for nonprofit strategy*. Paper presented at the annual meeting of the Academy of Management, Chicago, IL.

Singh, K. 2005. *The impact of strategic planning process variation on superior organizational performance in nonprofit human service organizations providing mental health services.*

Paper presented at the annual meeting of the Association of Research on Non-profit Organizations & Voluntary Action, Washington, DC.

Smith, D. 1999. *Make success measurable.* New York: John Wiley & Sons.

Smith, D. 2004. *On value and values.* New York: Prentice Hall.

Sowa, J., S. Selden, & J. Sandfort. 2004. No longer unmeasurable? A multi-dimensional integrated model of nonprofit organizational effectiveness. *Nonprofit and Voluntary Sector Quarterly* 33(4): 711–728.

Stauber, K. 2001. Mission-driven philanthropy: What do we want to accomplish and how do we do it? *Nonprofit and Voluntary Sector Quarterly* 30(2): 393–401.

Stern, G. J. 1999. *The Drucker Foundation Self-Assessment Tool process guide.* San Francisco: Jossey-Bass.

Stone, M., & W. Crittenden. 1993. Articles on strategic management in nonprofit organizations. *Nonprofit Management & Leadership* 4(2): 193–213.

Suàrez, J. G. 1992. *Three experts on quality management: Philip B. Crosby, W. Edwards Deming, Joseph M. Juran.* Arlington, VA: Total Quality Leadership Office.

Suàrez, J. G. 2009. Interview, June 24.

Thompson, K., W. Hochwater, & N. Mathys. 1997. Stretch targets: What makes them effective? *Academy of Management Executive* 11(3): 48–60.

Venture Philanthropy Partners. 2001. *Effective capacity building in nonprofit organizations.* Reston, VA: Author.

Walton, M. 1986. *The Deming management method.* New York: Penguin Putnam.

Welch, J. 1996. *To our share owners.* General Electric 1995 Annual Report. Fairfield, CT: General Electric.

Welch, J., & S. Welch. 2005. *Winning.* New York: HarperCollins.

AFP Code of Ethical Principles and Standards

ETHICAL PRINCIPLES • Adopted 1964; amended Sept. 2007

The Association of Fundraising Professionals (AFP) exists to foster the development and growth of fundraising professionals and the profession, to promote high ethical behavior in the fundraising profession and to preserve and enhance philanthropy and volunteerism. Members of AFP are motivated by an inner drive to improve the quality of life through the causes they serve. They serve the ideal of philanthropy, are committed to the preservation and enhancement of volunteerism; and hold stewardship of these concepts as the overriding direction of their professional life. They recognize their responsibility to ensure that needed resources are vigorously and ethically sought and that the intent of the donor is honestly fulfilled. To these ends, AFP members, both individual and business, embrace certain values that they strive to uphold in performing their responsibilities for generating philanthropic support. AFP business members strive to promote and protect the work and mission of their client organizations.

AFP members both individual and business aspire to:

- practice their profession with integrity, honesty, truthfulness and adherence to the absolute obligation to safeguard the public trust
- act according to the highest goals and visions of their organizations, professions, clients and consciences
- put philanthropic mission above personal gain
- inspire others through their own sense of dedication and high purpose
- improve their professional knowledge and skills, so that their performance will better serve others
- demonstrate concern for the interests and well-being of individuals affected by their actions
- value the privacy, freedom of choice and interests of all those affected by their actions
- foster cultural diversity and pluralistic values and treat all people with dignity and respect
- affirm, through personal giving, a commitment to philanthropy and its role in society
- adhere to the spirit as well as the letter of all applicable laws and regulations
- advocate within their organizations adherence to all applicable laws and regulations
- avoid even the appearance of any criminal offense or professional misconduct
- bring credit to the fundraising profession by their public demeanor
- encourage colleagues to embrace and practice these ethical principles and standards
- be aware of the codes of ethics promulgated by other professional organizations that serve philanthropy

ETHICAL STANDARDS

Furthermore, while striving to act according to the above values, AFP members, both individual and business, agree to abide (and to ensure, to the best of their ability, that all members of their staff abide) by the AFP standards. Violation of the standards may subject the member to disciplinary sanctions, including expulsion, as provided in the AFP Ethics Enforcement Procedures.

MEMBER OBLIGATIONS

1. Members shall not engage in activities that harm the members' organizations, clients or profession.
2. Members shall not engage in activities that conflict with their fiduciary, ethical and legal obligations to their organizations, clients or profession.
3. Members shall effectively disclose all potential and actual conflicts of interest; such disclosure does not preclude or imply ethical impropriety.
4. Members shall not exploit any relationship with a donor, prospect, volunteer, client or employee for the benefit of the members or the members' organizations.
5. Members shall comply with all applicable local, state, provincial and federal civil and criminal laws.
6. Members recognize their individual boundaries of competence and are forthcoming and truthful about their professional experience and qualifications and will represent their achievements accurately and without exaggeration.
7. Members shall present and supply products and/or services honestly and without misrepresentation and will clearly identify the details of those products, such as availability of the products and/or services and other factors that may affect the suitability of the products and/or services for donors, clients or nonprofit organizations.
8. Members shall establish the nature and purpose of any contractual relationship at the outset and will be responsive and available to organizations and their employing organizations before, during and after any sale of materials and/or services. Members will comply with all fair and reasonable obligations created by the contract.

9. Members shall refrain from knowingly infringing the intellectual property rights of other parties at all times. Members shall address and rectify any inadvertent infringement that may occur.
10. Members shall protect the confidentiality of all privileged information relating to the provider/client relationships.
11. Members shall refrain from any activity designed to disparage competitors untruthfully.

SOLICITATION AND USE OF PHILANTHROPIC FUNDS

12. Members shall take care to ensure that all solicitation and communication materials are accurate and correctly reflect their organizations' mission and use of solicited funds.
13. Members shall take care to ensure that donors receive informed, accurate and ethical advice about the value and tax implications of contributions.
14. Members shall take care to ensure that contributions are used in accordance with donors' intentions.
15. Members shall take care to ensure proper stewardship of all revenue sources, including timely reports on the use and management of such funds.
16. Members shall obtain explicit consent by donors before altering the conditions of financial transactions.

PRESENTATION OF INFORMATION

17. Members shall not disclose privileged or confidential information to unauthorized parties.
18. Members shall adhere to the principle that all donor and prospect information created by, or on behalf of, an organization or a client is the property of that organization or client and shall not be transferred or utilized except on behalf of that organization or client.
19. Members shall give donors and clients the opportunity to have their names removed from lists that are sold to, rented to or exchanged with other organizations.
20. Members shall, when stating fundraising results, use accurate and consistent accounting methods that conform to the appropriate guidelines adopted by the American Institute of Certified Public Accountants (AICPA)* for the type of organization involved. (* In countries outside of the United States, comparable authority should be utilized.)

COMPENSATION AND CONTRACTS

21. Members shall not accept compensation or enter into a contract that is based on a percentage of contributions; nor shall members accept finder's fees or contingent fees. Business members must refrain from receiving compensation from third parties derived from products or services for a client without disclosing that third-party compensation to the client (for example, volume rebates from vendors to business members).
22. Members may accept performance-based compensation, such as bonuses, provided such bonuses are in accord with prevailing practices within the members' own organizations and are not based on a percentage of contributions.
23. Members shall neither offer nor accept payments or special considerations for the purpose of influencing the selection of products or services.
24. Members shall not pay finder's fees, commissions or percentage compensation based on contributions, and shall take care to discourage their organizations from making such payments.
25. Any member receiving funds on behalf of a donor or client must meet the legal requirements for the disbursement of those funds. Any interest or income earned on the funds should be fully disclosed.

A Donor Bill of Rights

PHILANTHROPY is based on voluntary action for the common good. It is a tradition of giving and sharing that is primary to the quality of life. To assure that philanthropy merits the respect and trust of the general public, and that donors and prospective donors can have full confidence in the not-for-profit organizations and causes they are asked to support, we declare that all donors have these rights:

I.

To be informed of the organization's mission, of the way the organization intends to use donated resources, and of its capacity to use donations effectively for their intended purposes.

II.

To be informed of the identity of those serving on the organization's governing board, and to expect the board to exercise prudent judgement in its stewardship responsibilities.

III.

To have access to the organization's most recent financial statements.

IV.

To be assured their gifts will be used for the purposes for which they were given.

V.

To receive appropriate acknowledgement and recognition.

VI.

To be assured that information about their donations is handled with respect and with confidentiality to the extent provided by law.

VII.

To expect that all relationships with individuals representing organizations of interest to the donor will be professional in nature.

VIII.

To be informed whether those seeking donations are volunteers, employees of the organization or hired solicitors.

IX.

To have the opportunity for their names to be deleted from mailing lists that an organization may intend to share.

X.

To feel free to ask questions when making a donation and to receive prompt, truthful and forthright answers.

DEVELOPED BY
Association for Healthcare Philanthropy (AHP)
Association of Fundraising Professionals (AFP)
Council for Advancement and Support of Education (CASE)
Giving Institute: Leading Consultants to Non-Profits

ENDORSED BY
(in formation)
Independent Sector
National Catholic Development Conference (NCDC)
National Committee on Planned Giving (NCPG)
Council for Resource Development (CRD)
United Way of America

Index